Jumpstart!

Jumpstart! Grammar (2nd Edition)
Games and activities for ages 6–14
Pie Corbett and Julia Strong

Jumpstart! Talk for Learning
Games and activities for ages 7–12
John Foster and Lyn Dawes

Jumpstart! PSHE
Games and activities for ages 7–13
John Foster

Jumpstart! History
Engaging activities for ages 7–12
Sarah Whitehouse and Karen Vickers-Hulse

Jumpstart! Geography
Engaging activities for ages 7–12
Sarah Whitehouse and Mark Jones

Jumpstart! Thinking Skills and Problem Solving
Games and activities for ages 7–14
Steve Bowkett

Jumpstart! Maths (2nd Edition)
Maths activities and games for ages 5–14
John Taylor

Jumpstart! Spanish and Italian
Engaging activities for ages 7–12
Catherine Watts and Hilary Phillips

Jumpstart! French and German
Engaging activities for ages 7–12
Catherine Watts and Hilary Phillips

Jumpstart! Drama
Games and activities for ages 5–11
Teresa Cremin, Roger McDonald, Emma Goff and Louise Blakemore

Jumpstart! Science
Games and activities for ages 5–11
Rosemary Feasey

Jumpstart! Storymaking
Games and activities for ages 7–12
Pie Corbett

JUMPSTART! GRAMMAR

Fully updated to help teachers deal with the 2016 Grammar Tests and beyond, this second edition of *Jumpstart! Grammar* presents a collection of simple to use, multi-sensory games and activities that will jumpstart pupils' understanding of grammar in action.

It now includes coverage of the subjunctive and past progressive, selecting which tense is the most definite, identifying when a word is used as a subordinating conjunction/preposition, explaining how a comma can change meaning, and an increased emphasis on the passive.

Jumpstart! Grammar will prepare children for any grammar tests on the horizon in an engaging way so that they love playing with words and spinning sentences to make ideas dance. And, of course, they will be able to name the parts if that is what is required.

Fun games focus first on helping children to hear the difference various types of grammar can make followed by activities to help them understand what different effects you can create with grammar. Technical terms will only be introduced once the children have established what the various features can do, with a particular focus on those terms that really help children discuss what makes language coherent and effective.

This indispensable, practical book celebrates the joys of language and coherent expression; of finding just the right words or phrases to express what you want to say.

Pie Corbett, educationalist and bestselling author, is well known for his books on teaching creative writing, as well as many other educational books, schemes and anthologies. Pie writes widely in the educational press, provides training nationally and works as a poet and storyteller in schools.

Julia Strong is a former English teacher and deputy headteacher. She later became deputy director of the National Literacy Trust. She specialises in literacy across the curriculum and now works with Pie developing Talk for Writing.

Jumpstart! Poetry
Games and activities for ages 7–12
Pie Corbett

Jumpstart! Creativity
Games and activities for ages 7–14
Steve Bowkett

Jumpstart! ICT
ICT activities and games for ages 7–14
John Taylor

Jumpstart! Numeracy
Maths activities and games for ages 5–14
John Taylor

Jumpstart! Literacy
Key Stage 2/3 literacy games
Pie Corbett

JUMPSTART! GRAMMAR

GAMES AND ACTIVITIES FOR AGES 6–14

SECOND EDITION

Pie Corbett and Julia Strong

LONDON AND NEW YORK

Second edition published 2016
by Routledge
2 Park Square, Milton Park, Abingdon, Oxon OX14 4RN

and by Routledge
711 Third Avenue, New York, NY 10017

Routledge is an imprint of the Taylor & Francis Group, an informa business

First edition published 2014 by David Fulton Publishers Ltd

British Library Cataloguing in Publication Data
A catalogue record for this book is available from the British Library

Library of Congress Cataloging in Publication Data
Corbett, Pie.
Jumpstart! Grammar : games and activities for ages 6-14 / Pie Corbett and Julia Strong. -- Second Edition.
pages cm
Includes index.
1. English language--Grammar--Study and teaching--Activity programs.
2. English language--Composition and exercises--Study and teaching.
I. Strong, Julia, 1948- II. Title.
LB1576.C7182 2016
425--dc23
2015030731

ISBN: 978-1-138-18278-3 (pbk)
ISBN: 978-1-315-64622-0 (ebk)

Typeset in Palatino and Scala Sans
by Saxon Graphics Ltd, Derby

Printed and bound by CPI Group (UK) Ltd, Croydon, CR0 4YY

This book is dedicated to all those teachers who love the architecture of the English language and believe in its power to create and communicate.

Contents

	Introduction	xi
1	**The things: nouns, adjectives, pronouns and determiners**	**1**
	What are nouns?	1
	What are adjectives?	19
	What are noun phrases?	36
	What are pronouns?	39
	What are determiners?	46
2	**The actions: verbs, adverbs, adverbials and prepositions**	**51**
	What are verbs?	51
	How to help children understand tense, modal verbs and mood	63
	What are adverbs?	73
	What are adverbials?	80
	What are prepositions?	84
3	**The links: conjunctions and connectives**	**88**
	What are conjunctions?	88
	What are connectives?	101
	How connectives help link non-fiction activities	103
4	**Sentences: clauses, phrases and different types of sentences**	**111**
	What is a sentence?	113
	What is a clause?	123
	What is a phrase?	125
	How different text types require different sentence structures	154
	Varying sentences to achieve different effects	158

5 **Punctuation** **161**
What is punctuation? 161
Commas – understanding the pauses 162
Separating off subordinate clauses if they begin the sentence 163
Dropping in extra information 167
Direct speech (inverted commas) 169
Dashes, hyphens and ellipses 175
Understanding apostrophes 177
When to use colons and semi-colons 185
Avoiding ambiguity 189

6 **Cohesion: including subject and object, formal and informal, active and passive** **191**
What is cohesion? 191
How pronouns can affect coherence 193
Why understanding subject and object matters 196
Embedding understanding of cohesion 202

Grammar glossary and index to grammar games **207**

Introduction

In an article in *The Times* about grammar, Ted Hughes stated that 'conscious manipulation of syntax deepens engagement and releases invention'. At the time, I had been teaching for a few years and had already found that playing sentence and word games could be an effective way of developing both written style and creativity. We played the games both orally and by writing.

For instance, as a quick start to a lesson I would put on the board a list of dull sentences for the children to improve. Another game that we often played was 'make a sentence'. I wrote a word and they had to invent a sentence. What I noticed with this game was that starting from one word tended to produce rather dull sentences. However, if I wrote three words (eg *donkey – jelly – because*), the children produced much more inventive sentences. I realised that constraints actually helped the children to become creative.

- **Comparing** – comparing word choice, sentences and paragraphs in order to consider the effect of differing word choices, sentence construction and linkage.
- **Cloze procedure** – filling gaps in sentences with words or gaps in texts with sentences.
- **Discussing and using** – constant discussion of words, sentences and texts and the relationships between language construction and the impact on the reader.

Almost all of the games are blueprints and we expect that teachers will provide their own sentences that are related to the text being taught.

It is worth spending some time creating a school overview and system. Each teacher needs to know their contribution to the development of children's understanding about how the English language works but also their ability to accurately and powerfully use it. Teaching should not be through grammar exercises, rather teachers should help pupils 'exercise' their grammar through its constant use in writing and reading. A useful document for planning progression is 'How to plan year-on-year progression' which can be downloaded from http://www.talk4writing.co.uk/resources. It is linked to the Primary Curriculum in England but will be useful to anyone teaching English anywhere.

It might be worth having a grammar quiz every half-term across a school, though of course you will also be able to assess children's ability to use their grammar on a daily basis through their reading and writing. Any such quiz should strike a balance between questions that are about knowledge (eg underline the verb) and usage (eg which of these sentences is punctuated accurately). Remember – in itself, it is pointless to learn what 'modal verbs' might be. How will that help a child make their way through the world? However, what might be useful is to be able to use them effectively. For us, it is the application of grammar in action that not only really deepens understanding of the possibilities of the English language but also makes children more effective as language users.

English is a beautiful language that possesses a multitude of linguistic possibilities. It has been shaped by Shakespeare and many other wonderful writers and speakers. Across the world, the language has many variations and is used for international communication as well as great literatures and language variations.

Effective language users are like chameleons, adapting what they say and how they speak according to audience and purpose, shifting language use according to the context. We believe every child should be able to adapt their language in this way. This is not just about shifting into Standard English when they need to. It is about being able to argue your case, discuss, explain, inform, instruct, and talk about what has happened as well as enjoying storytelling and poetry. It seems obvious to us that understanding how our language works is not just interesting in itself; it is not just that this will help us understand and learn other languages; it is about helping children develop the ability to use language powerfully to understand themselves, their lives and make their way happily in the world.

Other useful books to help you build confidence with grammar are:

- *Rediscover Grammar with David Crystal*, published by Longman;
- *Teaching Grammar Effectively in Primary Schools* by David Reedy and Eve Bearne, published by UKLA;
- *For Who the Bell Tolls* by David Marsh, published by Guardian Books;
- Watch Pie talking about 'grammar in action' on the Oxford University Press website: https://global.oup.com/education/content/primary/experts/pie-corbett/?view=ProductList®ion=international.

There are useful resources relating to grammar that can be downloaded from www.Talk4Writing.com.

NOTES

1 Myhill, D., Lines, H. and Watson, A. (2011) *Making Meaning with Grammar: a repertoire of possibilities*. University of Exeter. Metaphor, Issue 2, 2011.

2 Andrews, R., Torgerson, C., Beverton, S., Freeman, A., Locke, T., Low, G., Robinson, A., Zhu, D. (2004a) 'The effect of grammar teaching (sentence combining) in English on 5 to 16 year olds' accuracy and quality in written composition'. In: *Research Evidence in Education Library*. London: EPPI-Centre, Social Science Research Unit, Institute of Education.

CHAPTER 1

The things

Nouns, adjectives, pronouns and determiners

WHAT ARE NOUNS?

Use these games to draw out from the children that a noun is a word that labels or 'names' something. Nouns name things, objects, people or places. You can put *a, an* or *the* in front of them – *the* ***storm***, *a* ***surprise***, *the* ***fear***, *an* ***umbrella***.

Most nouns can be either singular (only one) or plural (lots of them) – ***cloud, clouds***.

You can have an adjective before them – *the white* ***clouds***.

A collective noun is a word that refers to a group – ***shoal, herd***.

Proper nouns begin with capital letters and name people, places, organisations and unique things – ***Bob, London, Macdonalds***. Days of the week and months should also begin with a capital letter – ***Tuesday, March***.

All other nouns are called common nouns.

Concrete nouns are nouns that name people, places and things that can be experienced through the five senses – ***car, rain, bird***. Abstract nouns name feelings, ideas and concepts – ***hate, anger, jealousy***. A simple way to explain the difference between concrete and abstract nouns is to say that concrete nouns can be touched, like ***concrete*** whereas abstract nouns cannot be touched, like ***hunger***.

I spy

Play 'I spy'. Make it easy for very young children by suggesting that we only choose things that we can see. Vary this by inviting them to suggest things that you might see in different places, for example, a wildlife park, town centre, shopping mall, park. All the words they choose will be nouns.

Mime it

Someone is selected and comes to the front. This person has to mime something (a noun) and everyone else has one guess. It can help children if you give them categories like animals, things you find in a kitchen, eating something, something you find in the town, something in the countryside, etc.

The 'does it fit?' game

This game is quite a useful way of helping children get a feel for the grammatical properties of a noun. Provide the children with these two sentences:

> *The x is great.*
> *The x were great.*

Then provide a bag of words and the children have to try and work out which can be nouns, which are not, and which can be used as a noun and something else. A basic test to see if something is a noun is to see if it will fit into either of the above sentences. Let us take the word 'green', which at first glance might appear to be an adjective. However:

> *The green is great.*

This works as a sentence. This means that *green*, which is often used as an adjective, can also be used as a noun when it refers to the village green or a golf course or a colour itself. Here are some other words to test out:

> *fish, group, huge, stole, cars, question, branch, Susie* (careful with this one as you need to drop the – 'Susie is great'*), party, angry, hard, sun, laptop, potato, stars, shirt, shy, scissors, following, missing, bird, wave.*

Text marking

Begin using the term *noun* when discussing reading and writing – use a colour to underline the nouns in a text and then another colour for the adjectives and another for the verbs. The basic tests for a noun are – can you have lots of them (singular/plural), can you put *a/an* or *the* in front of the word? Give children sentences or paragraphs so they can be 'noun hunters'. Can they find the nouns?

Labelling

Everyone loves a Post-it note – and you can buy them in all sorts of colours, shapes and sizes. Play a simple labelling game, where Post-its are put on objects in the classroom and arrows are used to label objects in an image. The words are all called *nouns*. Nouns tell you the name of something.

Provide the children with a list of words on a board and get them to decide which are 'Post-it' words (*nouns*) and which are ones that tell us what something does (*verbs*):

> *cat, cup, jump, car, run, cow, walk, cap, tortoise, candle,*
> *hop, book, pencil, cheese, policeman, swim, guitar, computer.*

This is where grammar becomes tricky because you can never really tell what a word is until it is placed within a sentence. Most of us would say, at first glance, that *run, jump, walk* and *hop* are verbs. However, they can also be nouns – cricketers make a run; athletes might make a jump; most weekends we go for a walk; beer is made from hops!

I used a variation of the simple Post-it game with a Year 7 class several years ago. We wrote imaginative questions for the chosen objects and placed them around the room, leaving them there for future classes to look at and wonder:

> ***Crack in the ceiling** – are you a hiding place for spiders?*
> ***Light bulb** – do you ever get tired of staring down at our whirring brains?*
> ***Dictionary** – you have all the words but do you have any sense?*
> ***Door** – you seem to be silent but do you really think that we have not heard your squealing?*

Memory game

Everyone of a certain age remembers Bruce Forsyth helping winners in 'The Generation Game' trying to remember the items from the conveyor belt. Try your own version – playing the same memory game (known as 'Kim's game'). Place objects on a tray in front of children or use a collection of images on the interactive whiteboard (IWB). Give the class time to try and memorise the objects and then cover the tray or blank the screen. On their own, or in pairs, they can try and list the items on a whiteboard, draw them or just remember by memory.

Vary the game. For instance, you might select objects that are all one colour (red = adjective, a word that 'tells us what something is like') or for younger children use objects that all start with the same sound/letter.

Alphabet races

These races practise the alphabet and encourage children to generate ideas as well as reinforcing the nature of a noun. Create a simple grid for the children with the alphabet down the left-hand side. The children then have 5–10 minutes to complete as much as possible. The easiest categories are 'girls' names' and 'boys' names'. Another fairly easy one is to list fruit and vegetables or food. You could also try other categories such as 'things you can see in the room', 'things you can see in the countryside', 'things you can see in the town'. If you are engaged in a topic, then see if they can produce an alphabet of related words perhaps with glossary definitions.

Alphabet	Girl's name	Boy's name	Fruit and veg
A	*Alice*	*Ali*	*avocado*
B	*Beyoncé*	*Bill*	*banana*
C	*Carly*	*Clive*	*cucumber*
D	*Danni*	*Duane*	*dates*
E	*Elif*	*Eddy*	*endive*

Leave them out (cloze games)

Nouns are crucial labelling devices – without them sentences collapse. Find a few sentences (magpie them from a book) or a paragraph and omit the nouns, creating a simple cloze procedure. Get the children to read the cloze procedure aloud so they can 'hear' how the keystones of a sentence are missing – the things/nouns.

Cloze procedure	**One possible answer**
The … wheezed past the old. … The … tooted the … and waited while the … chugged along. Was it about to explode? After a while, a young … came out and poured cold … into the …. Everyone watched while it bubbled happily. … hissed.	*The car wheezed past the old garage. The driver tooted the horn and waited while the engine chugged along. Was it about to explode? After a while, a young man came out and poured cold water into the engine. Everyone watched while it bubbled happily. Steam hissed.*

Ask the children to fill the gaps. Then ask them to explain what 'sort' of word was missing. What is the 'job' of that type of word?

Replace with fruit and veg (cloze games)

Another version of cloze procedure involves taking out all the nouns and replacing them with a different word. This can produce much hilarity but is useful because it helps the children to revisit and deepen their 'feel' for the nature of the noble and humble noun – without which we do not know our surroundings. Try replacing nouns with fruit, vegetables or animals. Once again, begin by getting children to read aloud the text as this helps to draw their attention to the nouns that sound odd.

Cloze procedure version	**One possible answer**
As the banana chugged through the beans, she stared out of the cucumber. Tiny strawberries clung to the tomatoes and, in the melon, lemons grazed. A potato ran beside the lettuce, gurgling on its way to the radish. As she looked out of the cucumber, she noticed the dark pineapple drifting overhead.	*As the train chugged through the valleys, she stared out of the window. Tiny houses clung to the hillsides and, in the distance, sheep grazed. A river ran beside the train, gurgling on its way to the sea. As she looked out of the window, she noticed the dark clouds drifting overhead.*

Get children to prepare their own paragraphs using fruit or vegetables instead of nouns. They then swap their prepared paragraph with a partner.

Swapping

Another amusing game that focuses on nouns involves swapping them over in a text. You could do this yourself and provide the children with a paragraph or list of sentences with the nouns swapped and they have to sort it out. Once again, reading the text aloud is crucial. You may have noticed that if you are writing and a sentence doesn't seem 'quite right', you find yourself automatically reading aloud to 'hear' whether or not what you have written 'works' – grammar is not just knowing the function of the words in sentences but it is also about usage.

The original	**Swapped over text**
Bees are famous for making honey. They live in hives and spend most of their time in the summer flying round looking for flowers that contain pollen.	*Hives are famous for making bees. They live in honey and spend most of their pollen in the flowers flying round looking for summer that contain time.*

'Dead common' or 'Nice and proper'?

Present children with the list of words below. Can they sort the words into two groups and say what the difference might be? Don't prompt the children at all – see if they can notice the difference – and then explain the rule.

dog, Richard, cow, Leeds, cat, chair, December, frost, egg, Wednesday, donut, dust, Thames, sand, Folkestone, flea, Asda

What sorts of words in sentences have a capital letter and why? The key ones are months, days of the week, names of people, organisations and places.

In addition, capital letters are used to start the first word in a sentence and for the word 'I'.

The proper noun alphabet race

Hold an alphabet race in pairs – giving a common and a proper noun for each letter, as well as using alliteration:

A is for Archie, an amiable ant.
B is for Boris, a beautiful bear.

One way to play the game is for partner a to say the first part (*A is for Archie*) and partner b to add on the animal plus adjective (*an amiable ant*). Which pair reaches the end of the alphabet first?

The proper noun poem

Provide the class with a simple pattern that involves a day of the week, a month, a name and a place. Give a few minutes for them to create a simple 'day of the week' list poem. In pairs, let the children 'police' each other's sentences, checking for correct use of capital letters ... and of course full stops, for example:

On Monday in December, Ayse swam seriously to Swindon.
On Tuesday in January, Nick trotted timidly through Grantham.
On Wednesday in February, Tina tiptoed tenaciously by the Thames.

Name it

One of the key things that children need to consider about nouns is the impact they make on the reader. Show the children these two sentences and ask them which one creates a stronger picture and why.

The man came into the building with the dog.
The policeman came into the school with the poodle.

In the second sentence, the nouns are more precise so that the reader can build a stronger picture. Now compare these two sentences and discuss the impact on the reader:

The policeman came into the school with the poodle.
The policeman came into the school with the Rottweiler.

What sort of picture and what effect are created? To me, the idea of a policeman with a poodle sounds silly. However, the Rottweiler sounds like serious business.

Choosing nouns with care can help to build a picture for the reader. Now ask the children to consider the following. If you are writing about a character who is swimming and meets a fish, what do the following words suggest? What mood is created? What might the reader think?

He could just make out a cod swimming towards him.
He could just make out a shark swimming towards him.
He could just make out a sardine swimming towards him.

Try the same thing with these sentences.

> *Gary stared up at the tree. There was a budgie in it.*
> *Gary stared up at the tree. There was a bird of paradise in it.*
> *Gary stared up at the tree. There was a vulture in it.*

When writing, encourage children to choose nouns with care so that they 'name it'. It is not a cat – it is a Siamese. Nouns create pictures and also may have implications. If a shark is swimming towards the main character, then a sudden dash is called for! If it happens to be a sardine, we can relax. Try a game in which you provide a list of nouns that children have to 'name' in order to make them more specific. I have provided some suggestions.

dog	Alsatian
cat	Burmese
bird	eagle
fish	salmon
animal	tiger
tree	oak
flower	primrose
car	Mercedes
man	Mr Jobson
woman	Miss Welcome
vegetable	marrow

Try this paragraph below. The children have to underline the nouns and then 'name it' by changing the nouns to make them more particular. Point out that 'the girl' could become 'Beyoncé' or 'the man' might be turned into 'Harold'.

> *The girl, who came from a planet, soon reached the town and found the street. The school was empty except for the boy who was climbing a tree in the playground. They made their way to the market and wandered past stalls selling fruit, vegetables and sweets. They bought a fruit to eat and wandered to the shop. Inside there were cages. In one, a dog sat watching them. In another, a cat lay asleep. Insects swarmed in a small glass cage.*

On top of the counter was a huge tank where a fish swam round. The girl chose an animal to buy. Outside, a strange bird swooped overhead. A car pulled up. Inside, they could see a pile of glittering jewels.

You might want to share my version for their comments.

Jasmine, who came from Xargon soon reached Salford and found Cherry Tree Avenue. St Peters Primary was empty except for Jason who was climbing an oak tree in the playground. They made their way to the Carswell Market and wandered past stalls selling water melons, potatoes and liquorice. They bought an apple to eat and wandered to Pets 'R' Us. Inside there were cages. In one, a poodle sat watching them. In another, a Siamese lay asleep. Locusts swarmed in a small glass cage. On top of the counter was a huge tank where a goldfish swam round. Jasmine chose a gerbil to buy. Outside, a strange hawk swooped overhead. A Mercedes pulled up. Inside, they could see a pile of glittering diamonds.

Basic Writing Toolkit Ingredient

You may want to use name-it activities like these to contribute to a writer's basic toolkit that you co-construct with the class. The class might decide on a wording like the following:

- **Name it. Select precise nouns that name exactly what you are trying to include.**

Which works and why?

Provide children with sentences to compare in which you have altered the nouns to create different effects. What is the effect? It is not so much a matter that one sentence is 'better' than another – the point is that each one creates a different effect on the reader. Compare the effect of these three sentences.

The man sipped his drink as he stroked the dog.
The teacher sipped his cocoa as he stroked the poodle.
The politician sipped his wine as he stroked the Rottweiler.

Here are some clusters of sentences to discuss. It is worth remembering that you never really know how well a sentence works until it is in a paragraph.

The old man stood under the tree and stared at the bird.
Mr Granger stood under the willow tree and stared at the vulture.
Mr Grabbit stood under the oak tree and stared at the parrot.

The fish moved silently through the water.
The shark moved silently through the Thames.
The herring moved silently through the stream.

Noun explosion

This game is good for 'limbering up' the imagination. Choose a noun. Let's say the word *cat*. You might think words say exactly what they mean therefore we all know what a cat is. However, words also carry other echoes and shades of meaning. For instance, you might think of someone being *catty* or about seeing the musical *Cats*. Take another word, *cross*. This might make you think of a religious cross – or of being angry.

To play this game, choose your noun and put it in the middle of the page or whiteboard. Now explore different categories that produce echoes and shades of meaning. Don't forget too that words also make sounds – so include rhymes and alliteration. Here are some suggestions with examples for *cat*:

Memories – *my cat curled asleep at home, a kitten chasing shadows.*
Types – *Siamese, Burmese, moggy.*
How it is used/what it does – *purrs, hunts at night, has green eyes.*
Idioms and expressions – *it's raining cats and dogs, put the cat amongst the pigeons.*
Art works (music, art, songs, books, plays, films, TV, etc.) – *Cats, Cat Woman, Six Dinner Sid, The Mousehole Cat…*
Rhymes – *rat, bat, sat, fat, mat…*
Words that start with a similar sound – *car, cask, carriage, candle, cattle, casket…*

For *cat*, you might also include a category of words that start with cat – *catalogue, catastrophe, catapult, category*. As one child once said to me at the end of brainstorming the word *stone*, 'You'd never imagine there was so much in a word'.

Singular and plural riddles

Nouns can be either singular (only one) or plural (more than one). There are a few words that do not change their spelling such as *sheep, deer, salmon* and *scissors*. Play a riddle game by giving the children a clue to the noun that you are thinking about and they have to write the singular and plural. Here are several examples.

Clue	Singular	Plural
I am thinking of someone who steals.	*thief* *robber*	*thieves* *robbers*
I am thinking of something found in the sky.	*cloud* *sun*	*clouds* *suns*
I am thinking of a musical instrument with white and black keys.	*piano*	*pianos*

Gender

Some nouns are either masculine (*boy*) or feminine (*girl*). Many nouns are neither (neuter) – *wall, car, tree,* etc. Some nouns could be either (*baby*). It is worth noting that some people talk about objects as if they did have a gender. For instance, many teachers talk about their cars as if they were people! Several quick-fire games could be played along the lines of providing a list of people and the children have to give the male or female equivalent. I have given the answers.

Male	Female
actor	*actress*
lord	*lady*
policeman	*policewoman*
sister	*brother*
uncle	*aunt*
father	*mother*
queen	*king*
princess	*prince*

Play the same game with animals. Try listing these nouns to see if they know the male or female equivalent. Once again, I have provided the answers.

cow	*bull*
buck	*doe*
drake	*duck*
vixen	*dog fox*
mare	*stallion*
boar	*sow*
cockerel	*hen*
ram	*ewe*

Another version would be to list adult animals and ask the children to name the noun used for their babies. Here are some animals to use plus the answers.

wolf	*cub*
chicken	*chick*
cat	*kitten*
deer	*fawn*
dog	*puppy*
duck	*duckling*
goose	*gosling*
frog	*tadpole*
goat	*kid*
horse	*foal*

Knowing the names of baby animals and male/female focuses the children on the noun but is also, of course, part of children's growing vocabulary and general knowledge. This sort of work will pay dividends when children come to learn other languages where the notion of gender can become more important.

Compound nouns

Compound nouns are nouns that have been made by putting two nouns together. Over time, the convention has become, in many instances, to push the actual words together so that they form a single word. Provide a list of compound nouns and ask the children to invent a story about how each one became a word.

> *fireman, tablecloth, earthquake, schoolboy, bedroom, aircraft, toothpaste, alleyway, football, sunlight, crossword, spaceship, toothache, sheepskin, waterproof, fingerprint, downward*

The next game is to provide the following list and see who can pair up the words from each column to create compound nouns.

back	beam
bed	berry
book	board
dart	cake
farm	end
fire	ground
home	guard
wind	house
kid	light
life	light
moon	man

An alternative to the above game is to move on to pair up words that have never been put together before and create new compound words, eg *windberry*. The children then have to explain what their new compound noun might mean – *A windberry is only found in magical lands. It is a form of flying fruit that can only grow when the wind blows.*

Create new definitions by swapping the core ideas around. By this I mean that a *schoolboy* is a *boy* who goes to *school*. How about seeing it the other way round so that a *schoolboy* is a *school* made of *boys*? Present each one like a dictionary definition:

> ***fireman*** – *superhero who is made of fire*
> ***crossword*** – *angry speech*
> ***babysitter*** – *someone who sits on babies.*

For new definitions, these compound words work well – *understand, thunderclap, woodworm, lifeguard, peacekeeper, sleepover, rattlesnake, membership, childhood, manhole.*

Kennings

Kennings are a form of ancient metaphorical compound noun associated with Anglo-Saxon, Icelandic and Old Norse poetry. For instance, in the great poem *Beowulf,* written over a thousand years ago in Old English, the sea is described as a *sail road, swan road* and *whale road*. Death is referred to as *sleep of the sword*. Wonderfully, horses were described in Norse as *wind-racers*, snow as *feathers fall*, the moon as *ship of night*, night as *sky's black cloak* and an icicle as *winter spear*. Here are some other kennings and their source language. You can see that to make it obvious that both words work together to create one meaning, they have been hyphenated.

Kenning	Meaning	Language
blood-ember	axe	Norse
spear-din	battle	Norse
slaughter-dew	blood	Norse
sea-stead	ship	Norse
sky-candle	sun	Old English
sky's jewel	sun	Old English

Children love inventing kennings for everyday things and kennings lend themselves to the quick-fire lesson starter as you only need one or two ideas. A teacher might be described as a 'sum-ticker' or a 'punctuation-spotter'. Choose a simple subject such as a *cat*. Think about what they do and see if the children can invent a few kennings:

> **Cat:** *flea-trapper; door-scratcher*
> **Clown:** *smile-bringer; pie-slinger*
> **Dog:** *bark-biter; cat-fighter*

Noun riddles

This is quite a simple game. Play it with the class and then children can play in pairs or in a group. You provide clues and they have to guess the noun. The nouns should be fairly simple – *I'm thinking of something which can fly – it has white wings – it swims in rivers.* The winner is the first to guess correctly (swan). For children who have a broad vocabulary, make your clues more enigmatic:

I am seen by the thousand at a glance
And yet you cannot touch me –
I'll illuminate the darkness
And guide your ship home. (*stars*)

The colour of butter,
I'll appear in the Spring.
I am a trumpet
But I make no sound. (*daffodil*)

Beetle black,
I'll take you where you wish
If you cross my palm. (*taxi*)

Collective nouns

A **collective noun** is one that can be used to describe a group of people, animals or things. So, a *flock* describes lots of sheep whereas a *library* describes a place where there are lots of books. Provide a list of collective nouns and see who knows or can guess what they might be for.

flock, herd, shoal, swarm, litter, team, gang, crowd, bunch, string, pack, bouquet, gaggle, pride, army, crew, team, choir, pack, school, plague, bunch, cluster, forest, library, pack, suit, brood

Collective nouns often have a magical ring to them. Who cannot fail to be impressed by a *murder of crows*? In pairs, ask children to decide/invent the story that lies behind these collective nouns:

nuisance of cats
storytelling of crows
watch of nightingales
parliament of owls
bed of oysters
mischief of rats
bask of crocodiles
paddling of ducks
murmuration of starlings

Once children have a feel for the nature of a collective noun, then they can invent some of their own. Begin with something familiar like *teachers – a worry of teachers, a tick of teachers.*

Make a list of other possibilities and give children a few minutes to invent their own ideas. These nouns work well: *swans, clocks, clouds, snowflakes, sunbeams, flames, rings, lorries.*

Now invent ones that are opposites. So, *a slither of snakes* describes the snakes as sinister and moving rapidly. However, *a cuddle of snakes* is the opposite. These can be quite fun.

> *a stumble of trapeze artists; a silence of politicians; a frost of flames; a sloth of athletes.*

Abstract and concrete nouns

Concrete nouns are nouns that name people, places and things that can be experienced through the five senses – *car, rain, bird.* Abstract nouns name feelings, ideas and concepts – *hate, anger, jealousy.* A simple way to explain the difference is to say that concrete nouns can be touched like concrete whereas abstract nouns cannot be touched. Play a simple sorting game using the following words – which are concrete and which are abstract nouns?

bison, belief, rose, frog, thought, chair, king, curiosity, grass, reluctance, sunset, road, greed, digger, jealousy, duke, jam-jar, opinion, giant, thorn, agreement, sheep, cowardice, cattle

City of stars

A version of this game was suggested to me many years ago by the poet Philip Gross. This is a variant – though there have to be many ways to play the game. It is fun to play the game in pairs though not necessary.

Partner A makes a list of places or containers – *library, cathedral, zoo, garage, museum, hotel, music hall, theatre, beach, cave, rucksack, suitcase, sack, box, etc.*

Partner B makes a list of abstract nouns – *belief, thought, curiosity, reluctance, greed, jealousy, opinion, agreement, cowardice, power, discretion, fear, sorrow, wonder, envy, generosity, strength.*

Now the pairs work together to mix the two lists, creating remarkable new places and containers:

The library of belief
The cathedral of thought
The zoo of curiosity
The garage of reluctance
The museum of greed
The beach of cowardice

The game can be made even more interesting by working in fours so that partner C lists adjectives and partner D lists verbs. Let's say we have these adjectives and verbs:

adjectives	**verbs**
scarlet, soft, cruel, sharp, sensitive, cautious, sunlit	*investigates, flees, chuckles, whispers, cartwheels, notices, sleeps*

Select each adjective and verb in the random order in which they were listed. The list of poetic phrases now reads as follows:

The library of scarlet belief investigates
The cathedral of soft thought flees
The zoo of cruel curiosity chuckles
The garage of sharp reluctance whispers

Each idea could be extended or completed by tying the lines together:

> *The library of scarlet belief investigates the cathedral of soft thought that flees to the zoo of cruel curiosity that chuckles at the garage of sharp reluctance where whispers from the museum of sensitive greed cartwheel to the beach of cautious cowardice that notices the cave of sunlit power sleeping.*

Alternatively, each place could be turned into a verse of ideas by thinking about what might happen there:

In the library of belief

> *The books sprouted wings*
> *And flew out of the windows*
> *Many years ago –*
> *Silent stories are ghosts now*
> *Perched on dusty shelves,*
> *Poetry flits across the floor.*
> *Rusted facts shuffle for space.*
> *A full stop eyes the door.*

Mass and countable nouns

Most nouns can be 'counted' as either singular or plural (usually shown by adding an 's'). These are sometimes known as countable nouns. Some nouns you cannot count and these are often known as mass nouns. Mass nouns are words such as *dust, rubbish, money, gold, wheat, milk.* You cannot say, *Look at the dusts on the floor*. The word *dust* might mean one spec or vast heaps! An interesting activity for older children would be to see how many mass nouns they can find – a good homework challenge.

Apostrophes

Whilst you are thinking about nouns, you might want to consider the apostrophe for possession. This is a concept – understanding the idea of possession – and many teachers attempt teaching this too early with the end result of apostrophes appearing like tadpoles, scattered across the page. However, many children of about 9–11 years can begin to grapple with the idea. See pages 177–183 for apostrophe-related games.

Get those nouns moving

Try using a noun to start a verb race. Write a noun up on a board – let's say *car*. Now give the children one minute to list as many verbs as possible that might go with the noun. The winner of the race is the child who manages to come up with the largest number of verbs. Discuss how the noun is the *thing* and the verb shows *what it does*. The verb is the engine of the sentence – it gets things going.

With younger children, put the noun to the left of the page so that the verbs come after the noun to the right of the page:

	cruised
	rushed
	dashed
car	*drove*
	prowled
	trundled

Try using the following nouns – *the snake, the laugh, the sneeze, the volcano, the baby, the wind, the river*. Extend the game by placing the chosen noun in the middle of the board. List adjectives before it and verbs after to create simple sentences. Get the children to discuss the job of each type of word.

WHAT ARE ADJECTIVES?

Use these games to draw out from the children that an adjective is a word that describes somebody or something, adding extra information to a noun or completing a verb. Adjectives are placed before the noun: *The **red** flower*. But, when they complement a verb, they come after it: *The flower is **red***. (Verbs such as *to be, to look, to get, to seem* need to be completed to make sense.) Adjectives refer to the qualities that something or someone might have. They tell you what something is like. This is often referred to as 'modifying' the noun because an adjective changes the meaning of the noun slightly – it modifies what the noun is like. Sometimes I talk about how the adjective snuggles up to the noun.

You may need to use an adjective to compare things – *That dog is **taller** than my dog*. Generally, this is done by adding *er* onto the adjective – *small, **smaller**,* though sometimes for longer words you can use the word *more – that one is **more** amazing*.

If you are comparing more than two things, then you need a superlative which may well end in *est – My dog is tall and your dog is taller but that dog is the **tallest***. Again, for longer words, you can use the word *most* – *That handbag is expensive but this one is more expensive, and Jo's is the* ***most*** *expensive of all.*

It is worth noting that the position of the adjective in an English sentence is different to many other languages. This means that when teaching, it is important to use colour, human sentences and words on cards to make the position clear for those learning the English language.

Spot the adjective

Write up a few sentences and the children have to underline the adjective. Some are in front of the noun but others are complements so they come after the verb they complete. They all *add* to the noun.

> *Fred had a red hat and blue shoes.*
> *Lilly's scarf was blue.*
> *Mrs Snagglenose picked up the broken box, the damp coat and the dusty cloak.*
> *Gavin stared at the watery painting and gave a deep chuckle.*

Brainstorm

A simple way into understanding adjectives is to brainstorm possibilities. It can help if you use an image of an animal and then list as many describing words as possible. Begin by brainstorming as a class. Then choose another image and challenge the children – who can list the most in one or two minutes? This sort of activity helps children get a feel for the job of the adjective – to describe, to add new information and build a picture, etc. With younger children, you may find this works best if you use real objects. Obviously, this sort of game acts as a good precursor to writing. It is useful before describing characters or building up a setting in a story.

A variation of this game is to provide an object or image and a list of possible adjectives and ask which ones would work well and which would not. For instance, if you had on the screen an image of a lion roaring, which of these adjectives would work and which would not?

> *savage, hungry, desperate, cruel, gentle, friendly, frightening, comfortable, happy, whispering, roaring, singing, sleepy*

What is the job? Spot the odd one out

This is a handy game to play because you ask the children to work out what the underlined words have in common – what is their job? Can they explain their function? You have also included an 'odd one out'. Which is it and why? (*limped* – because it is a verb.)

> *Then something reared up in front of Tom. Its huge, leathery wings flapped like mighty sails. He stared up into its scarlet eyes and shuddered. Quietly, it placed an enormous claw in front of Tom and he could see that a golden ring was biting into the soft flesh of its lower leg. The dragon took a step nearer and limped. A vast tear splashed down its scaly cheek....*

Filling the gaps (cloze games)

The simplest adjective game is to provide a cloze procedure in which the adjectives have been missed out. But remember – it is worth discussing a few choices to consider which adjectives work most effectively and why. Here are some sentences to get you started. I have played this differently where I have just used the word 'nice' as an adjective each time.

The ________ dog barked at the ________ cat.

The ________ snake slipped through the ________ grass.

The ________ wall crumbled under the ________ weight of the ________ giant's ________ foot.

Mrs Snaggleworth rode her ______ bicycle through the __________ market.

She passed ________ stalls of ______ apples, _________ pears and ____________ pineapples.

Adjective riddles

This is a simple enough game. Play it with the class and then children can play in pairs or in a group. They have to guess the noun – and you provide clues – which are all adjectives.

This is –

alive,
silent,
slim,
cold,
scaley*... (snake)*

These are –

white
or black
soft
distant
cold
damp*... (clouds)*

The adjective generator

This is a quick-fire game that provides a variety of nouns while the children have a limited time – a few minutes – in which to list as many adjectives as possible. The ability to rapidly generate language is a crucial writing skill, otherwise children have limited choice – and writing is about selecting the right word for the job. Here are some common, proper, abstract and collective nouns to use.

cat, snake, tree, computer, bus, taxi, London, Paris, Betty, Bill, fear, greed, anger, hope, curiosity, swarm, flock, crowd, shoal

Swapping over (cloze games)

In this game, you provide a sentence or paragraph that is muddled. The adjectives have all been swapped round. Give a time limit to see who can sort them out into their rightful places. Hear several examples as there may be different ways to reorganise the adjectives that work equally well. Start with a few sentences such as these and work on them together before letting the children loose on a paragraph. I have provided the originals.

Original

Sian paused at the wooden door and peered into the dark room. In the sunlit corner, she could see the cowardly prince wearing his silky shirt and holding the rotting apple.

Swapped version

Sian paused at the cowardly door and stared into the rotting room. In the silky corner, she could see the wooden prince wearing his sunlit shirt and holding the dark apple.

Provide more extended examples to work on, for example:

Original

The crumbling walls were covered with wooden shelves that bowed under the stupendous weight of glittering crowns, steep piles of golden coins, rusted keys and gleaming bracelets. Wonderful strings of pink pearls and glowing necklaces of glistening jewels hung from carved hooks. Sitting on an empty shelf was a white owl. Suddenly, it blinked at her and muttered, 'Don't stare!'

Swapped version

The wonderful walls were covered with glowing shelves that bowed under the pink weight of empty crowns, carved piles of rusted coins, gleaming keys and steep bracelets. Crumbling strings of golden pearls and glistening necklaces of white jewels hung from stupendous hooks. Sitting on a glittering shelf was a wooden owl. Suddenly, it blinked at her and muttered, 'Don't stare!'

As you can see from the above example, there are many ways to reorganise the adjectives and sometimes the more unlikely combinations are the most interesting. All of this play with language provides children with a feel for the function and effect of the adjective. The games are not just about labelling and identifying but also about how adjectives can be used to achieve different effects.

Replacing

In this game, remove the adjectives from a piece of writing and replace them with the names of sweets. Here are some names of sweets I have culled from my memory.

> *toffee, colabar, mint, chocolate, wine gums, marshmallows, jelly baby, aniseed ball, chewing gum, liquorice, loveheart, sherbet, nougat, gob stopper, butterscotch, shrimps, fudge*

Can the children work out what the original might have been? Begin by reading the text aloud so the children can hear what it sounds like. There will be, of course, a variety of possible solutions. However, I am providing the original as a matter of interest.

Using sweets as adjectives	**Original version**
But at that moment, she noticed a fudge door that led into a spearmint room. She was standing in what she imagined was a toffee room in a gob stopper palace. Butterscotch curtains cut out the nougat daylight, sherbet candles flickered and the jelly baby carpet was a mint, chocolate colour. In a caramac corner, stood a fruit gum suit of liquorice armour.	*But at that moment, she noticed a silver door that led into a darkened room. She was standing in what she imagined was a perfect room in a fairytale palace. Silk curtains cut out the bright daylight, slender candles flickered and the ancient carpet was a soft, red colour. In a dusty corner, stood a metallic suit of shiny armour.*

Character descriptions

One purposeful approach to adjectives is to collect ones that would be useful when building a character description or a setting. These could be stored in children's writing journals. The simple idea is that everyone brainstorms possible adjectives that might be useful when writing.

Eyes – cruel, mean, sly, sharp, bright, red, yellow, green, thin, dangerous, dark, cold …

Hands – old, gnarled, withered, wrinkled, twisted, soft, gentle, creased, lined, knobbly, tough, strong, hairy …

Mouth – thin, mean, cruel, hard, bitter, swollen, tense …

Jabberwocky

Read, enjoy and learn by heart this wonderful poem which you can download from the internet. Ask the children to underline the adjectives in one colour. What do you think they mean? Create dictionary definitions.

Vorpal – dangerous, with a sharp and deadly edge that is guaranteed to slice through even the toughest of metals. Looking vicious.

Frabjous – joyous and fantastic. Often used to describe an event or time which demands celebration.

Tulgey – a place that is difficult to navigate through because the area is overgrown to the point where no one can pass through unless very strong.

Invented adjectives

Building on the previous Jabberwocky investigation, write a simple piece but instead of using real adjectives invent some of your own. This can be made quite simple by putting halves of two real words together.

There are three wontastic reasons for believing that generating power from the sun is a favourous idea. First, it will be worthsome for the environment.

Provide definitions for the invented adjectives.

Wontastic – wonderful and fantastic at the same time. Sometimes used as an exaggeration.

Favourous – said to be favourable and tremendous. Often used to persuade others to a viewpoint.

Worthsome – will do good and be beneficial. Used when referring to ecological aspects of life.

Trim

If you have children who tend to use too many adjectives, then play a simple game in which they have to 'trim back' an overwritten sentence, deciding how many adjectives to keep. Generally, if you use too many, they tend to clash against each other, reducing the impact through a conflict of description. Ask which adjective should be used – if any. Get the children to read aloud so everyone can hear their ideas – and then ask them to justify their choice.

The slim, graceful, elegant flamingo slipped through the fence.

The tired, weary, exhausted giant slumbered.

The scared, frightened, worried, anxious goblin shivered.

Adjectives have to earn their place and should not be just chucked into sentences. This leads to overwriting. A well-chosen adjective will add something new that the reader needs to know. For instance, *big giant* is rather silly as the word *giant* means *big*. However, a *shy giant* is something that the reader could not possibly know and may well influence or explain what will happen next.

Basic Writing Toolkit Ingredient

You may want to use this activity to contribute to a writer's basic toolkit that you co-construct with the class. The class may decide on a wording like the following:

- **Make every adjective earn its place by adding something useful and new.**

The superlative zoo

Sometimes adjectives are used to compare one thing with another.

*My dog is **bigger** than your dog.*

When comparing more than two things, a superlative is needed.

*Gerry's dog is the **biggest** in the world.*

Generally, the comparative has *er* added to the adjective and the superlative has *est*: *big, bigg**er**, bigg**est***

There are a few common exceptions to the usual pattern that children need to know.

Adjective	**Comparative**	**Superlative**
good	*better*	*best*
bad	*worse*	*worst*
far	*farther*	*farthest*
little	*less*	*least*
many	*more*	*most*

Play a game in which you say an adjective and the children have to write down the comparative and superlative forms. A more creative game is to produce sentences that use a superlative in a playful manner by creating a zoo and populating it with amazing creatures:

> *In the superlative zoo, there is –*
> *the finest monkey munching the best bananas,*
> *the coolest gorilla growling at the tastiest bacon,*
> *the coldest penguin snoozing on the warmest blanket,*
> *the calmest camel dancing to the loudest orchestra.*

Draw it

Put the children into pairs. They take it in turn to be in charge. The person in charge describes some one, something or a place using lots of adjectives and their partner has to draw what is being described. This can work well if they are describing, for instance, an ogre's face, a new toy or an invented machine for keeping a teacher happy or perhaps the ideal classroom.

Pairs

Ideally, for this activity you need two bags or boxes. In one, there is a pile of words that can be used as adjectives. In the other, there is a pile of words that can be used as nouns. If that sounds like too much bother, then you can brainstorm a list with the class and write them on a board.

To play the game, dip your hand in the bag/box to randomly select six adjectives and six nouns (or choose six of each from the list). Roll a dice to select an adjective and roll again to select a noun. Pair these up. The children then have to create a sentence – which of course may need to be ingenious or just plain surreal. Here is a bank of adjectives and nouns to get you started.

Adjectives	**Nouns**
angry, brave, cool, deadly, emerald, frosty, gorgeous, helpless, impressive, jealous, keen, lazy, moody, naughty, old, pale, quick, red, bad, tall	*cup, table, chair, grass, tree, bus, car, bike, computer, pencil, ruler, desk, bell, tower, forest, lake, banana, carrot, owl, parrot*

So, if you had selected six adjectives and six nouns and rolled the dice twice you might end up with *naughty* and *banana*. The challenge is to invent a sentence:

> *Mrs Cartworry stared at the* ***naughty banana*** *that had just stuck its tongue out at her!*

Adjective alphabet races

Simple race games provide a basic format such as the alphabet or counting one to ten. See who can think of the most adjectives in two or three minutes:

> *A is for angry*
> *B is for beautiful*
> *C is for crazy …*

You may want the children to use a dictionary. Or try a counting list using alliteration:

> *One is a white whale*
> *Two is a tiny turtle*
> *Three is a threatening thistle …*

This game is based on an old one that we used to play at home. It can be played as a memory game linked to the adjectives. In the game, you pretend that you have a cat or monkey or badger or newt and then the children take it in turns to repeat the ideas and add on a new one, saying what the creature is like by using an adjective:

> *Mr Corbett's cat is an adventurous cat.*
> *Mr Corbett's cat is a boring cat.*
> *Mr Corbett's cat is a calm cat.*

It doesn't have to be in alphabetical order.

Initials

My initials are PC – Pie Corbett, and Julia's are JS – Julia Strong. To play this game put the children into pairs. If I were playing with Julia, I would make a list of five adjectives that start with J, while Julia made a list of five nouns that start with S. We would then put the list together. This has to be done without looking at each other's list because it works best when the combinations are random. In the same way, we would then swap over and work on PC. We might end up in this fashion.

Julia Strong is	*Pie Corbett is*
a jubilant strawberry	*a proud cheese*
a jagged ship	*a powerful clown*
a jaded sunbeam	*a peeling cyclist*

Drop in

When children start writing, teachers encourage them to use adjectives. This can lead to a situation where they get into the habit of believing that there is virtue in chucking in any old adjective – they just bung them into sentences without really thinking about choosing carefully and some children (and teachers) seem to believe that the more adjectives, the better the writing. However, a good writer chooses each word with care. Remind children of their toolkit ingredient ***Every adjective should earn its place*** displayed on your writing wall/washing line (see page 25).

To begin opening this discussion up, list some weak sentences for the children to improve, focusing on inserting some adjectives. Discuss a few of their choices. Get the children to explain why their choice works and what it tells the reader. Here are some sentences to get you going. Ask the children to drop in adjective/s – or decide whether they actually need one.

- *The cat purred.*
- *The dog bit the postman's leg.*
- *I like to eat sandwiches with cucumber, ham and cheese in them.*
- *The car rushed past the donkey.*
- *On the moor, Jim could see the clouds drifting by and hear the skylarks singing.*

The adjective X Factor

Put up a similar sentence say three or four times but in each version use different adjectives. The children give each one a rating on a scale of one to ten, rather like in the TV show 'The X Factor', by holding up their fingers or writing a score on a mini whiteboard. Brief discussion in pairs can be useful. Choose several children to come out and explain their rating, justifying their choice as if they were judges. Here is one to get you going. Which is the most effective? Rate it and be ready to justify.

1. *Finally, the woman bent down, blew the feathers from Kinga's shoulders and picked up the shield.*
2. *Finally, the old woman bent down, blew the soft feathers from Kinga's bony shoulders and picked up the gleaming shield.*
3. *Finally, the wicked woman bent down, blew the furry feathers from Kinga's shallow shoulders and picked up the shiny shield.*
4. *Finally, the strange woman bent down, blew the swan's feathers from Kinga's tired shoulders and picked up the steel shield.*

Try and tease out conclusions about using adjectives:

- *choose carefully;*
- *think about their meaning;*
- *make sure they add to the description.*

How to use them?

Put up a sentence such as this one: *The cold, frozen, frosted, chilly icicle glittered.*

Get children to rate it on a scale of one to ten for effectiveness. Discuss the choice of adjectives – do you need one? If so, which? Aren't all icicles cold? Why tell the reader what they already know?

Begin to make explicit that when writing, it is crucial to choose with care. Do you always need an adjective? What happens if you use too many? Do the adjectives mean the same? Does the adjective tell the reader what they already know – or does it add something new?

A well-chosen adjective should add something new that the reader needs to know. Try using the sentences overleaf to develop the discussion about the choice and use of adjectives. I have completed the comment boxes for you but let the children discuss and begin to shape their own conclusions. These will be refined over time through constant reading, writing and discussion. Look out for other examples in their own writing to work on. One simple game is for children to select a sentence from their writing, read it aloud and explain why they think it works/does not work.

Original sentence	Comment
The tiny flea was impossible to see.	Do we need *tiny* if it was impossible to see?
The large, big, enormous, massive skyscraper exploded.	Skyscrapers are big by definition – don't tell the reader the obvious.
The sleepy, exhausted elf slept for a whole day.	Avoid repeating adjectives that mean something similar.
The red shoe was bright scarlet.	Repetition.
The cold ice had frozen.	If it is frozen, then it will be cold!
The kind giant knelt.	Well-chosen.

Comment

Play this game many times, and not just with adjectives. Writing is about choosing the right word for the job. In these four sentences, I have made some pretty poor choices. Can the children improve the sentences and explain what works and why/ what does not work and why?

a. *The slim, thin, slender, sleek snake slid by.*
b. *The ancient goblin was old.*
c. *The wet water drifted down the polluted stream.*
d. *The huge dog slipped through the catflap.*

It is worth noting that in 'c' the word *polluted* does add something new that might lead the story forwards.

Out of these games, children might draw the following conclusions.

1. *Only use an adjective to add something new that the reader needs to know.*
2. *Avoid telling the reader something obvious.*
3. *Do not use too many.*
4. *Avoid using adjectives that mean the same thing.*
5. *Avoid repetition.*
6. *Read your sentence aloud and listen to it to hear whether it works.*
7. *Collect and try using surprising adjectives.*

Basic Writing Toolkit Ingredient

Use this activity to add any useful new ingredients to the writer's basic toolkit that you are co-constructing with the class.

Label the effect

Provide a sentence in which you have used different adjectives and the children have to decide the effect that the writer is creating. The key to this sort of game is the quality of discussion that surrounds the choice and reasoning:

1. *Master Barnaby clambered up the rickety ladder, plucked the rotting apples and placed them carefully into the broken basket.*

2. *Master Barnaby clambered up the sky-blue ladder, plucked the juicy, red apples and placed them carefully into the ornate, wicker basket.*

3. *Master Barnaby clambered up the electronic ladder, plucked the luminous apples and placed them carefully into the computerised basket.*

To me, the first sentence sounds dangerous: something is going to go wrong! The second is much more upbeat and is at a place in a story when everything is going well. The third sounds as if it is from a futuristic story set in another world.

Change the mood

Divide the class in half – one half adds adjectives that will create a positive sentence and the other half adds negative choices:

> *The _______ girl sat on the ________ chair and stared at the _______ painting.*

The positive side might write:

> *The pretty girl sat on the comfy chair and stared at the delicate painting.*

The negative side might write:

> *The cruel girl sat on the broken chair and stared at the ruined painting.*

Now ask them to select a mood and rewrite their sentence, changing only the adjectives.

Mood	**My example**
Comic	*The ______ girl sat on the _______ chair and stared at the ______ painting.*
Frightening	*The ______ girl sat on the _______ chair and stared at the ______ painting.*
Heroic	*The ______ girl sat on the _______ chair and stared at the ______ painting.*
Threatening	*The ______ girl sat on the _______ chair and stared at the ______ painting.*
Calm	*The ______ girl sat on the _______ chair and stared at the ______ painting.*
Excited	*The ______ girl sat on the _______ chair and stared at the ______ painting.*
Gloomy	*The ______ girl sat on the _______ chair and stared at the ______ painting.*

Having played around with the sentences and seen how a change of adjective can influence the mood and atmosphere of a piece of writing, now try working on a paragraph. Take the example below and split the class in two – one half has to make the writing sound upbeat and the other side has to aim for a negative effect:

> *Barry stared at the ______ burger. Outside the ______ window, a ______ wind swept across the ______ town. ______ cars purred by and on the ______ promenade, ______ newspapers tumbled along, driven by the ______ wind. The ______ sea rolled up the _______ beach, crashing against the _______ rocks that fringed the ______ shoreline.*

Negative version

Barry stared at the stale burger. Outside the grimy window, a biting wind swept across the derelict town. Ominous cars purred by and, on the empty promenade, old newspapers tumbled along, driven by the cruel wind. The bitter sea rolled up the empty beach, crashing against the jagged rocks that fringed the polluted shoreline.

Positive version

Barry stared at the juicy burger. Outside the sparkling window, a warm wind swept across the tropical town. Colourful cars purred by and, on the bustling promenade, today's newspapers tumbled along, driven by the whispering wind. The warm sea rolled up the beautiful beach, crashing against the distant rocks that fringed the sandy shoreline.

Share my examples and ask the class to discuss the effect of the different pieces. What do they see in their mind? Draw attention to the fact that all I have done is change the adjectives – they can be great mood creators and changers.

For sale

In this little game, the impact of the adjective becomes obvious. Present something like the following for the children to work on. It is a *sale notice* for a house ... but the wrong adjectives have been used. Re-write it, changing the adjectives. Whose is the most persuasive?

Original

For sale

This is a filthy, tiny house with a crumbling balcony. Dreadful views of one of the ugliest gardens on the frightful estate. Damp walls, dirty carpets and peeling wallpaper throughout. The kitchen floor has rotten floorboards and damaged cupboards. In the cold bathroom, you will find a stained bath, cold water and a broken sink. The cracked lampshades in the shabby sitting room are a depressing feature and the soiled sofa provides a disastrous place to sit. Outside, there is a polluted pond, an uncared for garden and this is all rounded off by the deafening noise from the crowded beach and local amusement arcade.

My version

For sale

This is a bright, cheerful house with a well-placed balcony. Amazing views of one of the prettiest gardens on the brand new estate. Decorated walls, plush carpets and fine wallpaper throughout. The kitchen floor has wooden floorboards and spacious cupboards. In the ideal bathroom, you will find a deep bath, steaming hot water and a steel sink. The designer lampshades in the cosy sitting room are an attractive feature and the patterned sofa provides a comfy place to sit. Outside, there is a goldfish pond, a pretty garden and this is all rounded off by the soothing noise from the sandy beach and distant amusement arcade.

Three-word descriptive poems

Provide what you think might be a fruitful starting point for the children. For instance, you might put up an image of a football crowd/match on the screen. The children then make a list of things that they can see (nouns), provide a describing word for each one (adjectives) and an appropriate verb. You could use a three-column sheet. Here are some ideas I jotted down about a football match so you can see what I mean (I have included a rhyme just for fun though this isn't necessary and for some children becomes too much of a constraint).

Adjective	Noun	Verb
bright	*banners*	*wave*
desperate	*players*	*save*
sagging	*net*	*crashes*
leathery	*football*	*smashes*

Synonyms and antonyms

One key way to improve children's vocabularies is to build up a strong bank of synonyms so that children have a choice of words to use when writing. Synonyms are words that have the same meaning, eg *wet/damp*; antonyms are words that mean the opposite, eg *cold/hot*. This could just be a quick-burst activity where you provide a few words and the children list as many possible synonyms or antonyms. Here are some to get you going:

Chosen adjective	Possible synonyms	Possible antonyms
hot		
light		
big		
tired		
clever		
soft		
still		
funny		
weak		
sharp		
kind		
clean		
nice		

The spelling game

To create an antonym, some words just use the prefix *un*. A quick warm up might be to see who can list the most *un* words in a minute – *unhelpful, unkind, unwelcome, unpleasant*, etc. Make the game more fun by then seeing who can write a sentence using as many of the *un* words as possible:

> *Although Barry had been unhelpful about making the unkind parrot so unwelcome, Bernice decided not to make the situation any more unpleasant.*

The adjective generator

This quick activity is an adjective race. How many adjectives can be generated within a given time limit? The children are trying to think of different types of adjective. I've filled some ideas into the different sections so you can see what I mean.

Descriptive	Colour	Size	Feelings
frail, fragile, delicate, smooth, rough	*blue, yellow, green, orange, brown, purple, violet, indigo, emerald*	*small, tiny, minute, minuscule, large, huge, great, swollen, colossal*	*scared, happy, joyful, tearful, miserable, sad, angry, cross, irate*

Another way to play the same game is to list adjectives to do with the sense.

Touch	Taste	Look	Smell	Hear
smooth	*bitter*	*shiny*	*acrid*	*loud*
hot	*sour*	*gleaming*	*smoky*	*silent*
cool	*sweet*	*glittery*	*stale*	*rasping*

Nouns and verbs as adjectives

Eagle-eyed grammarians will have noticed that sometimes nouns can behave as adjectives – *the* ***school*** *boy, the* ***school*** *bag, the* ***school*** *hall, the* ***school*** *playground.* Verbs can also behave as adjectives – *the* ***racing*** *bike, the* ***running*** *track,* ***swimming*** *pool* (see participle in the glossary).

WHAT ARE NOUN PHRASES?

Nouns are one of the key building blocks of language and thought. They label the world and bring it into being. When writing, children can be shown how to make more of a noun by learning how to add to the noun and tell the reader more, adapting the meaning and building a clearer picture of the noun. A noun phrase works as a single unit of meaning.

You know that you have a noun phrase because it can be replaced by a pronoun:

> ***The tall man from across the road who grows pears*** *is ill.*
> ***He*** *is ill.*

You can build a noun phrase by placing modifiers before or after it. These help you build the picture bit by bit. They can help you be more descriptive. It is the difference between:

> ***The camel*** *slept.*
> *and*
> ***The ragged camel, which was weary after travelling so far****, slept.*

Noun phrases are also useful when writing non-fiction and you need to be precise. It is the difference between

> *Turn* ***the switch*** *carefully.*
> *and*
> *Turn* ***the blue switch at the top of the box*** *carefully.*

Play some games in which children start building noun towers.

- Start with one noun – ***ship***.
- Now add on a determiner – *a, the, some, my, that*. The determiners tell us which one, which ship – ***my ship***.
- Now add in an adjective to describe the ship more clearly – ***my red ship***. You now have an expanded noun phrase.
- Now try using a prepositional phrase to explain where the ship is located (*on the sea, at the end of the harbour, across the ocean, under the sea*) – ***My red ship on the boating pool***.
- Build the picture further with a subordinate clause – ***My red ship on the boating pool that is deep***.
- To complete the sentence add on a verb to the expanded noun phrase – ***My red ship on the boating pool that is deep*** *has crashed*.

Having worked through an example such as the one above, use a simple grid to help children build expanded noun phrases.

determiner	adjectives	noun	prepositional phrase	who/ which/ that, ing or ed clause
a, the, any this, that, my, our, your, those	*cool, cold, hot, strange, red, thin, bright*	*dog, car, house, sea, eagle, marble, bus*	*across the road, on the fridge, under the chair, beside the sea*	*who is hungry* *that is sinking* *which is heavy* *which is crafty* *hissing to itself* *stunned by the sun*

From the above grid a number of slightly surreal noun phrases could be created:

> *The cool marble on the fridge which is crafty…*
> *That thin car under the chair hissing to itself…*

Noun towers

Another way into noun phrase building is to use a sequence of simple questions:

What is it?	*dog*	noun
Which one?	*that dog*	determiner
What is it like?	*that savage white dog*	adjective
Where is it?	*that savage white dog in the road*	preposition phrase
What is it doing?	*that savage white dog in the road growling at me….*	clause

Of course, when writing, the danger of the noun phrase is that children overwrite. The answer to this concern is to read the writing aloud and listen – does it sound over elaborate? If in doubt, trim back. If there is a choice between a simple way of saying something and a complicated string of language, choose the simple way. The aim of writing is to communicate and not to befuddle or show off. However, playing around with building noun phrases can help children begin to add description into their writing as well as being more precise in their non-fiction composition.

In non-fiction, noun phrases are often used to provide accurate names – *the lesser-spotted Burgundian ridgeback dragon.* They are used to be precise – *only use fine-grained brown sugar from the Cayman Islands,* and exacting about a category – *Politicians who have voted for this bill.* Instructions and directions often have to use noun phrases in order to be exact – *Turn left at the red house on the edge of the pond where the reeds are overgrown.*

Noun phrase descriptions

Use children's experience of building noun phrases to write simple descriptive poems. These might be built around describing a scene or a character. Use an image to help the children spot the details. Begin by listing the nouns – the key things that you want to describe. Then build the descriptions. In the following examples, the noun phrases are in bold.

A city scene

The sturdy city clock at the side of the road *... ticks its way through the night.*
The thin willow trees on the distant hill *... stoop in the breeze.*

A character description

His red, swollen nose *... juts out.*
The thin hair on the top of his head *... straggles.*

What job does the word do?

There are some words that have several meanings or jobs in a sentence and often can be used as both nouns and verbs. Try collecting these. In this game, you provide the children with a list of such words and they have to use them in sentences showing both their meanings (a few words may have more than two meanings).

The ***waves*** *pounded the beach.* (noun)
She ***waves*** *goodbye.* (verb)

watch, ink, box, trip, arm, match, jam, bat, arm, bark, club, fan, lie, rock, saw, bear, lead

Words which are spelled the same but have different meanings are called homonyms – same spelling, different meaning. Can the children write a sentence with all the possible meanings for these words?

He picked up the ***bat*** *and tried to* ***bat*** *away the* ***bat*** *as it flew.*

WHAT ARE PRONOUNS?

Use the following games to help children understand the function of **pronouns. The clue to the job of the pronoun is in the word 'pro-noun' – at its simplest, it is a word that stands in place of a noun**:

> *The dog looked at the sandwich and then **it** ate **it**.*

It is a pronoun, standing in place of the nouns *dog* and *sandwich*. Pronouns can stand in the place of words, phrases and ideas. They are helpful because they help writers not having to repeat themselves.

When writing, be careful not to confuse the reader:

> *The dog looked at the cat and **it** chased **it** till **it** was tired and **it** had to lie down and sleep.*

In the above sentence, the reader might well be unsure about who became tired and had to sleep – the cat or the dog? The basic test for a pronoun is to decide whether or not it stands in place of a noun.

Relative pronouns – these are pronouns (such as *who, which, that, whom, whose*) used in a relative clause that relate back to something already mentioned: *The boy, **who** was crying, ran down the lane.*

Possessive pronouns – these are pronouns that show ownership: *mine, ours, yours, his, hers, its, theirs*

Sort it

This is a rapid sorting game. List the main pronouns in no specific order. The children have several minutes to organise them as they see fit.

I, you, we, he, she, they, you, it

Can they categorise them in any way? This might be best done in pairs. Some will manage to sort them by singular or plural –

I, you, he, she, it	*we, they, you*

Then see if they can pair them up – which singular one matches with which plural.

I	we
you	you
he, she, it	they

Ask the children to explain why the word *I* is always a capital letter (because we are special).

This sorting game is more demanding. Sort these pronouns into two groups by deciding which can be used as the subject of a sentence and which are used as the object of a sentence. I have presented them below split into their respective groups so muddle them up when playing the game.

Subject	**Object**
I, you, he, she, it, we, you, they	me, you, him, her, it, us, you, them

What you are

Roger McGough wrote a poem many years ago called *What you are*. The poem is a list of metaphors. I borrowed the idea and tried writing different versions with my first class. I found that children enjoyed listing ideas using a simple frame: *I am, you are, he is, she is, it is, we are, they are …*

In this first example, Matthew (seven years old) lists similes:

> *She is like a golden star,*
> *Slinking into the night.*
> *She is like a flower of light.*
> *She is like a silent pair of lips*
> *saying something unknown.*
> *She is like a brilliant spurt of love.*
> *She is like an ungrateful silence.*

In the companion poem, Tim changed tactic:

> *He is in a misty cloud*
> *That floats through a bewildered sky.*
> *He is in a swirling smoke*
> *That bows at his honour.*
> *He is in a sharp flash*
> *Of fierce lightning.*

He is the sharp blade
Of a golden knife.
He is a buzzing fly
That shimmers in a velvet web.

Improve it

Provide a short paragraph where there are too many pronouns so that the meaning is easily lost. What is the problem? How can it be fixed? Can the children get the balance between nouns/pronouns?

The unicorn flew down the lane towards the dragon. It stared at it as it landed and wondered if it was friendly. It snorted at it and it waited. It eyed it and it was uncertain what to do. It turned and flew off leaving it behind. It sighed, relieved that it was gone.

Try the game the other way round so that this time there are too many nouns. Young writers tend to pass through a phase when they overuse the noun and cannot quite hear that they can use a pronoun to help their writing flow. Here is an example for children to work on – what is wrong? How can it be solved?

On a tall, bare hill overlooking the camp, Steve lay and watched. Far below Steve, Steve could just make out the soldiers. The children were marching up and down. Mr Jenkins was barking out commands as the children plodded wearily up and down. The children looked tired beyond belief but Mr Jenkins did not seem to notice the children. Mr Jenkins shouted at the children. The children responded. Mr Jenkins shouted again, enjoying Mr Jenkins' control over the children. Steve gritted Steve's teeth and clenched Steve's fist. Steve knew that Steve had to rescue the children before Mr Jenkins went any further.

Cloze – insert the pronoun

Try a simple cloze where you omit all the pronouns. This is easily prepared with the advent of the computer and interactive whiteboard and makes a focused activity for the start of a session – here is one prepared for you.

The grin that crossed the orc's face was almost as wide as the tunnel in which ____ lived. Shuffling, ____ plodded into the underground lair. Steve decided to follow. ____ waited till the orc had disappeared and then _____ began to follow _____. Carefully, _____ entered the darkness. What ____ did not know was that Sharon had followed ____. ______ both tiptoed forwards but Steve was unaware that ____ was just behind ____. ____ paused in the darkness and listened. _____ could hear something breathing behind _____. Sharon waited, controlling her breathing. Had ____ heard ____? Was ____ safe?

Swap it

In this game, take a series of sentences or paragraphs and swap the pronouns around. The children have a few minutes to try and sort the meaning out. Here is an example:

Them walked for most of the day with the wind behind they. When her reached the camp, Sharon put up they tent. Clive and Derek put up I tent as well as Kim who had I own. Their snored and so no one would share with I. Him made sure that her was sleeping by the fire. Sharon cooked I own meal but the boys cooked it meal in the camp kitchen. I ate by the stream whilst my made he way into the forest. As their wandered into the darkness, his heard they.

Swap it – The silly vegetable game

In this game, the pronouns in a paragraph have been swapped with the names of vegetables. You can play this with younger children by just using sentences, as in the first example below. You will want to invent your own sentences.

While potato was feeding the cat, carrot purred.

Original: *While I was feeding the cat, it purred.*

When the cat chased the bird, Mrs Jenkins shouted at cauliflower. Then tomato ran across the lawn, chasing cucumber out of the garden. Tomato picked the bird up and stroked marrow. Marrow hopped onto bean shoulder and pecked bean cheek. Tomato thought that marrow was the friendliest bird that tomato had ever met.

Original: *When the cat chased the bird, Mrs Jenkins shouted at it. Then she ran across the lawn, chasing it out of the garden. She picked the bird up and stroked it. It hopped onto her shoulder and pecked her cheek. She thought that it was the friendliest bird that she had ever met.*

Whose is it?

Ask the children if they can work out what this group of pronouns has in common. They are all possessive pronouns. These are pronouns that show ownership – to whom something belongs. Can they sort the words into singular and plural?

mine, yours, his, hers, its, ours, yours, theirs

Singular	Plural
mine, yours, his, hers, its	ours, yours, theirs

In this passage, I have swapped the possessive pronouns around to cause confusion! First get the children to underline the possessive pronouns and then discuss the possibilities. Can the children sort it out? Say the passage aloud and weirdly it sounds right but if you look carefully, it cannot be.

'I own that computer game so it is yours not mine and the tennis racket belongs to Jack so it is hers not theirs. However, the tennis balls came from my family so they are his rather than theirs but the football has a team name on it so it must be hers,' said Joshua.

The original reads: *'I own that computer game so it is mine not yours and the tennis racket belongs to Jack so it is his not hers. However, the tennis balls came from my family so they are ours rather than yours but the football has a team name on it so it must be theirs,' said Joshua.*

Relative pronouns

Relative clauses use relative pronouns: *who, whom, whose, which, that*

These handy little fellows introduce a subordinate clause (a relative clause) telling us more about the noun that precedes it – they link one bit of the sentence to another:

> *Polly, **whose** feet were sore, stopped running.*
> *Jack stared at the running shoes **that** had been torn to shreds.*

***Which* or *that*?**

It can be hard to decide, when using the relative pronoun, whether to select *which* or *that*. A simple guide is to check whether the dropped in clause can be taken out of the sentence with it still making complete sense – in which case, use *which*:

1. *The cat, **which** was hungry, licked its lips.*

In the next sentence, the relative clause is vital to the sentence and therefore requires *that*.

2. *The teacher read the boy's story **that** was full of mistakes.*

In sentence 2, while you can take the relative clause away and the sentence still makes sense, the reader would be unaware of the key point that the story is full of mistakes.

Commas or no commas
The *which/that* dilemma holds the key to whether you need to put commas round the relative clause or not – if the clause is extra information that can be removed and the sentence still makes complete sense, then it needs commas to separate it from the main clause as in sentence 1 above. But, if the clause is vital to the sense of the sentence, then you don't use commas, as in sentence 2 above.

The drop-in game
It is worth teaching children to 'drop' relative clauses into sentences. It is a handy way to add in extra information about a character or object:

*Mrs Tinklenose, **who was tired of sneezing**, lay down to sleep.*

*The car **that was bright blue** stood at the roadside whereas the yellow one was parked on the playground.*

*Red kites, **which are on the increase in England**, were once almost hunted to extinction.*

Practise 'dropping in' relative clauses into simple sentences, model this in shared writing and encourage children to experiment in their own writing. Demonstrate when you need the commas to separate off the clause and when you don't. Here are a few sentences to get you going:

Mrs Hardy glared at the shark.

Sonny picked up the frozen carrot.

Whales are rare.

Reflexive pronouns
This little bunch of pronouns is known as reflexive pronouns because they reflect back to a previously mentioned noun or pronoun:

myself, yourself, himself, herself, itself, ourselves, yourselves, themselves

For instance: *Tom sat on the train wondering to himself if he would arrive on time.*

You could provide several such sentences and ask the children to link up the pronoun and the noun or pronoun that it relates back to. Here are some to get you going:

> *He had a secret and he knew to keep it to himself.*
> *Boris and his aunty kept the doughnuts for themselves.*
> *Sheila picked up the last custard cream without anyone seeing and decided it was best kept for herself.*

The I/me confusion

It is common in certain areas for children to say, *Me and my friend ran home* but grammatically the standard convention when writing formally should be to write, *My friend and I ran home*. Take the friend out of the sentence for a moment and you would be left with:

> *Me ran home.*

Most children can hear that this is an immature construction and, faced with the choice, would say that *I ran home* is the standard version. Now ask the class who should be put first in the sentence if we are being polite? This then gives you:

> *My friend and I ran home.*

Give the class a few simple sentences to correct like

> *Ed and I/me ate all the doughnuts.*
> *The doughnuts were eaten by Ed and I/me.*
> *Jo and I/me were frightened of the dog.*
> *The dog frightened Jo and I/me.*

See if they can come up with the solution for when to use *I* and when to use *me*.

WHAT ARE DETERMINERS?

Use the activities below to draw out from the children that **a determiner is like a special adjective that pins down precisely which noun is being talked about**. In most instances a noun cannot stand on its own in a sentence and needs, at the least, what is called a 'determiner' to help us know which particular thing is being referred to. We do not say:

Dog barked at man.

Rather, we specify which dog and which man by using determiners and say

That *dog barked at* ***this*** *man.*

So, determiners come before a noun (or noun phrase) and determine the number or definiteness of the noun:

articles – *a, an, the*

demonstratives – *this, that, those, these*

possessives – *my, your, his, her, its, our, their*

quantifiers – *many, few, some, any, no, much, both, all, every, each, none of, a little*, etc.

numbers – *two, three, second, first*, etc.

some question words – *which (which dog), what (what time), whose (whose handbag)*

Determiners help you pin down exactly what is being referred to:

a *spider*
two *spindly spiders*
which *spider?*
I'm looking for ***my*** *black hat.*
Is it ***that*** *gangster hat?*

A really useful aspect of determiners is that the articles *a/an* or *the* can tell you whether it is a particular thing that is being talked about or just any old thing.

Look at these sentences:

> ***A** dog bit me.* (It could be any dog.)
> ***The** dog bit me.* (This refers to a particular dog.)
> ***A** man walked down the road.* (This indicates an unknown man.)
> ***The** man walked down the road.* (This refers to a particular man.)

A and *an* are known as indefinite articles – this is because it is unclear/indefinite about which thing is being discussed.

The is the definite article because we know which particular thing is being referred to.

'The' is an important part of the English language and it is worth knowing that not every language uses a definite article in the same way. Languages like Punjabi, Urdu and Turkish do not have an actual word for *the* but use a grammatical construction instead. To develop the habit of using an article correctly, make sure that you model clearly sentences using *a, an* or *the* as well as recasting sentences if children omit *the/a/an.* For activities to help children know when to use *an* instead of *a* see pages 49–50.

Cloze – insert the determiners

A shift in the determiner can alter the emphasis in a sentence. Try omitting them and see how it changes what happens.

_____ *afternoon,* _____ *dog will bite* ______ *leg.*

This seemingly simple sentence can be changed considerably:

> ***Every** afternoon, **that** dog will bite **each** leg.*
> ***This** afternoon, **my** dog will bite **your** leg.*

Here are some sentences to play around with.

___ *soldier rushed to* ____ *road as* ____ *ambulance pulled up.*

Look at ______ *man stealing* ______ *handbags.*

I like ______ *scarf and* _____ *rings.*

_____ *dog growled at* ______ *cat.*

_______ *snakes swim.*

The determiner challenge

I have muddled up all the determiners in this paragraph. See if the children can reorder it so it makes good sense.

> ***Each*** *baker grinned as he turned* ***a*** *pies over. They were cooked on* ***a*** *sides.* ***Three*** *pie had* ***the*** *beautiful crust.* ***The two*** *cat sidled up to* ***our*** *safe hiding place,* ***the*** *eyes scanning for scraps.* ***All*** *passing dog stared in at* ***that*** *door.* ***Its*** *cook glared at* ***his*** *animals.*

Listen to several completed examples and discuss the different shades of meaning. At first, these seem like simple words – ones which we use all the time. After a while, you realise that they are crucial. This is one version:

> ***Our*** *baker grinned as he turned* ***three*** *pies over. They were cooked on* ***all*** *sides.* ***Each*** *pie had* ***that*** *beautiful crust.* ***His*** *cat sidled up to* ***a*** *safe hiding place,* ***its*** *eyes scanning for scraps.* ***A*** *passing dog stared in at* ***the*** *door.* ***The*** *cook glared at* ***the two*** *animals.*

Tricky pronouns/determiners

1. *It's* or *its*?

> *It's* = *It is* or *it has* – ***It's*** *raining.* ***It's*** *rained here.* (pronoun + apostrophe of omission)
> *Its* = belonging to it – *I have* ***its*** *collar*. (possessive pronoun/ determiner)

It is important to keep reminding children about this tricky point until they really know it. This can be done by occasional quick games where they have to decide whether to use an apostrophe or not. Try playing the game 'sentence doctor' in which they have some sentences that need correcting – or do they? Here are a few where I have omitted any apostrophes:

> *I wonder if its safe to go outside.*
> *Its going to rain on the dog so grab its collar.*
> *Its tiny feathers were coloured red.*
> *Do you know if its time to see its next programme?*

2. *Their* or *there* or *they're*?

Another tricky muddle comes about from these three customers. Once again, we can remember ***they're*** because it actually means *they are* and is therefore in the same category as *it's* and needs an apostrophe for the omitted letter.

Their and ***there*** are easily muddled unless children have developed the concept of ownership. *Their* is used when something belongs to someone else – it is a possessive determiner. *It is **their** dragon.*

There has two uses. It can be about place – it is related to the words *here* and *where*. *There* can also be used with the verb 'to be' (is, am, are, was, were), eg *There is a policeman.* In both cases, you can replace 'there' with 'here' and the sentence still makes sense. All three words are to do with place. I used to remember it when I was younger by thinking that *here* was inside ***there***.

> *Where is it?*
> *Here it is?*
> *Oh, there it is.*

Improve it

Again simple reminder games could be played where children have to decide which is right in a series of sentences, or they can act as 'sentence doctor' and correct sentences that contain errors. Here is a paragraph for sentence doctors where *there/their/they're* have all been spelled in the same way – incorrectly!

> *The camels stared at ther next meal whilst the riders picked up ther reward. Ther were three of them and they had travelled far to reach ther destination. 'Ther weary,' thought the chief as he gave them ther money and asked them to put ther bags down.' 'Over ther will do,' he said, catching ther glances. Ther a funny bunch, he thought. Ther camels chewed in silence.*

A *or* an?

One of the aspects of determiners that will concern many teachers of young children is the use of *a* or *an*. It helps if you recast what children say so that when they say *a apple* this is instantly recast by the listening adult and repeated as *an apple.* As children learn the basic rule that *an* is used before a vowel then you can shift to saying, *Should it be 'a apple' or 'an apple' – which sounds right?* The trick is to get them to hear and experience how much easier it is to say ***an** apple* than ***a** apple*. The *n* acts as a buffer to help us with the pronunciation.

When formally focusing on the concept, provide a list such as this and see if the children can work out the rule:

> *an ant; an apple; a balloon; a cup; a dog; an elephant; an engine; a frog; a giraffe; a horse; an ice cube; an igloo; a juggler; a kite; a lemon; a mouse; a newt; an orange; an owl; a parrot; a queen; a rat; a snake; a telephone; an underpass; an umbrella; a vest; a weekend; a yam; a zoo*

Every so often, provide a few sentences or a paragraph in which the *a/an* issue needs editing:

> *I have an ball and an bat.*
> *Can you see a eagle eating a ant?*

Playing with vowels and consonants

Of course, to understand whether to use *a* or *an*, the children will need to know vowels and consonants. It is easiest to teach the vowels and tell the class that the rest are consonants. This is simply a matter of endlessly talking about vowels/consonants in the context of other work. Have a display up that lists the vowels. Can anyone invent a sentence in which each word starts with the letters *a-e-i-o-u* that might act as a mnemonic? For example – *All Elephants Itch Offensively, Unsurprisingly* – *At Edinburgh I Often Undress.* A dictionary helps with this sort of activity! Once they have understood this, you can add that the consonant *y* is a bit of a hybrid as it sometimes functions like the vowel *i* as in *mystery, my, try, fry, cry, dry* and *rhythm*.

Games can be played where a bag of letters has to be sorted or words sorted by their initial letter. Plenty of good work on phonics should help to reinforce the notion of vowels as they are central to most words. Try altering vowels in cvc words (consonant-vowel-consonant): *cup, rat, top, sip, sat, pin*. Do any two consonants yield up five different words by changing the vowels? For instance, c/p yields *cap, cep* (type of mushroom), *cop, cup*. Experiment with ccvc words (consonant-consonant-vowel-consonant) such as *slip*.

CHAPTER 2

The actions

Verbs, adverbs, adverbials and prepositions

WHAT ARE VERBS?

The games below should help you draw out from the children that **a verb is a doing word that shows what someone or something** is, has or does: *It* ***is*** *hot today. He* ***has*** *a dog. She* ***walks*** *to school.* Verbs are like the engine of a sentence – they get things going. The activities help children understand that often several words form a verb phrase: *is leaving, was running, were waiting* etc and that verbs can be altered to show the time when the action took place. *I* ***run*** (present tense); *I* ***ran*** (past tense); ***I will run*** (future tense). There are also suggestions for how to help children understand the wide range of verbs created with auxiliary verbs like *have, be* and *can*: *I* ***am running*** (present progressive; *I* ***was running*** (past progressive). ***I have run*** (present perfect); ***I had run*** (past perfect/aka pluperfect) etc. (See glossary: **auxiliary** and **tense**.)

I Spy action

Once children have played *I Spy* to identify nouns (see page 2), ask them to choose things that they can see in the room (the nouns) and make each noun do, have and be something in turn – *The table* ***stands*** *on the floor. The table* ***has*** *four legs. The table* ***is*** *small.*

You could then suggest they look out of the window and carry on – *The tree* ***looks*** *beautiful. The tree* ***has*** *green leaves. The tree* ***is*** *very tall.* You may want to list the verbs they have chosen – *stands, looks, has, is* etc to help the class understand that doing words show what someone or something is, has or does and are called verbs.

Build on this by inviting them to suggest things that they might see in different places (the local town centre, shopping mall or park etc) and make these things do, have or be something. Help them see that all the things that they choose will be nouns but what the things do, have or are will be verbs and begin using the term verb when discussing reading and writing.

Now teddy is ...

This simple game involves any cuddly toy beloved by the class, eg a teddy. Make teddy move and get the class to tell you what teddy is doing. Then flip-chart all the actions they have identified and help the class to understand that action words are known as verbs.

Yesterday teddy was

Once the children are confident with saying what is happening to teddy now, help them know how to show that the action has already happened. Go back to your flip chart and see if the children can help you make all the actions in the past:

> *Teddy was walking* etc

Spot the odd ones out

This game helps children become confident at identifying verbs. The more the children are put in teacher role and have to talk about which words they have selected, the more confident they will become with grammar.

Choose the opening of any story that the class already knows well so that they are very familiar with the language they will be analysing. Highlight all the verbs (as illustrated below) but also highlight two or three different types of words that aren't functioning as verbs within the story (in this example, *your, square, but*). The class works in pairs/small groups to identify which highlighted words aren't verbs and how they know this.

> *Little Charlie*
> Once upon a time there **was** a little boy **called** Charlie who **lived** on the edge of a big city.
> Early one morning, when he **woke** up, his mother **said**, '**Take** this bag of goodies to **your** Grandma's.' Into the bag she **put** a slice of cheese, a loaf of bread and a square of chocolate.
> Next he **walked**, and he **walked** and he **walked** till he **came** to a bridge. There he **met** a cat – a lean cat, a mean cat.
> 'I'**m** hungry,' **said** the cat. 'What **have** you **got** in your bag?'

The missing verb detective (cloze game)

This game helps children see that verbs are key to understanding what is happening – without them meaning begins to collapse.

Find or write a paragraph related to a current class topic and omit the verbs, creating a simple cloze procedure. The children work in pairs or small groups to fill the gaps – the discussion around what words would fit is key here. Remind them that it is not a question of coming up with exactly the same choice of words as in the original, but of making certain that the words they choose make good sense. The children decide what 'sort' of word was missing and what is the 'job' of that type of word.

Cloze procedure	**One possible answer**
Mr Wiggle and Mr Waggle	***Mr Wiggle and Mr Waggle***
Once upon a time there … two friends – Mr Wiggle and Mr Waggle. Mr Wiggle … in this house and Mr Waggle … in that house.	*Once upon a time there* ***were*** *two friends – Mr Wiggle and Mr Waggle. Mr Wiggle* ***lived*** *in this house and Mr Waggle* ***lived*** *in that house.*
Early one morning, Mr Wiggle … ***to*** *… and … Mr Waggle. So he … up the door – eeeeeee! – … outside – POP! and … the door – eeeeeeee!*	*Early one morning, Mr Wiggle* ***decided to go*** *and* ***visit*** *Mr Waggle. So he* ***opened*** *up the door – eeeeeee!* ***popped*** *outside – POP! and* ***closed*** *the door – eeeeeeee!*

Make it happen now

Nouns are easier to pin down than verbs, which keep altering because they can change tense. Help children become more confident with tense by asking them to change the tense. Revisit a text you have already worked on to identify the verbs, for example *Little Charlie* (see page 53), but now ask the children to make it happen in the present.

Initially, it is probably best to model this as a whole-class activity. Through shared analysis, book-talk style, help the class to tell you that you can't begin a story in the present with the words *Once upon a time* because this immediately places the action in the past. Get them to tell you that the words actually spoken in a story (the direct speech) have to stay in the tense they are in for the story to make sense. Once you have worked together on the opening lines, as illustrated below, ask the class in pairs or small groups to finish recasting the story into the present tense. Then invite one group to come out and explain the changes they have made to the whole class.

> ***Little Charlie***
> **There is** a little boy **called** Charlie who **lives** on the edge of a big city.
>
> Early **in the** morning, when he **wakes** up his mother **says**, '**Take** this bag of goodies to your Grandma's.' Into the bag she **put** a slice of cheese, a loaf of bread and a square of chocolate.
>
> Next, he **walked**, and he **walked** and he **walked** till he **came** to a bridge. There he **met** a cat – a lean cat, a mean cat.
>
> '**I'm** hungry,' **said** the cat. 'What **have** you **got** in your bag?'

Spot the irregular verb

Children like spotting the verbs that don't follow the regular pattern, for example, *I go* = *I went* (not *I goed*); *I run* = *I ran* (not *I runned*). If the local dialect in your area uses a different version of a verb, for example, *go/goed*, explain that this is fine for informal speech but that they must use the standard form for formal speaking and writing, and recast their verbs for them so they practise using Standard English. You may want to explain that a form of south-eastern dialect became Standard English because it was the English used locally when the printing press was first developed in England. Challenge the class to see how many irregular verbs they can come up with. Create a poster of these and build them up as the children find them in their reading.

Irregular verbs

Present	**Past**
I go	I went
I run	I ran
I do	I did
I have	I had

Rhyming irregular verbs

This game helps older children remember irregular verbs and can also be a good source of words for a nonsense rhyme. As illustrated below, provide the class with a list of irregular verbs, a matching list of regular verbs that rhyme with the irregular ones in the present tense, and the present tense of the regular verbs. Ask the children to work out what the past tense would be if it rhymed with the past tense of the irregular verb and place the made-up word in a sentence, modelling what to do for the first few verbs.

Irregular verbs		**Regular verbs that happen to rhyme with the irregular verb**		
Present	**Past**	**Present**	**Past**	**Made-up past**
bleed/s	bled	need/s	needed	ned – I ned to go home.
blow/s	blew	glow/s	glowed	glew – It glewed in the dark.
catch/es	caught	hatch/es	hatched	haught – It haught out of the egg.
deal/s	dealt	heal/s		
dig/s	dug	rig/s		
eat/s	ate	heat/s		
fall/s	fell	call/s		
freeze/s	froze	breeze/s		
get/s	got	jet/s		
make/s	made	fake/s		

Alphabet action races

Help extend the children's vocabulary by setting an alphabetical alternative-words-for-x challenge. Use common verbs in the past tense like *said* or *walked* and set a short time limit. You may want to turn the children's words into posters, display them and then add to them later by asking the children to raid their reading and writing over the next few weeks and see if they can add to the lists.

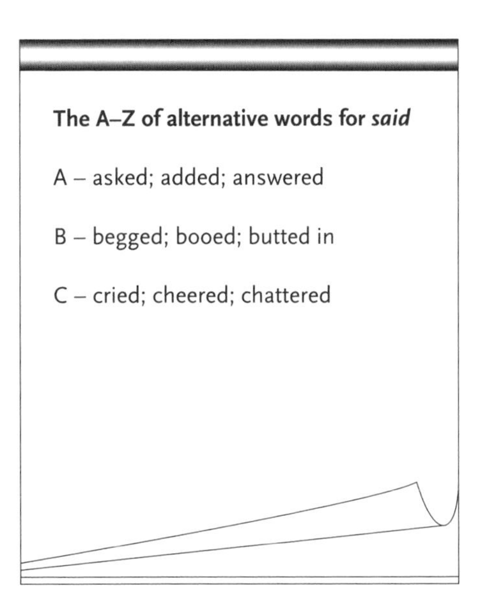

Make the verbs work

This game helps children consider the impact well-chosen verbs can have on the reader as well as helping build their vocabulary, so it makes a good follow-up activity to the alphabet game. It shows the children how choosing verbs with care can help the reader or listener build a picture and can be more powerful than adjectives or adverbs.

Take any everyday, much-used verb like *walked* or *said* and write your chosen word in the middle of your flip chart. Use the corners and the space above and below the word to draw out different shades of meaning, as illustrated below. Then model how to build alternatives showing how you can refine your choice of alternative word so that the verb chosen does the describing for you.

The alternative verbs for 'said' poster

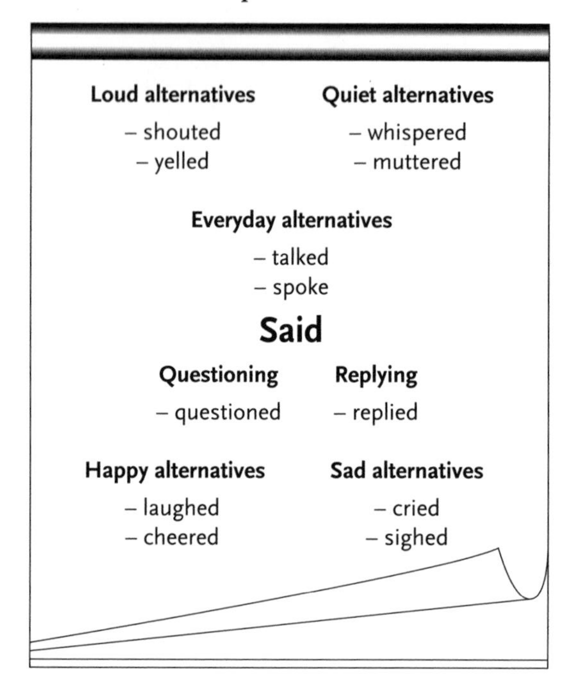

An alternative way of presenting this is to ask the children to place the words on a graph.

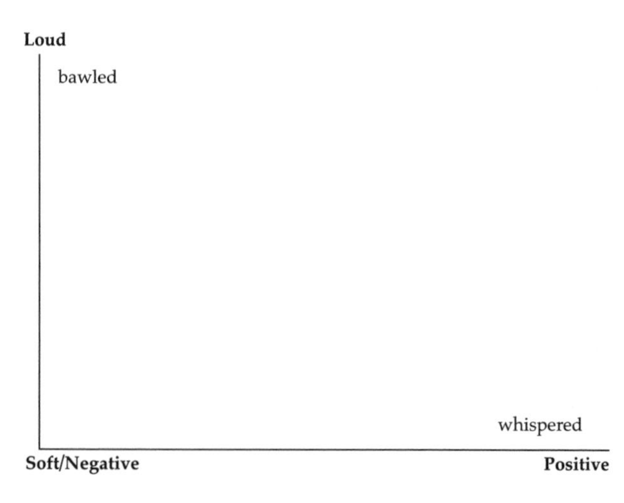

The alternative words can then be displayed to sharpen up the children's use of verbs in a wide range of writing activities. Add verbs to the lists from their reading and writing. Such posters could begin simply and be developed across a year and then go up the school with the class so that, term-on-term and year-on-year, they are building their vocabularies.

Basic Writing Toolkit Ingredient

You may want to use this activity to contribute to a writer's basic toolkit that you co-construct with the class. The class may decide on a wording like this:

- **choose powerful verbs that describe the action precisely.**

Bring-things-to-life game (personification)

Because personification (giving objects the feelings and attributes of living things) helps the reader picture what is being described, it is a good way of helping children select powerful verbs. It also helps them reflect on which words work best. This is a useful starter activity to warm up the children's imagination before writing related poems or descriptive writing.

Select the topic – for example, stormy weather – and provide the class with a short list of stormy weather conditions and a longer list of possible powerful verbs that are normally used for the actions of living things. Ask the children to select one verb for each weather condition and then compare their ideas and decide which is the most effective and why. Ask one group to feed back their ideas, getting them to explain their choices.

The things – nouns (in this example, different types of weather)	**The actions – verbs** (associated with living things)
wind fog rain mist	whispers; whistles; roars; shivers; screeches; groans; clasps; hugs; drowns; screams; creeps; blinds; dances; riots; rebels

Repetition doctor

Children like improving other people's writing. Help them remember to select an effective verb by writing or adapting a passage that has been ruined by the repetitive use of a verb like *said*. If you select a text the class is already familiar with, reading should not be a problem.

In pairs or small groups, give the children a copy of the story and ask them to read it aloud and replace the word *said* with a more effective verb so that there is only one *said* left in the story. You may want to display your *alternative-words-for-said* poster to help them.

> ***How long will it take?***
> One day the Hodja was chopping wood close to the road. After a while, a man came along the road walking towards Konya, and **said** to the Hodja, 'Can you tell me how long it will take to get to Konya?'
> The Hodja heard him and looked up from his work but **said nothing**. So the man **said again**, louder this time, 'How long will it take to get to Konya?'
> Still the Hodja **said nothing**. This time the man **said like a lion**, 'How long will it take to get to Konya?'
> When the Hodja yet again **said nothing**, the man decided he must be deaf and so he started walking rapidly toward the city. The Hodja watched him carefully for a moment and then **said**, 'It will take you about an hour!'
> 'Well, why didn't you say so before?' the man **said angrily**.
> 'First I had to know how fast you were going to walk,' **said** the Hodja.

Basic Writing Toolkit Ingredient

You may want to use this activity to contribute to a writer's basic toolkit that you co-construct with the class. The class may suggest an ingredient like the following:

- **Don't repeat words except for effect.**

Advanced alternative verb challenge

With older classes, challenge the children to come up with as many alternative verbs as possible for trickier verbs like '**shows**'. Give the pupils a sentence with the verb *shows* in relation to a story they have just read so there is a real context for their work, eg *This **shows** how sad the character is feeling.* The children then see how many alternatives they can think up in two minutes. You may want to display the words to support evaluative work.

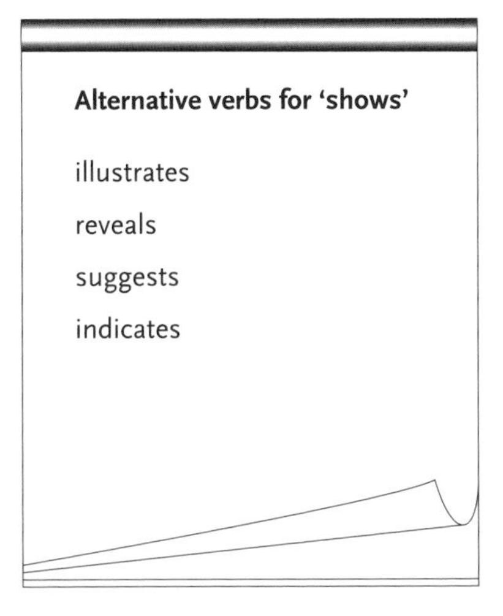

Is it a noun or is it a verb?

This game helps children see that language is a living thing. As new things are invented, so are new words – nouns to name them and verbs to help us express what they can do. The new thing tends to be named first and then the action. Often the same word can be the name or the action – it just depends on how it is used in the sentence. Help pupils understand that it is the way a word functions within a sentence that determines which word class it is. Make up sentences for the children to consider like the ones below and ask them to decide which is the noun and which is the verb in each case and how they know.

1. Ask Google. I always Google things I don't understand.
2. If I get a text from her, I'll text back.
3. I want to hoover the lounge but the hoover isn't working.
4. Now I've got my own blog, I blog every day.
5. Email him and explain that his email arrived too late.

The noun/verb challenge

Look back at any verb posters you have created and see if the same word could function as a noun. The children try to make up a sentence using each word from the poster twice, once as a noun and once as a verb.

1. The man said, '**Hop**!' and with one **hop** the rabbit was free.
2. The horse fell at the last **jump** because it couldn't **jump** that high.
3. The **iron** may burn my shirt if I **iron** it.

You may want to discuss that words are included or not included in dictionaries depending on whether they start to be used in written text. Commentators at the London Olympic Games in 2012 regularly shouted things like, *'He's medalled again!'* Many people felt this wasn't the correct use of the word but the Oxford Dictionary cites its first written usage as being in an American newspaper in 1966.

What difference a prefix can make

A good way of extending the children's vocabulary and the range of verbs they can use is to ask the children to work out the meaning of common prefixes that alter the meaning of verbs. Use a grid like the one below at the right level for the class.

Prefix	**Verbs including this prefix**	**Meaning of the prefix**
re	return; revisit; reappear	
dis	distrust; disappear; discontinue	
over	overturn; overtake; oversee	
un	undo; unfasten; unwrap	
mis	mistake; misunderstand; misspell	
co	co-operate; co-construct; co-exist	
de	deport; depose; depress	
pre	preposition; preheat; preview	
sub	subtract; subdivide; subdue	

Through discussion, help the children establish the following meanings: re – again/back; dis – reverses meaning; over – too much; un – reverses meaning; mis – badly/wrongly; co – together; de – do the opposite of; pre – before; sub – under/below.

HOW TO HELP CHILDREN UNDERSTAND TENSE, MODAL VERBS AND MOOD

The tense of a verb indicates the time at which an action takes place – whether in the present, the past or the future. (Technically the future is not a tense in English but is usually formed by using the auxiliary verb *will*. However, it is practical to call it the future tense, otherwise you may end up confusing everyone, including yourself!) Sorting activities are a useful way of helping children understand how the basic past, present and future tenses are formed. With the help of a few auxiliaries, verbs can indicate whether the action happened further in the past, is planned to happen in the future or whether it is likely to happen at all. Tense in all its possible forms is best understood in context via reading.

Teddy walks or Teddy is walking?

It's always a good idea to internalise the language patterns before naming the parts. First make sure that the children, when speaking or writing, have become confident automatic users of the simple present and past (*walks/walked*) and the present progressive and past progressive (*is walking/ was walking*) – sometimes known more usefully as the present/past continuous because the tense indicates that the action is continuing. The present/past tense are key terms and once the children implicitly know the difference, they should be introduced to these terms. Sometimes the use of more obscure grammatical terms, rather than aiding understanding, can just cause confusion. You may want to refer to the *is/are* present and the *was/were* past until the children are very confident users of the present/ past progressive.

Once the children are older, this game will help them explicitly identify the different tenses and what they help us express.

Construct a group of four sentences, preferably related to work the class is currently doing, structured like the ones below. The task works best if presented as a sorting activity as this encourages real discussion. Ask the class in pairs or small groups to match the sentence to the type of tense and its purpose:

A. **Simple present** (This tense allows us to talk about things that don't change like facts, habits or regularly repeated actions, for example the things we like or don't like.)

B. **Present progressive** (This tense allows us to talk about things that are happening now and haven't finished yet.)

C. **Simple past** (This tense states the action has already happened.)

D. **Past progressive** (This tense is often used to refer to things that happened at a particular moment in the past.)

1. *Sam often reads, plays on the computer and goes cycling.*

2. *Sam often read, played on the computer and went cycling.*

3. *Sam is playing on the computer.*

4. *Sam was playing on the computer when the front door bell rang.*

Ask groups to feed back and then ask them in pairs to write two more examples for each type of tense about anything they are currently working on. Reinforce understanding by referring to the use of these tenses in any text being read with the class. In particular, look out for examples like the one below where the simple past and the progressive past are used together in the same sentence:

> *As I **was walking** to school this morning, a man **ran** past quickly **pursued** by another man.*

Here the past progressive describes the context and the simple past describes the actions or events. Model this type of sentence in shared writing.

Tense doctor

Find pieces of text related to work you are doing with the class that move between the past and the present tense. Remove ***was/were, is/are*** from these sentences and ask the children in pairs to work out what the correct version should be. The children should be prepared to be in role as tense doctors and explain how they know they are right.

1. *Wolves … once very common in Britain but now they … only seen in zoos.*
2. *In the past, wood … often used to heat houses but today it … not so usual.*
3. *Smoking ... a much more widespread habit fifty years ago than it … today.*
4. *Although the Pyramids … built over 4,000 years ago, they … still standing.*
5. *Rats … the cause of plagues in the past and … still spreading diseases today.*

When did it happen?

Provide the children with sets of sentence cards with shaded headings like the ones below, preferably focusing on a topic they are currently working on. Ask the children in small groups to place each sentence under the appropriate heading by asking if:

The action is in the **past** – already happened eg *The dog ate the bone.*	The action is in the **present** – happening now eg *The dog is eating the bone.*	The action is in the **future** – has not happened yet eg *The dog will eat the bone.*
*The parrot **sat** in its cage.*	*The parrot **sits** in its cage.*	*The parrot **will sit** in its cage.*
*The parrot **was sitting** in its cage.*	*The parrot **is sitting** in its cage.*	*The parrot **is going to sit** in its cage.*
*The parrot **had sat** in its cage.*		
*The parrot **had been sitting** in its cage.*		
*The parrot **was told to sit** in its cage.*		
*The parrot **used to sit** in its cage.*		

Once they have sorted the sentences, explain that most of the sentences in each group are almost identical in meaning but some do have a different meaning. Ask them to discuss if they can see any differences in meaning in all the sentences in the past. Then do the same with the sentences in the present and the future. When reading with the class, help the children to notice these differences and the meanings they infer.

The 'had' and the 'have' past

As long as children hear and read good English, using the full range of tenses on a regular basis, they will quickly pick up how to automatically use what some grammarians refer to as the perfect forms of the past tense. These tenses are used to indicate whether the past action is continuing or whether something happened even earlier than the past time being considered. Children will understand how these tenses work if you call them *the have* or *the had past* since it is these common auxiliary verbs that feature in this tense. Many excellent teachers feel that this is sufficient as sometimes the more complicated terminology gets in the way of understanding. Primary teachers in England, where children will be confronted by questions about the perfect tense, may want to use the following activity.

To move from implicit to explicit understanding of the perfect tenses, explain to the children that in English we often use 'helper' verbs (auxiliary verbs) like *to have* to support the main verb in expressing additional meaning. Then construct a group of four sentences, preferably related to work the class is currently doing, structured like the ones below. The task works best if presented as a sorting activity as this encourages real discussion. Ask the class in pairs or small groups to match the sentence to the type of tense and its purpose:

A. **Simple present** (This tense allows us to talk about things that don't change like facts, habits or regularly repeated actions, for example the things we like or don't like.)	B. **Simple past** (This tense states the action has already happened.)
C. **Present perfect – the *have* past** (This tense suggests either that an action has been completed – 'perfected' – or that an action that started in the past now continues in the present.)	D. **Past perfect/pluperfect – the *had* past** (This tense is used to refer to something that occurred earlier than the time being considered, when the time being considered is already in the past.)

I eat cakes.

I ate two cakes and then I felt sick.

I have eaten all the cakes and now I feel sick.

By the end of the party, I had eaten all the cakes and felt very sick.

Ask groups to feed back and then ask them to construct some further examples of their own. Reinforce understanding by referring to the use of these tenses in any text being read with the class and model this type of sentence in shared writing. Ask the children to discuss why the different tenses are being used.

The modal verb puzzle

The trickiest tenses are the ones that allow us to speculate on the possibility of things happening or to insist that things happen. Use this activity to help children see that modal verbs are a special type of auxiliary verb ('helper' verbs), which enable us to express possible actions that may be within or beyond our control or which we may be required to do. Present the children with a few sentences using a range of modal verbs, like the examples below, preferably linked to a meaningful context they are currently working on.

1. *I can understand this now.*
2. *I could understand this.*
3. *I may be able to understand this if I talk about it.*
4. *I might have understood this if I had talked about it.*
5. *I will understand this.*
6. *I would have understood this if we had talked about it.*
7. *I shall understand this when we get chance to talk about it.*
8. *I should have understood this when we talked about it.*
9. *I must understand this.*

Ask the children to identify all the helper verbs and to discuss what difference the helper verbs make to the meaning of each sentence. You may want to draw out from the children the various shades of meaning that these verbs suggest, including how likely, necessary or definite the action is as well as whether it can be done at all. Explain that these sorts of auxiliary verbs are known as **modal verbs**.

Is it really going to happen?

To help children understand how modal verbs can be used to speculate on the likelihood of something actually happening, provide them with a sentence full of various modal verbs like this one:

> *I **would have** ice cream if I **could** but there isn't any so I **will have** chocolate instead.*

Ask the children in pairs to discuss what difference the highlighted verbs make to the meaning of the sentence. Through shared discussion, draw out from the children the difference the modal verbs *will, would; can, could; shall, should; may, might* and *must* make to the meaning of sentences and whether the action is definitely going to happen, may possibly happen or just has the potential to happen.

Then give the pairs of children sentences on strips of paper using different modal verbs. Ask them to place the sentences under the two headings.

Group 1: The event is actually going to happen or has already happened

Group 2: The event is possible but it has not happened yet

*a. The aliens **can land** without warning.*

*b. The aliens **could land** at anytime.*

*c. The aliens **might land** this evening.*

*d. The aliens **will land** tomorrow.*

*e. The aliens **would have landed** last night.*

*f. The aliens **must have landed** last night.*

Ask the children to feed back their conclusions.

The trickier tenses challenge

This is a useful way of helping children build their understanding of how many different ways verbs can express action. Devise ten simple sentences which show how auxiliary verbs can affect the meaning of the basic verb and display them for the class:

1. *The parrot* ***can sit*** *in its cage.*
2. *The parrot* ***might have sat*** *in its cage.*
3. *The parrot* ***will have to sit*** *in its cage.*
4. *The parrot* ***must sit*** *in its cage.*
5. *The parrot* ***should have been sitting*** *in its cage.*
6. *The parrot* ***does sit*** *in its cage.*
7. *The parrot* ***was just about to sit*** *in its cage.*
8. *The parrot* ***would have been sitting*** *in its cage.*
9. ***If only*** *the parrot* ***had sat*** *in its cage.*
10. *The parrot* ***wanted to be left to sit*** *in its cage.*

Ask the children to discuss the different meaning of the sentences – what can be inferred from the verbs. Help embed this understanding by referring to such sentences when they occur within texts the class is concurrently reading and model these types of sentences in shared writing so the children develop a feel for how tenses work in practice. The more they read, the more they will come to understand how tenses work and be able to manipulate them effectively.

The multi-tense challenge

Once the class is more confident with using a range of tenses, display a short text with a wide variety of tenses related to the same verb, like the one below. After reading it to the class, ask the children to discuss the differences in meaning of the different verb phrases. You may want to ask one group to lead the class discussion.

> *Inspired by the Olympics, the parrot woke up determined to change his routine. Today he would not sit in his cage. Recently, he had sat in his cage for most of the time. He realised he had been sitting for most of his life – he had become a couch parrot. Even when he was little, he had used to sit endlessly. 'Why am I sat here?' he thought. 'From today, instead of sitting upright, I will sit upside down, hanging by one foot after another.' So, as he sat on his perch, he resolved to sit no more. 'No more sitting! No more sitting!' he squawked, wildly flapping his wings.*
>
> *A cross voice from the sofa, irritated by such interruptions to the athletics, shouted, 'Sit down and shut up!'*

Each-one-teach-one

Children enjoy being in teacher role, which is fortunate since explaining to others is the best way of consolidating learning. Once you think the class has understood how verbs can change tense, challenge them to work out how to explain this clearly to their partner. Let them choose any of the examples that they have already worked with or they can devise their own. Once they have each had a go at teaching their partner, you may want to ask them to swap partners and explain to someone new.

Mastering the subjunctive!

The subjunctive is a mood, not a tense, that is used to indicate wishes, conditions and other non-factual (hypothetical) situations. As the name suggests, it is subjective and expresses uncertainty. The subjunctive is very important in some languages – eg French, Spanish, Polish, Turkish and Latin – but it is dying out and somewhat archaic in English. Our advice would be not to attempt to teach children how to tackle this one unless their grammar is really secure. You have to have the tune of the English language clearly in your head to grasp this one!

There are three types of subjunctive in English:

- The hypothetical subjunctive (the *were* subjunctive):
  If I were to do that again, I would try harder.
- The mandatory subjunctive (the *bossy* subjunctive):
  We require that he return the money immediately.
- The formulaic subjunctive (for certain set exclamatory phrases)
  God save the Queen!

If I were to understand the subjunctive ...

Use the sentences below to help children understand that sometimes, often in more formal situations, a special mood of the verb is needed to express wishes, conditions and non-factual situations. Ask the children to look at these four sentences and decide what is unusual about three of them:

1. If I were Prime Minister, I would deport the Daleks.
2. If you were Prime Minister, what would you do?
3. If she were alive today, she would sort the Daleks out.
4. If just one Dalek were to invade, we would have to find The Doctor.

Draw out from the children that sentences 1, 3 and 4 sound odd (unless your family are regular users of the subjunctive). You would normally expect it to be *I was …*; *she was …*; *a Dalek was* …. Explain that this is the hypothetical subjunctive (the *were*-subjunctive) that is used when you are imagining what might happen. This change only affects the first and third person singular as in *If I were … If she/he/it were … If we were …*; *If you were … If they were …* sound normal.

Then ask everyone to make up three different sentences about anything that might be wished for beginning:

> *If I were …*
> *If you were …*
> *If he were …*

Put a few of these on a flip chart so the children can see that the subordinate part of the sentence begins with *If* and then includes *were* (regardless of whether it is *I*, *you* or *he*), and the main clause has *would* in it.

Were there to be a question in a test on the subjunctive, and you were feeling confused, the best-guess solution would be to select the choice including *were*!

Mastering the bossy subjunctive!

Since the bossy subjunctive can be entertaining, you might want to use an activity like this. Ask the children to discuss which of the sentences below sound normal and which sound strange and why:

1. *I want him to start work tomorrow.*
2. *He starts work tomorrow.*
3. *Start tomorrow!*
4. *Can you start tomorrow?*
5. *I require that you start work tomorrow.*
6. *I require that he start work tomorrow.*

Draw out from the children that the first two sentences sound normal. In the language of grammar they are in the indicative mood (the straightforward factual) that is the standard way of speaking. The next two also sound normal – sentence 3 being in the imperative (bossy) mood and sentence 4 in the interrogative (questioning) mood, which are both everyday English.

Explain that the last two sentences are in the mandatory subjunctive (the bossy subjunctive) that sounds very formal and the last sentence sounds particularly weird because, in the third person (*he/she/it*), the subjunctive verb doesn't agree in the normal way – the sentence says ***he start*** not ***he starts***.

The new head teacher

Tell the children that they are now in role as the new head teacher, who has decided to issue new rules for all the teachers. Ask them to devise four more rules in the mandatory subjunctive mode:

1. *The head teacher requires that each* ***teacher accept*** *all school rules without question.*
2. *The head teacher expects that each teacher …*
3. *The head teacher demands that each teacher …*
4. *The head teacher insists that each teacher …*
5. *The head teacher wishes that each teacher …*

Flip-chart the best of the children's ideas. Then point out the subjunctive in practice should it appear in a text you are reading – but you may have to wait quite a long time to find an example!

WHAT ARE ADVERBS?

The games below have been designed to help you draw out from the children that **adverbs** are describing words that give added meaning to verbs. They are, to borrow Sue Palmer's useful phrase, roving reporters that can move around sentences telling us how, where, when or why something happened: ***slowly, surprisingly, near, far, tomorrow, next, sometimes, never***. They can also describe adjectives, another adverb or the whole sentence:

> *The* ***extremely*** *cute cat slept.*
> *The cat purred* ***rather noisily***.
> ***Usually***, *the cat is sleeping.*

Adverbs often end in *ly*.

How is teddy doing things?

Try revisiting some of the verb activities and relate adverbs to these. For example, go to your flip chart of 'Now teddy is ...' activities (see page 52) and ask the children to think up as many words as they can to tell you more about how teddy is doing all of the actions. Display all the ideas on a flip chart as illustrated below so they can see that the adverb is describing the action.

Teddy is sleeping ... *soundly* ... *happily* ... *etc.*
Teddy is walking ... *quickly* ... *slowly* ... *etc.*

Ask the class why they think the words that tell you how, where, when or why the action happened are called adverbs – draw out from them that they add to the verb and often end in *ly*.

Engaging adverbs

Provide the class with a list of adverbs used to engage the reader, eg *unfortunately, intriguingly, weirdly, scandalously*. Model for the class how each term can be used to introduce information about an entertaining topic, for instance, hedge giants.

Person 1: *Surprisingly, hedge giants are rarely seen near hedges.*
Person 2: *However, intriguingly, on Hallowe'en they always celebrate next to a hedge.*
Person 1: *Weirdly, many hedge giants have recently joined the Simon Cowell fan club.*

Then provide them with some engaging topics to practise with, for example, *Head teachers, Daleks, Aliens*, and ask the class in pairs to create their own sentences.

Adding meaning

Each word has to earn its place. Revisit your *alternative-verbs-for-said* poster (see page 58). Remind the class that powerful verbs don't necessarily need anything to describe them because each verb chosen tells you more about the action than the verb *said* can tell you.

Explain that sometimes it can be useful to add an adverb to a powerful verb to help the reader to picture precisely how something is being done. Take the first few verbs and ask the children to think of two alternative adverbs to describe each verb to make it more precise, using different adverbs each time.

1. *asked* ***hurriedly****/asked* ***slowly***
2. *added* ***entertainingly****/added* ***rudely***
3. *answered …*

Does it make the writing better?

The aim of this game is to help children see that a powerful verb may not need an adverb at all. Take a powerful verb like *whispered*, and explain that if all you want to do is to express that something was said quietly then you don't need an adverb, but there are all sorts of ways that you can whisper. The children discuss the range of alternatives and decide which ones could be effective and which ones just tell us what we already know. Here are some examples to get you going:

1. *He whispered slowly.*
2. *He whispered threateningly.*
3. *He whispered quietly.*
4. *He whispered sadly.*
5. *He whispered comfortingly.*

Ask groups to compare their findings and decide which words add value.

Change the mood

Providing one powerful verb and some alternative adverbs (each of which is potentially effective), helps children to reflect on what makes writing effective. Ask the children in pairs or small groups to try to describe the difference in mood and meaning that each adverb makes. Then ask them to make each sentence longer by continuing the mood set by the adverb.

1. *She stared sadly.*
2. *She stared sullenly.*
3. *She stared greedily.*
4. *She stared threateningly.*

Basic Writing Toolkit Ingredient

You may want to use these activities to contribute to a writer's basic toolkit that you co-construct with the class. The class may decide on an ingredient like the following:

- **Make adverbs earn their place by telling the reader something they don't know but that has real impact.**

Make the adverbs redundant

This game is a useful way of embedding understanding of the role of verbs and adverbs within sentences and helps extend vocabulary. Provide the children with a series of common verbs strengthened by adverbs that help define what the verb tells us. Model for the children how to replace the verb and its adverb with one powerful verb that says the same thing more effectively and then ask them to work in pairs finding powerful verbs.

1. *... she said angrily.* – *... she fumed / she exploded*
2. *He walked slowly.* – *He ambled. /He strolled.*
3. *... she said certainly.* –
4. *... she said commandingly.* –
5. *... she said weepily.* –
6. *He walked confidently.* –

The roving reporter

Illustrate how adverbs can move around a sentence by creating sentences that are often identical except for the position of the adverb. Point out that when the adverb starts the sentence (a fronted adverbial!) it is followed by a comma. Ask the children to discuss whether all the sentences in each group mean the same or are there some differences. Here are some examples to get you going:

Group A

A1. *The bear climbed up the tree* ***swiftly***.
A2. *The bear climbed* ***swiftly*** *up the tree.*
A3. *The bear* ***swiftly*** *climbed up the tree.*
A4. ***Swiftly***, *the bear climbed up the tree.*

Group B

B1. *The man was watching* ***happily*** *as his child fed the ducks.*
B2. *The man was* ***happily*** *watching as his child fed the ducks.*
B3. ***Happily****, the man was watching as his child fed the ducks.*
B4. *The man was watching as his child fed the ducks* ***happily****.*

Then ask the children to see how many different places they can place the adverb in some sentences and decide if the sense is the same in each case:

1. *The girl texted her friend* ***immediately****.*
2. ***Only*** *that boy gave the dog a biscuit.*
3. *Daleks* ***just*** *rest in the afternoons.*
4. *The teacher looked up* ***slowly*** *as the inspector entered the room.*
5. *She* ***even*** *knows where the bag was hidden.*

Through book-talk style discussion, draw out the fact that with adverbs like *only, just, even, also, mainly, almost* it is important to place the adverb immediately before the word that you want them to modify.

Word families – where many adverbs come from

This activity helps children investigate how one root word can lead to lots of other related words that perform a slightly different function within a sentence. So a noun can lead to a verb to an adjective to an adverb. Provide the class with a word-family ladder like the one below and ask the children (in pairs) to see if they can complete the ladder. Remind them that if you want to add *ly* to a word that already ends in *y* they must change that *y* to an *i* (eg *angry + ly = angrily*).

	noun	**verb**	**adjective**	**adverb**
	use	*to use*	*useful*	*usefully*
	anger	*to be angry*	*angry*	*angrily*
1.	hope	to hope	hopeful	
2.	dream	to dream	dreamy	
3.	care	to care	careful	
4.	health	to be healthy	healthy	
5.	help	to help	helpful	
6.	repeat	to repeat	repetitive	
7.	a hurry	to hurry	hurried	
8.	shock	to shock	shocking	
9.	interest	to interest	interesting	
10.	touch	to touch	touching	

Once the children have completed the grid, challenge them to work out what the rule is about words that add the suffix *full* and what happens when you add an additional *ly*? Point out that not all adverbs end in *ly* and not all adjectives just add *ly* to form an adverb.

The alternative adverbs expert

Use this game to help older classes increase the range of adverbs they can use appropriately. Present the class with an *alternative-verbs-for-x* poster like the one for the verb *show* below and ask them to think of a different adverb to describe each verb so that it could fit into the base sentence. Demonstrate that the adverb can come before or after the verb it describes:

> *This shows* ***clearly*** *how sad the character is feeling.*
> *This* ***clearly*** *shows how sad the character is feeling.*

See how many alternatives they can think up in say two minutes.

1. *This shows* ***precisely*** *…*
2. *This* ***reveals*** *…*
3. *This* ***suggests*** *…*
4. *This* ***indicates*** *…*
5. *This* ***hints*** *…*

Discuss that adverbs are more effective if you use them sparingly and that powerful verbs often don't need an adverb to describe them. You may end up with a poster, like the one below, that will be useful to display whenever you want the class to do evaluative work relating to a wide range of topics.

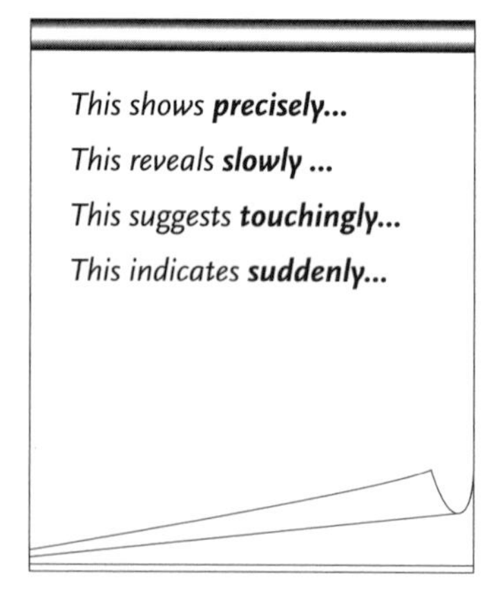

Change the adverb, change the mood, change the meaning

This challenging game engages children because of the different moods they can create and the different meanings that result. Demonstrate how, when you use general verbs, it is easy to change the mood of a piece of writing by changing the adverb. Devise two sentences as an example, for instance:

> *The man watched **fearfully** as the child balanced **precariously** on the edge of the pool.*
>
> *The man watched **proudly** as the child balanced **skilfully** on the edge of the pool.*

Then devise a range of sentences for the children to change from positive to negative. Depending on the age of the children, you can use simple or more sophisticated vocabulary.

1. *The child paddled **happily** watching the water flow **lazily** over the weir.*
2. *Elif ran **slowly** along the beach as the waves rolled **gently** in.*
3. *The boy listened **hopefully** as the footsteps came **reassuringly** closer.*
4. *The woman waited **expectantly** for the number 59 to arrive **punctually**.*

Adverb doctor

Children like the opportunity to wield the red pen and correct the work of others. Provide the class with a short piece of text where adverbs have been used well, preferably from a text the class is already familiar with to provide purpose and context, and highlight all the adverbs. Remind the class of their basic writing toolkit ingredient relating to adverbs: **Make adverbs earn their place by telling the reader something they don't know that has real impact.**

Now ask whether all the adverbs have earned their place, or whether the writing would be better if you deleted some of them or replaced them. The children should be prepared to present their conclusions to the class. Below is a light-hearted recount of a science experiment to illustrate the approach:

Smugly, I had pictured myself **expertly** growing the best cress seeds in the class – mine tall, green and healthy-looking while all the others were wilted, thin and mangy. **Sadly**, this turned out **not exactly** to be the case. **Apparently**, we were supposed to set up four different dishes and treat the little blighters **differently** to illustrate some point or other. **As usual**, I wasn't **really** listening and **just** set up one dish. **Enthusiastically**, I overwatered this and **somewhat** drowned the seeds. **Perhaps** I should cross 'Follow in Einstein's footsteps' off my career list.

The each-one-teach-one challenge

Once you think the class has understood what adverbs are and how to use them effectively, challenge them to work out how to explain this clearly to their partner. Explain that they can choose any of the examples they have already worked with or devise new examples.

Once they have had a go each at teaching their partner, ask them to swap partners and explain to someone new. See if any child wants to rise to the visiting-grammar-professor challenge and explain to the whole class.

WHAT ARE ADVERBIALS?

Use the following games to help children understand that an **adverbial** is a catch-all term for any word, phrase or clause that gives extra meaning to the main verb or clause within a sentence.

> *The cat slept **peacefully**. (adverb)*
> *The cat slept **in a peaceful manner**. (adverbial phrase)*
> *The cat will be sleeping **by the time we get back**. (adverbial clause)*

In roving reporter style, adverbials give additional information about the where, when, why or how of the action. A single adverb is also an adverbial. Often a number of adverbials join together to provide such additional detail:

> *We were sitting **happily**. (manner – how)*
> *We were sitting **happily on the beach**. (manner and place – how and where)*
> *We were sitting **happily on the beach when the giant wave appeared**. (manner, place and time – how, where and when)*

The important thing is not to be able to spot an adverbial from a hundred yards but to be able to add extra information into sentences effectively depending on the purpose of the sentence.

Once the children are comfortable with the concept of adverbs you may want to revisit some of the work they have done on adverbs and this time change the adverb into an adverbial phrase or clause. For example, revisit *Does it make the writing better?* (see page 75).

Ask the class to add information to each sentence to enhance the manner, place or time of the main action. Model the first sentence for them.

1. *He whispered slowly, glancing anxiously at the door of the room as the clock struck twelve.* (manner, place and time)
2. *He whispered threateningly ...*
3. *He whispered quickly ...*
4. *He whispered sadly ...*
5. *He whispered intently ...*

The fronted adverbial challenge!

Despite the name, children may even enjoy this linguistic challenge. Explain that the rather ghastly term *fronted adverbial* just refers to placing an adverb or an adverbial at the beginning of a sentence to engage the reader in some way: *Interestingly, ... Strangely, ... Suddenly, ...*. Model how the fronted adverbial could be a phrase or clause that lets you know the manner, place or time of the main action.

Without looking to the right or left*, the wolf ran straight home.*

As the clock struck midnight*, the wolf reached the front door.*

From the safety of home*, the wolf rang the police.*

Ask the children to create their own examples by adding adverbials to simple sentences to tell the reader more about the manner, place or time of the action:

> *The Daleks approached.*
> *The dragon woke.*
> *The final whistle blew.*

You may want to display some of the more entertaining sentences as examples of the effective fronted adverbial in action!

The great ed/ing/ly fronted adverbial challenge

Ed/ing/ly sentence starters (fronted adverbials) are a useful way of making some sentences more engaging. Return to the base sentences above, if these had worked well with your class, and now see if they can enliven each sentence with *ed/ing/ly* fronted adverbials. Model the first sentence for them.

Undaunted by the gunfire*, the Daleks approached.*
Entering in precise v-formation*, the Daleks approached.*
Menacingly*, the Daleks approached.*

The children then have a go at writing their own examples.

Spot the adverbial

The more the children can feel confident using basic grammatical terms, the more easily they will be able to discuss what makes writing effective, and the more they will be able to take disembodied grammar tests in their stride. A good method of building such confidence is to use discussion leading to explaining to others. The sort of questions below can be adapted to help embed any grammatical feature. Here the approach is applied to adverbials.

Ask the children in pairs to decide how to answer each of these questions and to be prepared to explain their choices.

1. Do all of the following sentences include adverbials?
1a. *As soon as he reached the safety of home, the wolf rang the police.*
1b. *The wolf rang the police, as soon as he reached the safety of home.*
1c. *Exhausted, the wolf decided to watch the football.*
1d. *The wolf, exhausted by a day learning grammar, decided to watch the football.*

2. Which of these fronted adverbials do you think is the most effective?
2a. ***As soon as he reached the safety of home****, the wolf rang the police.*
2b. ***Reaching the safety of home****, the wolf rang the police.*
2c. ***Exhausted by his efforts to reach the safety of home****, the wolf rang the police.*
2d. ***Exhausted****, the wolf rang the police.*

3. Which of the following does not begin with a fronted adverbial?
3a. *Not even waiting for midnight, the prince turned into a frog.*
3b. *The prince, deciding not to wait until midnight, immediately turned into a frog.*
3c. *Immediately, the prince turned into a frog.*
3d. *Deciding not to wait until midnight, the prince turned into a frog.*

The where, when, how and why detective

See if the children can add all these features into sentences and still have a sentence that is worth reading. Provide the children with some sentences of three like the ones below.

The boy woke up late, jumped out of bed and dashed out.

The dragon heard a noise, stood up and guarded the entrance to its cave.

The aliens landed, checked the outside temperature and took off.

In shared-writing style, demonstrate for the children how to complete the first one:

The boy woke up late ***that morning****, jumped out of bed and dashed* ***madly/ out to school/to avoid yet another detention.***

Now ask them to compose their own versions.

Each-one-teach-one

Once you think the class has understood what adverbials are and how to use them effectively, ask them to work out how to explain this clearly to their partner. Explain that they can choose any of the examples they have already worked with or devise new examples. Once they have had a go at teaching their partner, you may want to ask them to swap partners and explain to someone new. See if any pupil wants to rise to the visiting-grammar-professor challenge and explain adverbials, including fronted adverbials, to the whole class.

WHAT ARE PREPOSITIONS?

The games in this section have been created to help you draw out from the children that **prepositions** are the little words that join (glue) the phrases of a sentence together often showing how they are related in time (*at, during, in, on*) or space (*to, over, under, in, on*). As the name suggests, they tell you something about the position of things but they don't link clauses which is the job of conjunctions. They usually help you know where and when the action is taking place.

> ***In the morning**, the cat often hides **under the table**.*
> *The train leaves **at three o'clock from platform four**.*

As you may have spotted when looking at the examples of prepositions above, although the underlined words are prepositions, the phrases that they are a part of are adverbials. Just to keep us all on our toes, all prepositional phrases are also adverbials because adverbial is an umbrella term that includes all phrases that tell us where, when, how or why action takes place.

Where's teddy?

Small children enjoy saying where a favourite character from a picture book is now. They will probably have become familiar with the function of prepositions from reading books like *Where's Spot?* which can be a useful starting point.

Demonstrate the role and variety of prepositions to the children with a well-loved character like teddy. Place teddy *on, beside, below, near* or *next to* the table etc and then find other places for teddy to be so you can build up as many everyday prepositions for place as you can think of. Flag these up on a poster and display this when children are writing to help encourage them to use a wide range of prepositions. Add to the poster as more prepositions emerge from children's reading and writing. Over time, explain that these sort of words are called prepositions, because they tell you the position of things or actions.

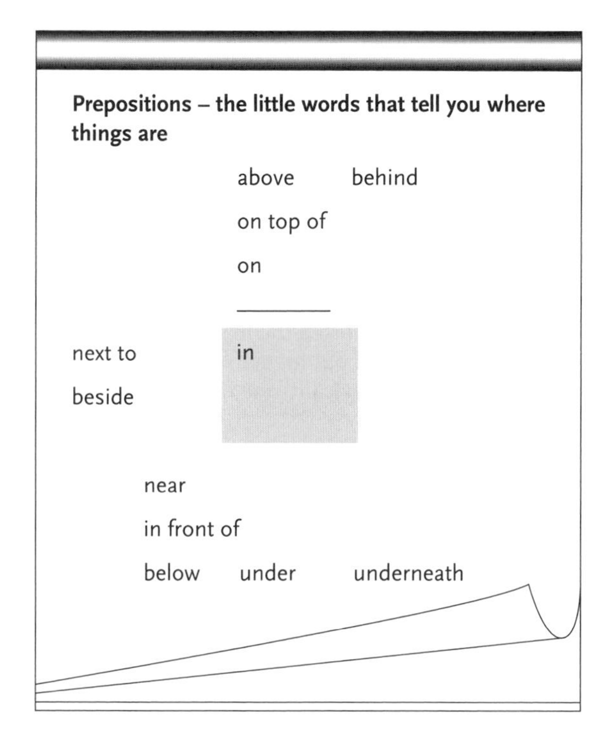

Spot the odd ones out

This process is less threatening than having to spot the prepositions yourself and encourages discussion about function, which is key to understanding.

Select a passage from a book you are reading with the class that is full of prepositions. Highlight all the prepositions and one or two words that are not prepositions, as illustrated below. Discuss the function of the first few highlighted prepositions and remind the class that these are prepositions if no one volunteers this. Then ask the class to discuss the function of all the remaining highlighted words and warn them that there are two words that shouldn't have been highlighted. See if they can identify them (*also*, *bit*). Then discuss what sort of words have been correctly highlighted and what their function is within the sentences. Add any additional prepositions from the work to your poster.

The Hodja and the missing grapes
One day, the Hodja put two big baskets of grapes **on** his donkey and set off **to** the market. **On** his way, he stopped to rest **under** the shade of a large plane tree, **beside** a stream, **near** where other men and their donkeys were **also** resting. While the men were dozing, the Hodja started to take grapes **from** their baskets and put them **into** his. One of the men woke up and angrily demanded to know what he thought he was doing.

The Hodja quickly replied, 'Don't mind me. I'm a **bit** mad and often do strange things.'

'**In** that case,' retorted the man, 'why don't you take grapes **out** of your basket and put them in someone else's?'

Looking **up** quizzically, the Hodja replied. 'I'm not that mad!'

How many prepositional phrases?

Display a simple passage that contains a number of prepositional phrases, preferably related to a current topic, for example:

The cat sat on the mat in front of the fire. Out of the corner of its eye, it could see that there was still fish in the dish. The humans were relaxing after a lovely meal. No one was looking at the cat: perhaps his big chance had come at last.

In pairs or threes, ask the children to identify all seven prepositions in this passage and the phrases that they introduce into the text. As the children feed back, highlight them on the text:

The cat sat ***on the mat in front of the fire***. ***Out of the corner*** *of its eye, it could see that there was still fish* ***in the dish***. *The humans were relaxing* ***after a lovely meal***. *No one was looking* ***at the cat***: *perhaps his big chance had come* ***at last***.

Now ask them to see if they can innovate on the passage orally so that all the prepositional phrases have been replaced by alternative prepositional phrases, for example:

The cat sat upon the shelf above the fireplace. Between its half-closed eyelids, it could see that there was still fish on the serving plate. The humans were relaxing following a large feast. No one was looking towards the cat: perhaps his big chance had come for this evening.

Ask different groups to feed back their alternatives and flip-chart all the possible alternatives. Use this list to show how the preposition is the head word of each prepositional phrase.

Prepositional phrases

- *upon the shelf*
- *above the fireplace*
- *between its half-closed eyelids*
- *on the serving plate*
- *following a large feast*
- *towards the cat*
- *for this evening*

Now ask the children to explain to the person next to them what a preposition is and how it usually introduces a phrase that adds meaning to a sentence. Once they can do this, they will have a secure understanding of prepositions. In the language of new curriculum speke in England, they will have 'mastered' it!

Primary children in England are now required to answer questions identifying whether a word like *before* has been used as a preposition or a subordinating conjunction. If this is useful to you, see the ***great conjunction/ preposition competition*** on page 97 in the next chapter.

CHAPTER 3

The links

Conjunctions and connectives

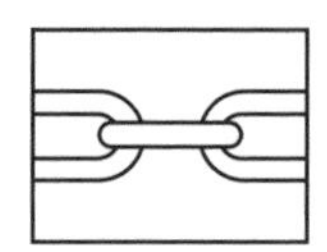

This chapter contains fun ways to help children understand how to link phrases, clauses and sentences effectively. Because conjunctions join things together, oral rehearsal is the ideal way to help children internalise the pattern of language they will need for coherent speaking and writing.

WHAT ARE CONJUNCTIONS?

Use the activities below to draw out from the children that **conjunctions** link things or actions within sentences. They are like glue – they help join words, phrases and clauses. By joining the parts of sentences together they can turn simple sentences into compound or complex sentences:

> *The girl looked for her lost Dalek* ***but*** *she couldn't find it anywhere.* (compound sentence)
>
> *The girl waited* ***until*** *she could visit the magic mountain* ***because*** *the pathway only appeared* ***when*** *the moon was full.* (complex sentence)

- **Co-ordinating conjunctions** (the main ones are *and, but, or, so*) join clauses of equal weight – ie each clause could be a standalone sentence.
  - *It will rain in the morning* ***and*** *it will rain in the afternoon.*
  - *I loved eating all the chocolate* ***but*** *now I feel sick.*

- **Subordinating conjunctions** (*when, if, although, because, after, until* etc) introduce a subordinate clause.
  - *We will light the fire **when** it gets dark.*
  - ***Because** it is cloudy, we can't see the moon.*

If the subordinate clause begins the sentence, the end of the clause is signalled by a comma. The comma is optional if the main clause begins the sentence, which is the normal order in English.

You may want to tell the children that the word conjunction comes from Latin (*con* – with; *iunctus* – joined).

The and/but game

This little activity helps children understand the difference in meaning signalled by *and* as opposed to *but*. Since these key coordinating conjunctions are in the top 50 most frequently used words in English, it makes good sense to start with these.

Ask the children to think of several foods that they love and some that they hate. Model for the children how to use *and* and *but* in sentences – *I like tomatoes **and** carrots **but** I hate sprouts.*

Ask a few children to tell their sentences to the class so that the children start to internalise the pattern of the sentence. Next, ask them in small groups to see if everyone can come up with at least two different *and/but* sentences about food. Flip-chart a few of these and ask the children if they can explain what *and* does and how *but* is different.

Once they have established the different functions of *and* and *but*, explain that these are called conjunctions because they link (join) words and phrases together just like a road junction links roads. For a short while, you may want to emphasise the *ands* and *buts* in text when you are reading and speaking to the class and encourage them to follow suit.

Next try the game with names, but make the sentence a little harder. Ask the children to think of some names that aren't the names of any child in the class and model a sentence for the class:

> *There are children called Mehmet **and** Jane in our class **but** there is no one called Sasha.*

Ask a few children to follow suit. In groups, the children in turn come up with at least two different *and/but* sentences about names in the class. Encourage the children to explain that these little joining words are called conjunctions. Understanding what conjunctions can do, and not being afraid to use the term, is really useful so time spent on this is time well spent.

What do conjunctions do?

Explain that coordinating conjunctions are so common because they can join all the bits of sentences together – words, phrases and clauses. Write a few linked sentences that illustrate this, preferably related to a topic you are focusing on:

> *The cat* ***and*** *the kitten had both disappeared. He thought they would be in the garden* ***or*** *in the house* ***but*** *he couldn't find them anywhere.*

Ask the children to explain the function of *and, but* and *or* in these simple and compound sentences. Get some feedback and, if necessary, model for the children how to explain that these words are conjunctions.

The conjunction detective

This game helps children to understand that conjunctions are key to linking ideas and actions together within sentences, without them sentences quickly lose coherence. Find a few sentences (magpie them from a book or write your own paragraph) and omit the conjunctions, creating a simple cloze procedure.

The children fill the gaps with, for example, *and, but* or *so*. Remind the class that it is not a question of coming up with exactly the same choice of words as in the original, but making certain that the words they choose make good sense. Then ask them to explain what sort of word is missing and what is the job of that type of word.

> ***The Enormous Turnip***
> Once upon a time there was a little old man who grew an enormous turnip. Early one morning he decided to pull up the turnip to make turnip soup. …, he pulled … he pulled … he pulled. … the turnip would not budge. Next he asked his wife to help. …, the woman pulled the man … the man pulled the turnip. … still the turnip would not budge. Next he asked his son to help.

Now ask the children to be the visiting-grammar-professor who can explain the difference between *and, but* and *so* and tell us all about these conjunctions. If you have any budding professors, get them to explain to the class.

The little so-and-sos

Playing the what-do-conjunctions-do game with *so* or *yet* is tricky because they can have different meanings and function differently within sentences. In the following pairs of sentences, *so* and *yet* initially function as adverbs and then as conjunctions.

> *I don't want* **so** *much cake.*
> *It's a sunny day* **so** *let's go for a picnic.*
>
> *Are we there* **yet**, *dad?*
> *In the end, I didn't go,* **yet** *I really wanted to.*

It's probably not a good idea to go into the detail of this but you may find this game useful to help children use *so* and *yet* as conjunctions. Devise two pairs of sentences like the ones below using *so, because, yet* and *but* to help the children see that *so* often functions somewhat like *because,* and *yet* often functions somewhat like *but.*

1a. ***Because*** *it's getting cold now, let's go inside.*
1b. *It's getting cold now,* **so** *let's go inside.*
2a. *It's getting cold now* **but** *let's stay outside.*
2b. *It's getting cold now* **yet** *we can still stay outside.*

The children decide which pairs of sentences are fairly similar in meaning.

The explanation game (subordinating conjunctions)

Subordinating conjunctions are key to children being able to write complex sentences because they link two clauses together: one being the main clause; the other being dependent on it (the subordinate clause). For example, ***As*** *the inspector entered the room, the teacher looked up nervously.* Since all explanation relies on complex sentences, explanation text is a good starting point. Write a short narrative explanation, like the one below, leaving out all the subordinating conjunctions. (Factual explanation text is harder for the children to recreate because they have to know a lot about something to be able to explain it.)

> ***The boy who liked sleeping***
> Lee didn't like getting up in the mornings and so he was often late for school. … the alarm went off, he would just turn it off and go straight back to sleep. His father tried to make him get up but he just kept on returning to bed. … everyone else was busy getting washed and dressed, he just slept. '… you don't get up immediately, I'm going to come in with a bucket of water,'

threatened his older sister. Such threats did not worry him ... he had wisely locked his door.

The children fill in the gaps so that the passage makes sense. You may want to read the passage aloud to the class, pausing appropriately at the gaps, so the children can hear the tune of the text. Once the task has been completed, ask groups to feed back their suggestions and flip-chart the words that can be used to fill the gaps. You will probably end up with a list like this:

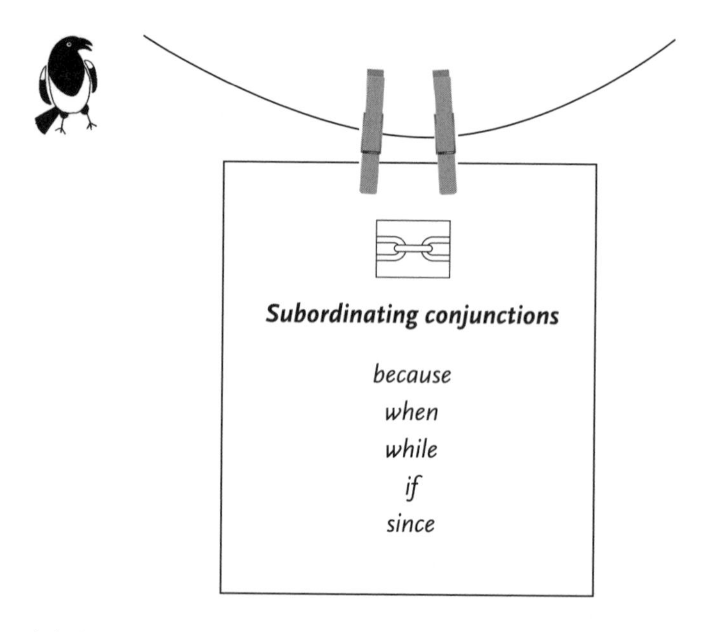

Ask the children to discuss the function of these words and establish that they join the actions in the sentences together. If you have already taught the difference between compound and complex sentences, this is a good opportunity to draw out from the children that these conjunctions introduce an action that is dependent on the rest of the sentence so they are known as subordinating conjunctions. Ask the children to see ***if*** they can add to this list of subordinating conjunctions from their reading. You might want to encourage the children, for a short time, to emphasise the conjunctions ***when*** they speak, ***as*** highlighted in this paragraph!

See *The intonation game* on page 163 to help teach the punctuation alongside this structure.

Spot the odd one out

Asking children to identify all the conjunctions in a passage tends to open up a Pandora's box of problems as children may identify words and phrases that link but which aren't technically conjunctions. Instead, highlight all the conjunctions in a passage but include one word that isn't a conjunction and which doesn't have a linking function within its sentence. (Preferably choose a short text they are already familiar with.) The children, in pairs, spot the odd one out (*that*) and justify their choice.

> *The man who could tell the future*
> One autumn day, the Hodja was sitting on a branch of a tree cutting wood, **because** he wanted fuel for the winter. **When** he started sawing away at the branch he was sitting on, a man passing by shouted, 'Excuse me, Hodja, **if** you carry on cutting that branch, you will fall with it.'
> **Since** the Hodja suspected the man was a passing fool, he took no notice of his warning **and** continued sawing away. Suddenly the branch gave way **and** it **and** the Hodja fell to the ground.
> 'My God!' exclaimed the Hodja, '**that** man can see the future.'
> **Although** his ankle hurt from the fall, he limped after the man **because** he wanted to ask him how long he was going to live.

Ringing the changes

This game shows children how subordinating conjunctions can subtly change the meaning of sentences. Divide the children into small groups and provide each group with a set of subordinating conjunction sentence strips to sort, preferably related to a topic you are working on:

1. ***As*** *it rained, we didn't go to the park.*
2. ***When*** *it rains, we don't go to the park.*
3. ***If*** *it rains, we don't go to the park.*
4. ***While*** *it rains, we won't go to the park.*
5. ***Unless*** *it stops raining, we won't go to the park*
6. ***Although*** *it's raining, we'll still go to the park.*
7. ***Because*** *it is raining, we won't go to the park.*
8. ***Since*** *it is raining, we won't go to the park.*
9. ***Until*** *it has stopped raining, we won't go to the park.*
10. ***Even*** *if it rains, we'll go to the park.*

The children sort the sentences so that any sentences that have the same meaning are in the same group. They should be prepared to explain all the different meanings they have identified. If you want to make the task easier, you can provide them with headings for the different shades of meaning:

Gives a reason	Suggests what may happen	Tells you when the action happens or what typically happens	Changes the direction

Improve it

This is also a useful way of helping children recognise how boring *and then* can be. Rewrite a familiar text so that it is full of *ands* and *and thens*, which have been highlighted. Model for the children how to recast the sentences so they include subordinating conjunctions rather than relying on *ands* to coordinate everything; then ask them to improve the writing, recasting the sentences where necessary.

Once they have improved the story, ask the children to share their version with a partner and explain the changes that they made.

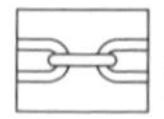

Combination games

The following three activities provide useful ways of building up children's confidence in using conjunctions appropriately to create complex sentences.

Combining two simple sentences into a complex sentence

Provide the children with a range of key subordinating conjunctions.

even though	*unless*	*because*	*until*
if	*as soon as*	*although*	*while*
when	*before*	*after*	*as*

Eating too much chocolate is bad for you.
Most children love it.

Ask the children to discuss how many of these conjunctions they can use to join the two sentences while retaining the same meaning. Ask one group to present the conjunctions they think work, explaining why the others won't fit in this context.

What a difference

Provide the class with a sentence starter and a range of subordinating conjunctions as illustrated below. Model for them how the clause introduced by the conjunction could begin the sentence, or continue the sentence.

Because *Daleks had landed in the area, all the schools were closed.*
All the schools were closed ***because*** *Daleks had landed in the area.*

even though	*unless*	*because*	*until*
if	*as soon as*	*although*	*while*
when	*before*	*after*	*as*

Ask the children to write sentences including the main clause *all the schools were closed* using each conjunction in turn to show how the conjunction can change the direction of a sentence. Remind them that if the subordinating conjunction begins the sentence, the end of the clause it introduces should be marked by a comma. You may want to ask one or two children to present the difference the conjunction can make.

Changing the combination

Provide the class with the range of key subordinating conjunctions and give them two sentences to link.

even though	*unless*	*because*	*until*
if	*as soon as*	*although*	*while*
when	*before*	*after*	*as*

The crowd was nervous. Mr Toad approached in a new shiny sports car.

Ask the children to try to use these conjunctions to join the sentences, making certain they make sense. Explain that they can add or delete words as necessary to fit the meaning of the conjunction. Using a visualiser, or any method that enables the children to see the text being discussed, ask one or two children to present their sentences to the class in teacher style, explaining the difference the conjunction makes.

The function of the conjunction

The following sorting games help children think about what key conjunctions signal to the reader or listener. Make a set of sorting cards like the ones below. Ask the children in small groups to see if they can place each conjunction under the heading that best explains what it signals. You may want to help them by saying that there are up to six examples for one category but only one for another.

Introduces an explanation	Suggests a possibility or a condition	Helps you know at what time the action happens	Introduces a change of direction	Introduces an addition	Presents a choice
because	*if*	*when*	*but*	*and*	*either*
since	*as long as*	*before*	*although*		*or*
so	*whether*	*after*	*despite*		
as	*unless*	*as soon as*	*however*		
	until		*rather than*		
	provided that		*yet*		

When they have finished, you may want to ask them to compare their conclusions with another group and then ask one group to explain their conclusions. A good way to embed children's understanding of the different things conjunctions can signal is through shared reading and writing. Any explanation text will be perfect for this as explanation relies on complex sentences where one clause is subordinate to another.

The conjunction cloze challenge

Challenge older children to complete an explanation text like the one below. If possible, select an explanation passage that they have actually used in say science or history, and remove all the conjunctions as illustrated.

Why do we change the clocks twice a year?
Many of us get confused about why we change the clocks twice a year. We often can't remember ... the clocks move backward ... forwards an hour in the spring ... in the autumn.

... we make the clock go forward an hour in the spring, known as British Summer Time (BST), this maximises the amount of useful summer daylight. This means that in summer the sun rises an hour later, ... most people are still asleep, ... the evenings stay light an hour later. BST was originally introduced ... a wartime measure in 1916 ... the government wanted to use daylight efficiently.

In wintertime, ... there is much less daylight, the clock goes back an hour. This causes the mornings to be lighter ... the evenings darker. This is a return to what is known as Greenwich Mean Time (GMT).

... you want an easy way of remembering which way the clocks move, remember: Spring forward; fall (autumn) back.

The each-one-teach-one conjunction challenge

Once you think the class has understood what conjunctions are and how to use them effectively, challenge them to work out how to explain this clearly to a partner. Explain that they can choose any of the examples they have already worked with or devise new examples. See if any pupil wants to rise to the Professor Glue challenge and explain to the class all about how conjunctions link the parts of sentences.

Also see the cohesion chapter (Chapter 6) for sequencing activities in which conjunctions are key to cohesion.

The great 'Is it a conjunction or a preposition?' challenge

Once you have a room full of professors of conjunctions, see if they can rise to this challenge. First of all, give them a sentence (related to work they are currently doing) with one clause in it and a couple of prepositional phrases like the sentence below:

> *The boy waited miserably* ***at*** *the bus stop* ***in*** *the rain.*

Ask the children what the function of the two **bold** words is and what those words are called. Hopefully, they will remember that they are **prepositions** – the little words that usually introduce a phrase that tells us a little bit more about when or where the action is happening. Remind them that they can't join two clauses together. If they are vague about this, do a little revision on prepositions – see pages 84–87.

Next give them two sentences like the ones below and ask them to discuss this with a partner: Which **bold** word is functioning as a preposition and which is functioning as a subordinating conjunction? How would they explain their decision.

a. He always goes for a run ***before*** *breakfast.*
b. ***Before*** *you have breakfast, you could go for a run.*

When the children explain their choices, help them to see that the key to understanding whether the word is functioning as a preposition or a conjunction is to recognise if the word is introducing a clause or not.

- If the word introduces a clause (ie a clump of meaningful words with a verb in it), it's functioning as a subordinating conjunction.
- If it just tells you the position in space or time of something, it's functioning as a preposition and can only introduce a phrase.
- Warning! They can both spin the sentences round because prepositional phrases are adverbials and adverbials can rove around sentences so it's no good thinking that if it's at the beginning of the sentence, it must be a subordinating conjunction.
- *When, after, until, before* and *since* can all function as subordinating conjunctions or prepositions.

Now provide the class in pairs or small groups with some sentences on separate bits of cards with two shaded headings like the ones below.

Ask the children to place all the sentences with a **bold** conjunction under the conjunction card, and the sentences with a **bold** preposition under the preposition card. They should be prepared to explain their choices.

Preposition	Conjunction

*I was in the queue **before** you.*
***Before** you go to bed, you should brush your teeth.*
***When** it stops raining, we will go.*
***When** will it stop?*
*I added my name **after** yours.*
***After** he saw the dragon, he felt afraid.*
***As** you've been so good, you can eat all the chocolate.*
***As** a start, we could try looking in the bin.*
*Do not open the door, **until** the train has stopped.*
*She read the book **until** break time.*

Then ask the children to be the visiting-grammar-professor who can explain why the words are sometimes conjunctions and sometimes prepositions. You may want to ask any budding professors to explain to the whole class.

Noughts and crosses – subordinating conjunction style

This is a great game to play once the children understand subordinating conjunctions and it will really build their confidence while being an engaging challenge.

Find an entertaining picture. Just Google 'Mouse in a helmet' and grand images of a mouse in a crash hat approaching a mousetrap loaded with cheese appear.

Provide the class with a noughts-and-crosses grid of subordinating conjunctions.

if	**although**	**while**
because	**as**	**before**
since	**when**	**after**

Warm up with the easy version of the game. The children should work in pairs. Each child in turn selects a conjunction and creates a complex sentence using that subordinating conjunction to describe the picture in some way. (The child who starts the game, if wise, will pick ***as*** for their starter word.) The first child to achieve a diagonal, horizontal or vertical row of correctly structured sentences wins.

Now the real game begins. Challenge the whole class to see if they can come up with one multi-clause sentence that contains all the three words in any of the rows. Their sentence has to make complete sense and describe the picture in some way. They have to be able to say whether they have used the words as conjunctions or prepositions.

The ultimate challenge is to see if you can use all three words as subordinating conjunctions in one coherent sentence.

If you are struggling for a possible answer, here's one for you:

> ***Although*** *the mouse put on a crash hat* ***when*** *approaching the cheese in the trap, it was still hurt* ***because*** *the hat was faulty.* (This claims the middle vertical line.)

A final challenge

If the class is really confident with this, then present this next challenge:

> Is the word *before* in the sentence below a preposition or a subordinating conjunction? You must be able to explain your decision.
>
> *The cat I owned* ***before*** *never hunted birds, so I'm rather cross with this one.*

Answer: It's a preposition.

Explanation: Although this is a two-clause sentence, the word *before* is not joining the clauses (*so* is). The expanded form of the sentence would be: *The cat I owned* ***before this one*** *never hunted birds, so I'm rather cross with this one.* The full phrase is 'understood' from the context of the sentence. Therefore the word *before* is functioning as a preposition.

WHAT ARE CONNECTIVES?

The games below have been designed to help you draw out from the children that **connective** is a general term for linking words and phrases. They are like clues or **sentence signposts**, helping the reader or listener to understand the direction in which the text is heading. Connectives can link whole sentences together and make text coherent as well as joining the bits of sentences together. All **conjunctions** are connectives. The term connective also includes adverbials that signal to the reader the direction in which text is going by introducing paragraphs or joining one sentence to another. For example, they can signal:

- **a list** – *first, secondly, finally, a result;*
- **addition** – *also, in addition, moreover;*
- **opposition** – *on the other hand, from a different point of view;*
- **explanation** – *for example, that is to say, in other words.*

The activities below are useful for warming up the type of connectives that will particularly feature in whichever sort of writing you want the children to focus on, both in English and across the curriculum. The more children have internalised these sorts of phrases for a wide variety of purposes, the more easily they will be able to craft coherent text for any topic.

Highlighting the connectives in exemplar text

A simple way of helping children understand the function of connectives is to provide them with a copy of the exemplar text you are currently focusing on and ask them in pairs to highlight any phrases that help join the text together. Build up flip charts of these phrases and display them (a washing line is useful here) and regularly refer to the lists and add to them so the children use the lists to support their own talking and writing. You may want to display all the connectives that help recount things chronologically (temporal connectives) separately from those that explain things (causal connectives) and so on.

Children as teaching assistants

Most children enjoy being in the role of 'teaching assistant'. It is a great teaching aid if a child can flag up the connective phrases on the flip chart for you, while you focus on teaching the class. In addition, nothing will sharpen up thinking faster than being put in this teaching assistant role, so the more children you can involve in the process, the better.

The biggest problem for anyone flagging up phrases is that they might not know how to spell the words. Remember to encourage children and adults alike to put a dotted line under any word they are uncertain about. This allows anyone adding words to the flip chart to get the phrases down quickly and the spelling can be checked later. Before displaying the posters for future use, just check the spelling is right. This is also a wonderful method of freeing children up when drafting writing, so that they don't interrupt their flow and can extend their vocabulary into words they are not certain of spelling.

Demonstrate for the class how to add each connective phrase identified on to a flip chart. Model how to put a dotted line under any word that you are not certain how to spell. Ask any child who you think will be good at this task to start adding additional connectives to the flip chart, supporting them as necessary to begin with. Over time, build up the range of children who can act as teaching assistant at the flip chart. If possible, include everyone.

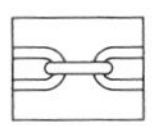

HOW CONNECTIVES HELP LINK NON-FICTION ACTIVITIES

Below are a number of warming-up-the-connectives games for non-fiction text types.

The alibis game

The alibis game is good for warming up time connectives for recount writing. Ask the children to make up an alibi for where they were between the hours of say 4 pm and 6 pm the previous day, making certain to include time connectives like *after, before, at the end of, a few minutes later, finally* etc. (They can tell the truth but making it up is much more fun.) Model this for them by emphasising all the connectives as you talk, for example:

***At the end of** school, I stayed in my classroom for about 30 minutes, tidying up **and** sorting things for the next day because I am such an excellent teacher. **Before leaving** the classroom, I collected all the work that I was taking home to mark that evening. **After that**, I went to the staffroom to check if there were any messages for me **and then** I went to the car park to drive home. **On my way** home, I stopped at FoodIsUs to get some cat food **and** a few things for our evening meal. **At about** 5 pm, I arrived home. **When** I got in the front door**, the first thing** I did was to make a cup of tea and feed the cat. **A few minutes later**, I settled down to marking **until** 6 pm **when** I turned on the evening news.*

Place the time connectives you have used on the flip chart and ask the class to take it in turns to tell their partner their alibi, emphasising all the connectives they use. You may want to get one or two volunteers to tell their alibi to the class and get your 'teaching assistant' to add any additional connectives to the flip chart. Over the next few weeks draw attention to time connectives in any other work you are doing and add new ones to the flip chart.

A word of warning: Remember that an overuse of time connectives can be dull. You might want to illustrate this by asking the children to think of a time when something frightened them and tell it to their partner using time connectives to help link what happened. Then ask them to retell their story trying to make it as engaging as possible. You may want to record some of the resulting most engaging stories. The chances are that only a few time connectives will have been used if any.

The how-to-make X game

Children enjoy making up instructions for fantastical products. The fact that the product is made up also allows them to focus on useful time connectives for instruction writing without having to worry about accuracy. Select any entertaining fantastic product, for example, *How to make monster porridge*. Learn the passage together Talk-for-Writing style so the children hear the instructions and internalise the connecting phrases. Then display the text on your whiteboard:

> *First, find a gigantic cooking pot.*
> *Next, half fill the pot with the juice of red berries.*
> *After that, add five kilos of best oats and a bag of salt.*
> *Then bring the mixture to the boil stirring it all the time.*
> *Finally, simmer it for five minutes.*

Ask the children to identify the time connectives while your child 'teaching assistant' adds the time connectives for instructions to the flip chart. Then ask the children to make up their own recipe orally using similar connectives and tell it to their partner. You may want to get some children to present their recipes and add any additional time connectives to the flip chart.

For a few weeks draw attention to time connectives suitable for instructions in any other work you are doing and add them to the flip chart.

The excuses game

This is a good way of warming up causal connectives for explanation text because it sidesteps the problem of having to know a lot about something to be able to explain it. Provide the children with a poster of causal connectives (*because, as a result, therefore, when, since*). Devise an activity based on situations familiar to children, for example, being late for school, not doing homework, not having the correct uniform on. Model for the children what the child might say and how the teacher might respond, emphasising any causal connectives that you use. Ask the children to take turns in being the pupil and the teacher in the role play. Then ask a few children to present their role plays to the whole class and get the class to identify any causal connectives used while your 'teaching assistant' adds any additional causal connectives to your poster.

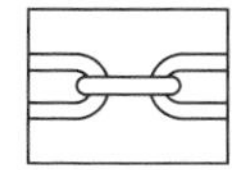

Explanation connectives

because

as a result

therefore

when

since

so

consequently

Should X be banned?

This is a useful way of providing children with the change-of-direction connectives they will need to join in debates on issues and to express themselves effectively when writing discursive text. Provide the children with a poster of change-of-direction connectives that are useful for argument and discursive writing.

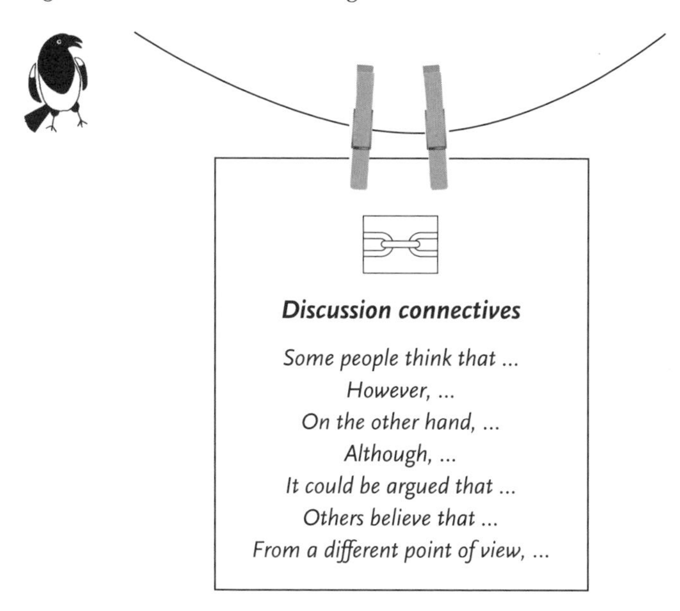

Think of any school-related issue that arouses strong opinions, for example, what the children are allowed to eat, wear or do. Model for the children how to present the different sides of the argument. Then ask the children to discuss the issue in pairs, with one child being *for* whatever it is and the other *against*. You may want to get some of the pairs to present their arguments to the whole class and add any additional change-of-direction connectives to your list.

What does it signal?

Deciding what the different sentence signposts signal can really get the children talking about the meaning of the phrases. Select a range of connective categories that are relevant to the work you are focusing on. For example, if you are focusing on discursive writing you may want to select the four categories chosen below. Present the following grid as a sorting activity so that the children in pairs or small groups have to sort all the phrases into the four categories.

Connectives signalling additional points	Connectives signalling change of direction	Connectives and signposts signalling cause and effect	Sentence signposts signalling uncertainty
Furthermore,	*but*	*because*	*It is possible that ...*
Additionally,	*However,*	*As a result,*	*It has been suggested ...*
In addition,	*Although*	*Therefore,*	*It could be argued that ...*
Moreover,	*On the other hand,*	*So that*	*whether or not*
Also	*Unfortunately/ unfortunately*	*This led to/ caused*	*Perhaps ...*

There are additional conjunction and connective games on pages 129–135.

What does my phrase signal?

An alternative and more active approach is to give each child a card with one connective phrase on it (see bullet points below) and then ask them to sort themselves into the appropriate clump using each corner of the room, plus the teacher's desk to represent one clump. When all the children have decided where they should be, ask each child to say their phrase to their group so that the group can agree that they are in the right clump. Then ask each group in turn to say their phrases to the whole class in the appropriate tone of voice. This engaging approach helps children internalise the phrases that signal the arguments for and against something.

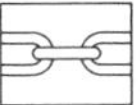

Introductory remarks • A much discussed question is ... • We are discussing whether or not ... • It's a well-known fact that ... • Let us look at ... • I intend to talk about ...	**Concluding remarks** • In conclusion, ... • In the final analysis, ... • Eventually, ... • Finally, ... • To sum it all up, ...
One side of the argument • First, let us examine ... • One side of the argument, ... • In my opinion, ... • On the one hand, ... • Many people think that ... • I believe that ...	**The other side of the argument** • On the other hand, ... • Some people would argue that ... • However, ... • Whereas, ... • Yet/Although, ... • From a different perspective, ...
Additional points • In addition, ... • One could add that ... • Furthermore, ... • Also, ... • Secondly, ...	

When the children return to their seats, give a copy of the completed sheet to each pair to support them in their task. Then show the children how to box up the plan for whatever is being discussed as below:

Simple boxed-up plan for discussing issues

Introduction to question	
• Arguments in favour ○ and any additional points	
• Arguments against ○ and any additional points	
Conclusion	

Now ask the children, in pairs, to present their argument to their partner using some of the phrases.

Raiding the reading

A useful way of helping children understand what connectives are good for is to draw their attention to the connectives in texts that they encounter across the curriculum. Look at any text that you will be using within a unit and think about the phrases that the children could magpie from this to use in their own work. Devise ways of drawing attention to useful phrases for the children to note down to use later. You may want to put these phrases on the flip chart as the class comes across them.

The know-it-all versus the thinking professor

Once children have begun to use a range of connectives effectively, introduce the idea of presenting arguments tentatively as opposed to with certainty. Our sound-bite world increasingly encourages people to present interpretations of events as if they were the absolute truth. This game strengthens children's use of the language of debate while helping them to be tentative about issues where the absolute truth is not known. Begin with a simple sorting activity where the children in pairs have to sort sentence signposts into those that signal certainty and those that signal uncertainty.

Uncertain versus certain (theory versus fact) signposts

It could be argued that ...	*It is clear that ...*	*It is worth considering ...*
The main cause is ...	*A key reason why ...*	*Another possible cause ...*
Research has established that ...	*Research suggests that ...*	*A possible cause of ...*

Think of any mythical creature or events for the children to discuss, then lack of factual knowledge cannot get in the way of crafting discursive sentences. For example:

> *Does the Loch Ness monster exist?*
> *Did Alice really visit Wonderland?*

Model how to debate the issue in pairs (with one person arguing adamantly for the existence of whatever is being debated and the other arguing strongly against) using phrases like:

> *'Research has proved that ...'*
> *'It is a well-known fact that ...'*

Now ask the children in pairs to practise arguing strongly, with one child representing each side. Get one or two pairs to present their debate so the children can hear what this sort of debate sounds like. Then ask them to be the thinking, reflective professor who considers the arguments that the other side might make and recognises that they could have a good point. Model for them how to argue reasonably and reflectively with the focus on being tentative and provide them with a range of tentative phrases like:

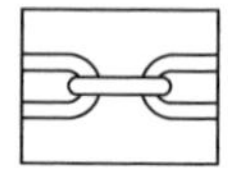

Phrases signalling uncertainty

It is not certain if ...

It is possible that ...

It might be worth considering ...

The evidence suggests ...

Then ask the children in pairs to practise being thinking professors. You may want to ask one pair to present their tentative debate to the whole class. Add any additional useful tentative phrases to your poster.

CHAPTER 4

Sentences

Clauses, phrases and different types of sentences

This chapter contains a bank of games that should be played on a regular basis as syntactical gymnastics, so that children enjoy a developing ability to create, manipulate and vary sentences to create different effects. Many pupils find writing hard because they are not skilled at writing sentences. Being able to write a sentence is as important to writing as kicking is to football. Weaker writers nearly always struggle with handwriting, spelling and sentence construction. The following games can be played by the whole class – or with groups or individuals who have a specific need. The games help children develop the ability to construct, control and vary sentences, and to choose language for effect. The following principles are important:

- **Daily** – it is repetition that helps children acquire skills automatically so that they are using language features with an automatic ease.
- **In relation to text type** – the words and sentences used in the games should relate to the text type that is being learned. So the children are hearing the language, saying it, seeing it, reading it and, ultimately, writing it.
- **In relation to progress** – practise the features and sentence types needed for progress. Marking should lead to direct feedback and action – otherwise it is pointless.
- **Hear it and say it** – in order for the children to be able to comfortably and fluently use different syntactical patterns, they need to have heard how the sentence 'goes'. The teacher has to model purposefully and repetitively the sentence types being taught by saying them aloud. The children then need to be put into a situation where they have to imitate, saying that sentence type. Many of the games therefore begin with 'hear it' and 'say it' before 'write it'.

- **Multi-sensory** – begin by speaking/hearing sentences, but reinforce this by using kinaesthetic methods – put words on cards, create washing line sentences, add words in and take words out and move words about. The principle is – hear it, say it, see it, move it, make it!
- **Colour** – to draw attention to specific structures or words, use colour to make the features stand out.
- **Explore** – use an investigative approach so that children are working things out for themselves with the teacher's guidance. Collect other examples of the sentence feature. Create class labels and put them on a wall chart to make them visible.
- **Model it** – before the children 'have a go' on their whiteboards, model examples. Start orally then use examples on card (visually) and then model construction in writing. Explicitly 'say it aloud' before writing – rehearsing the sentence in your mind. Also model rereading once you have constructed a sentence. You are trying to reinforce the idea that when you write you should think and rehearse, write and, finally, reread.
- **Discuss impact** – all this work is not just about writing sentences – it is also about becoming a writer. Think about the impact and effect. Keep discussing sentences in a 'readerly' and 'writerly' manner!
- **Practise** – practise sentence construction and variation as a matter of course, probably daily, for genuine control to develop. Otherwise, an illusion may be created whereby the children seem to be able to do things well on their whiteboards but when it comes to writing a longer text, they are not able to use the features that you have practised. Of course, writing stamina has to be developed but, for instance, the ability to simply punctuate without a second thought is something that comes only after a long time. Sentence construction needs to become a habit.
- **Grammar for the imagination** – the aim is for grammar to be taught creatively.
- **Relate the games to self-evaluation and marking** – remind children to use features that have been taught in their writing. They could underline or use a colour to show where or tally how many times they have used a feature. Mark **for effective usage, where the feature adds to the meaning.**
- **Hear, say and see it** – the following games can be shown on the IWB but remember that the children need to hear, say and see before they try writing.
- **Customise** – the games presented here are the main types of game, so all you need to do is add in more examples, customising them to the text type and anything that will help the children make progress.

WHAT IS A SENTENCE?

Spoken language is different to written language. One key difference is that because the speaker can use body language and there is a shared context, words may be omitted and a shrug imply what remains unspoken. In writing, there is no conversational partner and generally no shared context. The writer has to spell things out. This calls for sentences. The 'feel' for what constitutes a sentence is something that children begin to develop in nursery and continues throughout their lives. It is a conceptual understanding that gradually grows in particular through reading because spoken language is often not in complete sentences. If children are read to a lot and the teacher uses shared writing, most children soon begin to 'hear' what makes a whole sentence. In this way, you begin to make explicit some of the basic rules of a sentence such as it starts with a capital letter, ends with a full stop and makes sense on its own.

Spot the sentence

Try playing this simple game by providing a list of possible sentences. The children have to spot which are sentences and which are not, discussing how to turn them into sentences. Here are some to start you off:

I like to banana
the dog is barking loudly
The old ate all the doughnuts.
Fish like in water.
The tractor was painted bright red

Leave out the verbs

Of course, reading massively influences everyone's sense of what makes a sentence – so too does trying to write them. Try simple games where you omit all the verbs from the sentences or a paragraph so children can see and 'hear' that it is the verb that drives the sentence. Verbs are the engines of sentences – without them the sentence does not work. Here is a verbless paragraph to use.

Gravella out at the football pitch and. A moment later, her wish. Twenty players onto the field and soon the most extraordinary game. They a large Christmas pudding around the pitch. The pudding and but it no good. The players from one end of the field to the other.

Here is the original:

Gravella gazed out at the football pitch and wondered. A moment later, her wish was granted. Twenty players ran onto the field and soon the most extraordinary game began. They kicked a large Christmas pudding around the pitch. The pudding kept yelling and shouting but it was no good. The players ran from one end of the field to the other.

Draw up a toolkit poster with 'What we know about sentences'/'What can we say about a sentence'.

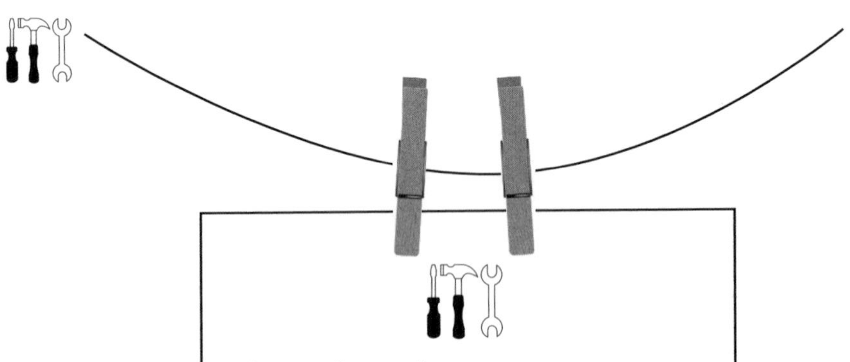

What we know about sentences

A sentence:

- is a group of words that creates a unit of meaning;
- is separated from other sentences by punctuation;
- starts with a capital letter and ends with a full stop, question or exclamation mark, or ellipsis;
- consists of one or more clauses, one of which will be the main clause;
- is built around a verb;
- can be a single word but is usually several words or more that make sense together.

Of course, there are all sorts or exceptions and provisos – however, young writers do not need to be bothered by anything too fancy. Little children have done very well for years on the notion that a sentence makes sense on its own, starts with a capital and ends with a full stop. With older pupils provide sentences or paragraphs in which some of the punctuation is missing or some of the sentences have key words omitted. This is a form of 'sentence doctor' (see example on page 144). Remember to get children using their sentence doctoring skills when editing their own work.

Mr Copycat (sentence imitation)

This game is ideal for nursery, reception classes and to use with children who are struggling with language. The idea is simple – the puppet says a sentence and the children have to 'say what the puppet says'. They have to listen and repeat. Sounds simple enough! Try varying HOW you say the sentence:

- loudly;
- softly;
- rhythmically;
- musically;
- word-by-word;
- syllable by syllable – like a ro-bot.

Try different sentence types, eg:

- long;
- short;
- complex;
- *when, how, where* starter;
- instructional;
- question.

If you have children who struggle with language, the game can be revealing. Use the list of sentences provided. Start with very short, simple words and then simple sentences. You will notice that the sentences increase in complexity. Eventually, you will get to a point where the child cannot imitate the sentence exactly. This will suggest something about their language development and may indicate to you what sorts of syntactical structures they might need to hear more often.

This sort of game is used by speech therapists to assess children's stage of language development. The errors let you know which syntactical patterns are not yet part of the child's linguistic competency. If the child finds it hard to repeat or makes an error, that may mean that the pattern needs constant modelling in a range of situations as well as helping the child repeat and innovate upon the pattern in order to internalise the structure.

The Mr Copycat game can be deployed to help children get ready for storytelling or writing other text types. For instance, when you are warming up the class before story writing, it might be a good idea to practise certain sentence structures. You might practise openings, *suddenly* sentences, exclamations, questions and so on.

When playing the game, notice the children's errors. But also remember that just because they can repeat what you are saying may not mean that they can use that sentence structure automatically in their everyday speech – they might just be good copiers!

1. Dog
2. Cat
3. Sheep
4. Big car
5. My friend
6. Go over there.
7. The bus is late.
8. Stop doing that.
9. Where is your reading book?
10. The ship sailed across the sea.
11. I can see a table and a chair.
12. I ate a doughnut last week.
13. The puppet is writing a list with a pencil.
25. The teacher gave the boy a letter.
26. Ali had a toy and Hamza had a banana.
27. The giant walked across the cave and then he ate his breakfast.
28. The princess cried when she saw the sad farmer.
29. After the king ate his breakfast, he had a cup of tea.
30. While Sal ran home, Bill dug the garden.
31. The bumblebee was caught by the crafty cat.
32. Jo ate the apple that the queen had given to her.
33. The king, who was waiting in the castle, ate a sandwich.
34. Aunty Mabel, running as fast as she could, soon came to the lake.
35. Because he had not slept, Bill went home.
36. The bumblebee, the eagle and the old shark soon became the best of friends.
37. While the teacher was talking, the two boys, who had just finished cleaning up the mess, asked if they could help her when she went out to her car.

Children speaking and writing sentences

Of course, every teacher knows that the trickiest part of teaching writing is to get children writing in sentences that flow into each other, driving the meaning forwards – demarcated with accuracy. One of the key aspects of Talk for Writing (www.talk4writing.co.uk) is that children learn stories and non-fiction texts (and poems) orally, using a text map and actions to support the retelling. This powerful tool helps many children internalise sentence patterns that they can then draw upon when writing.

Children learn language partly through 'imitation' – copying the patterns and vocabulary that those around them use. This store of language is added to and enriched through constant reading. However, language learning is more than copying. The young brain has the extraordinary ability to work out the underlying pattern of the home language and use these patterns to create new utterances that they have never heard before. In other words, if many of a child's early stories start by using this pattern, *Once upon a time there was a farmer who lived near a forest*, it may ultimately mean that the child can invent a totally new opening for a story by using the same underlying pattern – *Once upon a time there was a soldier who lived by a stream*. This ability, known as 'generative grammar', helps children create new utterances on the back of familiar underlying patterns. However, generative grammar only works if the children understand what the sentences mean. Language is acquired through memorable, meaningful repetition.

One simple way to help children develop the ability to write in sentences is to learn texts orally or to reread a picture book so often that the child knows it word for word. This sort of intense reading and learning is supported by daily 'shared writing' where the teacher leads the children in composing and writing sentences. This can begin in the nursery where the teacher makes up a sentence and writes it in front of the children, with the children helping as best they can. Sentence writing of this sort should be daily and, during the early years in school, can be increased gradually so that every day short paragraphs, stories, messages, letters and information are written in front of the children to help them with spelling, punctuation, vocabulary and ideas.

As children acquire phonics for basic spellings and for a few tricky words they can soon begin to orally invent and then write their own simple sentences using the sounds that they know, eg *I can see a cat*. Daily sentence writing is important and soon this develops into more fluent composition. All of this work develops children's understanding of sentences and their ability to independently construct and vary them to create effective compositions.

Early sentence games

- Use a selection of colours to write a story in 'rainbow sentences' where each sentence is in a different colour. Let children try the same activity.
- Write sentences in two colours, remembering to swap coloured pens.
- Every day children have to write a sentence. When they can write one sentence with a capital letter and full stop then they get a certificate and move to two sentences.
- Use guided writing from the beginning so that teaching writing words and sentences is directly linked to teaching phonics and tricky words. The teacher starts by dictating known sounds that the children write down. Once there are enough sounds (c-s-a-o-t-g-i-n-e-d) then simple words can be written or made using magnetic letters (*cat, sat, see*). Once there are enough sounds – and a few words – then the teacher can dictate simple sentences for writing, eg *I can see a dog.* Be vigilant at this stage so that children acquire the right habits at an early age.
- Make a fuss about full stops by making them special, eg instead of using full stops, provide stickers such as footballs to use.
- Perform a poem or read a story and clap every full stop or stamp a foot.
- Write on the flip chart a simple text with no full stops or capital letters.
- Write on a flip chart a text with no punctuation and then add it in the wrong places by using Blu-tack full stops. Read it aloud as directed by the punctuation to hear how odd it sounds. Then move the Blu-tack till it sounds 'right'.
- Have fun making up alliterative sentences about animals – *The slow snake slipped silently by the slimy staircase.*
- Early on it is worth remembering that you have to emphasise that the full stop does not come at the end of the line but at the end of the chunk of meaning.
- Try writing a simple story but miss words out so the sentences do not make sense. Children suggest what is missing and then reread to hear how they sound and make sense.
- Provide a list of characters – these could be toys or cards with pictures on them. Then make sentences up about each one. Try this with objects or by taking several words from a bag and see if you can make up a sentence using both words.
- After a while, move on to making up sentences using 'and' or 'but' to extend the ideas.
- Provide dull sentences and bring them to life by adding in extra detail.

Silly writer

The teacher writes in front of the children but keeps making silly mistakes – these might be spelling errors, missing out words, muddling words up, omitting capital letters or punctuation. The children have to help the poor old teacher!

Billy and Betty

Years ago, I invented two characters called Billy and Betty. The idea was quite simple. On some days Billy or Betty (they were twins) would sneak into our classroom and write the next part of our story on the flip chart. The trouble with Billy and Betty was that they kept making the same sorts of mistakes that the class made so the children had to help Billy and Betty by rereading their writing and editing. One teacher actually overheard two seven-year-olds saying one day, 'It's funny, but I think Billy is getting better at writing!'

The writing agony aunt

Older pupils can role-play at being a writing agony aunt. It can help if you cook up a piece of writing yourself that has many of the sorts of weaknesses that are typical in the class's writing but also include some real strengths. The children have to edit the writing – perhaps using polishing pens (see below) – but also write a message to the writer, advising on how to improve. This might be as a message, letter or a list of ideas. Develop a sense of the children being 'experts' so that writing well is not an instinctive activity but often discussed so that children have explicit understanding about how good use of grammar can create an effect on the reader.

Polishing pens

Provide children with polishing pens. These can be fine coloured highlighters. When you 'mark' children's writing use a certain colour to indicate what is effective, eg pink for perfect. Then use a different colour to indicate where the writing needs improving, developing or is inaccurate, eg green for growth. When the writing is returned, the children then use their polishing pens (any fine highlighter pen that they only use to polish their writing) to improve anything marked in green by the teacher. Some schools use various symbols to indicate where a punctuation error has been made (p) or a spelling error (sp) or an improvement or change is required (I). This sort of habit means that children's errors do not slip by unnoticed. Of course, the polishing pens are popular. If you use a visualiser, project a child's work and model how to read through a piece of writing, discussing 'what works', 'what does not' and 'how to improve'. Children can eventually work as response partners, editing and developing in pairs. It is crucial that they share and discuss the writing rather than just swapping books – it is the discussion about 'what works' and 'why' that helps the children to learn about what makes effective writing and how to improve their own compositions.

Build a sentence

I have often wondered why it is that so many children can have been in school for seven years and still cannot write sentences. Of course, a very small number of children find it difficult to grasp the concept but the truth is that almost every child can ... but yet they do not. Perhaps we need to make sure that, every single day, we play sentence games to help children acquire the automatic habit of punctuation. This should be a rigorous basic in all primary education – daily sentence work in relation to the text type. Of course, the other side of the coin relates to 'marking'. Perhaps we should avoid 'ticking' children's writing if it lacks capital letters and full stops and sentences. It may well be that it is crucial to insist on the habit from the very start of writing so that children gain the right habits rather than constantly writing without demarcation.

Building sentences is a key game and should be played on many occasions. There are endless possible permutations. Quite simply, the teacher provides an instruction and the children have to create sentences. This could be orally or in writing on a mini whiteboard. With strugglers and younger children use words on cards and create a washing-line sentence – or have children holding each card and standing in line to form a 'human sentence'.

- Start by writing one word on the board. The children make up a sentence. If spoken, they should use an action and sound to show the punctuation. If writing, insist on capital letters and full stops.
- Remind children to double check before showing – 'Don't show me until you've checked your own sentence.'
- When you can catch no one out, move on to two words and then three.
- Experiment with different word combinations, eg *shark, jelly, because.*
- As they become confident with capital letters and full stops, begin to intervene with the quality.
- Try using images on the IWB and asking the children to write sentences triggered by the image.
- Move on to writing two or more sentences so that mini paragraphs begin to appear. The aim is to be able to do this swiftly, accurately and, eventually, effectively.
- Try other forms of the game, varying the challenge:
    - a short sentence; a dramatic sentence;
    - exclamation or question;
    - adverb at the start;

- long sentence;
- sentence with three things happening;
- sentence with 'because' in the middle;
- opening line to a story;
- factual sentence about dragons;
- advertising sentence starting with, *'Buy…'*;
- a sentence to present a persuasive point starting with, *Most people believe that …*;
- a sentence with three adjectives or powerful verbs.

Adapt the types of sentences and the language challenges according to the text type that you are working on – and whatever will help the children make progress.

Statement, question, command, exclamation

There are four basic types of sentence. The statement usually has a subject before the verb and provides information about something. Most children's early writing consists of statements – *The dog is barking at the park keeper.*

Most teachers start work on questions early on – both posing them and answering them! This informal work soon leads into noticing them in shared reading and trying them out in shared writing. Many young children enjoy the spectacular possibilities of a curly question mark in their writing. Questions, of course, ask for something. They usually use what is called an interrogative pronoun – known in school as 'wh' words – *who, when, where, why, what, how*. The subject often follows an auxiliary verb – ***Can** you see the shop?* Of course, to use questions effectively, the young writer does not need to know these things – just be able to do them. Questions are handy in writing as they often seem to involve the reader – *Have you ever wanted to fly?*

Commands feature in instructional writing. They tell the reader or someone or something what to do. They use what small children call 'bossy' verbs or the 'imperative' – *Run to the end of the road.*

Exclamations differ slightly from commands because they use exclamation marks and may just be a dramatic statement – *It was huge!* (See glossary, page 217, for DfE's definition for Y6 examination purposes only in England.)

This is a silly but fun game and could be played in pairs. Select a topic, eg bananas. The children have to write four sentences, one for each type:

statement – *The monkey ate the bananas.*
question – *Why do bananas curve like the moon?*
command – *Peel the green banana.*
exclamation – *The banana exploded!*

Silly questions

Working in pairs, partner A writes a question using *why* – *Why do clouds not fall from the sky?* At the same time partner B writes an answer WITHOUT seeing the question using *This is because …* – *This is because they find that exercise keeps them fit.* A list of questions and answers can be put together:

- *Why do clouds not fall from the sky? This is because they find that exercise keeps them fit.*
- *Why did the mouse hide in the hole? This is because the sea reflects the blue sky.*
- *Why do trees have leaves? This is because wheels are round so they spin round.*

Fantasy commands

Neil Gaiman has written an interesting book called *Instructions* (Bloomsbury, 2010) which is literally just that – but they are magical. Try writing a set of fantasy instructions, using commands, eg:

a. *Walk to the distant mountain.*
b. *Pick the first feather that falls from the sky.*
c. *Stroke the surface of the purple rock as dawn breaks.*
d. *Ride the black unicorn till you come to the bridge made of rainbows.*

Instructions

Here are some quick-fire ideas for talking games and activities to practise using instructional sentences. Children could be in a small group or pair and have to say a distinct sentence each:

- create class instructions, eg how to care for class hamster/pet;
- role-play imaginatively, eg how to care for a goblin or gnome, catch a mermaid or journey to the end of a rainbow;
- instruction game, eg how to put on a pullover; how to get to the door;
- model instructions when moving in the hall;
- invent magical recipes;
- teach others how to play a playground game;
- design new board or card games;
- create instructions based on a map – real or invented;
- bring in a game and instruct others;
- show and tell – instructing the class.

Do what I say

This is a version of 'Simon says' – best played in the hall. Children choose a card with a bossy verb on it and have to invent a sentence to boss everyone around.

run	*hop*	*stand*	*walk*	*turn*
jump	*move*	*curl*	*stretch*	*touch*
crawl	*nod*	*shake*	*bend*	*blink*
tiptoe	*open*	*close*	*wave*	*bunny hop*

Provide a simple challenge such as, 'Walk to the door'. Dish out the cards. Children put up their hands when they think that their card needs to be played and they say the sentence.

first	*secondly*	*before*	*as soon as*
next	*to begin with*	*while*	*finally*
after that	*then*	*just as*	
now	*when*	*as*	

WHAT IS A CLAUSE?

Clauses are the basis of sentences. A clause is a group of words built around a verb that make sense together. They are rather like little sentences. They have a subject and a verb, though in some sentences the subject is implied and not actually stated. There are different ways to look at the role of clauses in sentences.

- **Simple sentences** – these are made up of one thing happening so they have one clause: *The curious cat purred all day.*
- **Compound sentences** – these are made up of two clauses of equal weight, both being main clauses and are linked together by co-ordinating conjunctions such as *and, but, or, so*: *The curious cat purred all day* ***but*** *the dog growled.*

- **Complex sentences** – these sentences have a main clause supported by one or more subordinate clauses: *The cat ran indoors because the dog barked.* In this sentence the main thing that happens is *the cat ran indoors* and that forms a sentence on its own so it is the main clause. It can stand on its own. The other clause is *because the dog barked.* This cannot stand on its own as a sentence and in order for it to make sense has to be attached to the main clause. The subordinate clause is less important – it is an extra piece of information that is added on to the main clause – the main event. Most subordinate clauses can move around in a sentence, placed at the front, dropped into the middle or tagged on at the end. This can cause slightly different effects and impact on the reader.

Some children find defining clauses as simple, compound and complex muddling because some simple sentences can be quite complicated and many complex sentences are actually quite straightforward. Perhaps a simpler way to think about clauses and sentences is to focus on the notion of single or multiple clause sentences. Single clause sentences have one clause (simple sentence) and will only have one thing happening – one verb. These are all single clause sentences:

The dog barked.

The dog barked at the fish and chip van.

The dog with the red collar barked at the fish and chip van at the side of the road.

In multi-clause sentences, there will always be a main clause and one or more other clauses, eg:

The dog barked and the cat purred.

The dog barked while the cat crept under the car where it waited patiently.

Here *The dog barked* is the main clause. *While the cat crept under the car* and *where it waited patiently* are both subordinate clauses as they sound odd if said aloud on their own and obviously need a main clause.

Spot the main clause

Play simple games where children underline the clauses in a sentence and decide which is the main and which are subordinate clauses. The main clause will stand on its own like a sentence. The subordinate will not make sense on its own and needs the main clause in order to make sense. It helps if you say them aloud and listen to which chunk makes sense on its own. Work on sentences that relate to the text type that you are working on. Look at good examples and select elegant sentences for children to play 'Spot the main clause'. Ask them to underline the subordinate clauses in one colour and the main clause in a different colour. Here are a few:

The shark, which is found around the world, generally lives in sea water.
That night the twins went home, hoping for a good meal.
After boiling the water, stir the soup gently.
The car slows down as soon as the brakes are applied.
Excited by the golden crown, the prince sat down.

What happens if you take out the subordinate clauses? Could these be added as an extra sentence? How does the writing now sound?

WHAT IS A PHRASE?

A phrase is a bunch of words that go together and are built around a single word that they develop. They do not make full sense on their own. For instance, *the huge, angry dog* is a phrase built around a noun (*dog*). It can be fun building noun phrases (see pages 36–38). They are useful for describing things.

- **Prepositional phrases** tell the reader 'where' something is. They are built around a preposition, eg *beyond the city wall.* Try writing simple list poems using a repeated prepositional phrase:

  Beyond the city wall, there is a cloud drifting.
  Beyond the city wall, a mouse scuttles across the wall.
  Beyond the city wall, sunlight lingers.
  Beyond the city wall, a hawk soars high and calls …

- **Verb phrases** are a collection of words built around a verb, eg *will be running.*
- **Adverbial phrases** work in the same way, modifying an adverb, eg *unusually late.*
- **Adjectival phrases** also can be built up, eg *beautifully green.*

It is quite handy to be taught how to add in extra information into a sentence about a character's relationship:

Mr Rustynose, the colonel's son, ran down the road.
Mrs Snaggletooth, Boris's sister, sat down.
John, the doctor's father, smiled.

Retell a story phrase by phrase or word by word

A popular game used in drama groups is to pair the children up (or play this in threes or round a small circle). Each child takes it in turn to say the next word, or chunk, creating a simple story. So it might begin like this:

Child A: Once
Child B: upon
Child A: a
Child B: time
Child A: there
Child B: was ... etc.

Use this to invent a new and playful story in which anything happens. Or pupils might retell a story (or other text) that is well known. A third option would be to provide ingredients such as a character, setting, object and dilemma. Build in adding in punctuation by using actions or speaking aloud, 'full stop'.

A variation of this game is to play in the same way but instead of building the sentences word by word, build stories 'sentence by sentence'. This is actually quite hard and children have to think carefully. Once they have developed an idea, pairs could come out and perform in front of the class.

Five-sentence stories

This simple game can be quite challenging. Put the children into groups of five and provide them with five key connectives, eg *Once upon a time/one day/unfortunately/luckily/finally*. Each group has to create a story using the basic story mountain structure, starting each sentence with the given connectives. These can be spoken orally or even written down.

Once upon a time – there was a princess who lived in a tower.
One day – she climbed down the tower and escaped.
Unfortunately – the wicked King chased her.
Luckily – she grew wings and flew away.
Finally – she found a little village where everyone had wings.

It is worth collecting any simple story ideas from this activity that seem to have potential as fully-blown tales. These could then be embellished so that each sentence becomes a paragraph.

Word by word

In this game, children are selected one at a time to add another word to a sentence. This could be done by using their mini whiteboards or by writing the next word on a flip chart, IWB or whiteboard. The game is to try and avoid ending the sentence. You can spice the game up by providing ingredients – these could be different words or objects that have to be included.

Imitation

Look carefully at the text type being studied and at the children's writing. What sentence patterns will they need to use that might be new, provide a challenge or will help them make progress? Isolate these sentence patterns and then daily use them for simple innovation. Let us imagine that the class is working on discussion writing. It is likely that the phrase 'whether or not' will be new to many young children but it is also something that is almost essential when introducing a topic for debate. Write up a sentence on the board and then use it for innovation. How many can the children create in a minute or two minutes. Here is the model sentence and some innovations:

> *We are discussing whether or not a new shopping mall should be built in our town.*
> *We are discussing whether or not a skateboard ramp should be built in the playground.*
> *We are discussing whether or not dragons exist locally.*

This basic idea is crucial for helping children develop their repertoire of sentences. Before writing the sentences, work a while on saying them orally. This speeds the process up – but is also crucial because children cannot write sentences unless they can say them ... And they cannot say them unless they have heard them so the teacher has to be in the habit of constantly modelling sentence patterns for the class. Good teachers know that when they are talking with the class, it is not any old chit chat. They are modelling eloquent talk. They are modelling sentences.

Opposites

Provide a list of sentences and then get the children to 'say the opposite'. This will involve a negative, eg:

> *The fireman climbed the ladder.*
> *The fireman did not climb the ladder.*

Sound and action sentences

This game is fun and helpful. It can be played in various ways by children of any age. It is a powerful strategy that helps children remember punctuation. Punctuation is not like spelling. Words make sounds when spoken aloud – they are more tangible than punctuation. Punctuation is more to do with meaning, expression and pause.

Using a sound effect and action whenever you punctuate makes it more obvious. If children's writing is not punctuated effectively, then embed this idea into your teaching for a term or two – and, as if by magic, punctuation will begin to appear in their writing! Agree with the children on actions and sound effects for punctuation. (Older pupils can use instruments.)

Punctuation mark	Sound effect	Action
.	Bang	Punch forwards
!	Whee bang	Move hand down and punch
?	Ugh?	Scratch head as if unsure or make question mark in the air
,	Eeeek	Flick of wrist in comma shape
Capital letter	Just use action	Hands over head, like a cap

- With young children, start with just the full stop.
- Play the game with action and sound many times before writing. Reinforce by using colour for punctuation when writing.
- Try reading and putting in sound effects and actions. This can be used by groups or pairs to perform stories, poems or impart information.
- Try the game so that you say a sentence and then children have to add in the appropriate sound and action.
- Invent sentences and put in sound and action.
- Add sound and action punctuation to whole stories or poems. This can be useful if the children in Year 1 learn several stories in this way as a precursor to writing. You will find that it virtually ensures correct punctuation!

Punctuation mark	Sound effect	Action
.		
!		
?		
,		
" "		
: or ;		
Capital letter		

Young children can find basic punctuation hard. However, orally learning stories by using Talk for Writing is a simple way of helping children internalise sentence patterns. Get them to say a text aloud and stamp the ground whenever they get to a full stop – that soon helps them internalise a strong sense of when to use one!

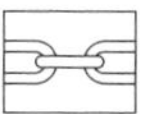

Louisa's connectives game

Louisa is a Year 2 teacher in North Wales whose class invented this game. It is important to note that the class spends 10–15 minutes every day on storytelling. Each class in the school does storytelling while the children are having their milk! When I visited, they were working on *The Magic Porridge Pot*. Louisa provided a large story map on a coat hanger. Because the children have heard and told many stories using connectives, they are therefore familiar with the syntactical patterns those connectives produce. They have heard it and said it. And in shared reading and writing, they have seen it and watched it being written. All this experience helps them play the game.

- Put a range of connectives that might be used in a story (or any other text type) on cards.
- Begin by making up a simple story.
- Pause at a point and select a connective.
- The children (or chosen child) have to continue the story using the connective.
- Through playing the game, you will discover that certain connectives are easier to use than others. For instance, most Year 2 children will find 'so' or 'when' not too hard. However, 'before' may prove more problematical.

- This all depends on their familiarity with the connectives. You may have to prompt them or model how to use a connective. It can help to provide the opening of a sentence. For instance, if you hold up 'when', you might help by saying 'when she ...'.
- Start with a simple range of connectives. Over time, add more. When a new connective is added, model how to say the sentence before expecting the children to be able to invent their own.
- Try stopping mid-sentence and use a conjunction that can introduce another clause.
- Try stopping at the end of a sentence and hold up a connective that could open a new sentence. Try using 'when' words (temporal connectives), 'how' words (adverbs) and 'where' words (prepositions).

Openings	Once upon a time Early one bright morning It all began when Once there lived Once there was
Build ups	First Late one night One day When Next One afternoon/morning/night/day While Since So Till As Before Until
Problems	Suddenly Unluckily Unfortunately At that moment Without warning However To her/his amazement

Resolution	Luckily So Amazingly Unexpectedly Fortunately
Ending	At long last So it was that … Finally Eventually In the end

Finish

This is a simple game to play. All you do is provide a chunk from a sentence and let the children complete it – either orally or in writing. Use sentence chunks from the sort of writing that you are working with.

- Start with openers – *The old king …*
- Then move on to the ends of sentences – *… covered with red plants!*
- Hardest of all, select a chunk from the middle of a sentence – *… made up of all the …*
- A variation that helps children use conjunctions is to provide an initial clause with the conjunction attached for the children to complete – *Jenny ran away rapidly* ***because*** *…*

When playing this game, get the child to say the whole sentence.

Starts	Ends	Middles to muddle you!
He must have …	*… and sat down.*	*… boasted that he …*
If you try hard, you …	*… down the hill.*	*… shadow fell across …*
The moment he had …	*… came into his head.*	*… owls and foxes …*
Once they had …	*… stay here.*	*… wanted to make …*
She turned from the …	*… the edge of the sofa.*	*… closer to …*
Encouraged by the giant's smile, Sally …	*… twisted her ankle.*	*… way of his …*

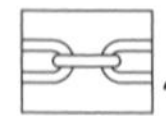

Joining games

There are various games that can be played with the idea of sentence combination, at different levels. The first can be used with younger children and the less confident. This involves you saying an opening clause, such as, *The king picked up the doughnut ...* Then provide a few conjunctions on cards. The children select – or you choose for them – a conjunction and have to complete the sentence.

and	*since*	*but*	*or*	*so that*
because	*if*	*though*	*when*	*while*
where	*wherever*	*in order to*	*as*	*as soon as*
before	*after*	*until*	*although*	*to*

The king picked up the doughnut and ate it.
The king picked up the doughnut but not the carrot.
The king picked up the doughnut because he was hungry.

What you notice will inform you directly about what needs to be modelled. Some young children will only be comfortable with using 'and'. This means that they need to hear other conjunctions being used. Remember, you can prompt by adding in an extra word or two as a clue as to how the sentence might run on, eg *The king picked up the doughnut which was ...*

A different way to play the game is to provide the bank of conjunctions and then provide lists of opening clauses and ending clauses. All the children have to do is join the two bits together using a conjunction. Again, notice which child is comfortable with which conjunctions. Challenge them to use new ones and see what happens.

The troll hid under the bridge

The big goat was angry

The baby goat was afraid

The troll lived under the bridge

The baby goat was hungry

The big goat butted the troll

it tried to cross the bridge.
it fell into the water.
it managed to cross the bridge.
the troll appeared.
waited for the goats.
it had no home.

Many children get stuck using *and* as their primary strategy for joining sentences. This either makes for dull writing with no sentence variation or, if you 'ban' the use of *and*, they end up writing lots of short, simple sentences so that their writing sounds like machine gun fire! Try playing the following game frequently to broaden their range of strategies for combination. In the game, the children are provided with a pair of sentences that they have to 'join' in order to make one sentence. Provide them with conjunctions on cards or make a list. Notice how the conjunction either falls at the start of the sentence or in the middle. Note too where the comma falls. As ever – start orally before moving into writing. For example:

The bus stopped.
The old lady got off.

This might be joined in two basic ways – using the conjunction at the front of the first sentence or in between:

As *the bus stopped, the old lady got off.*
The bus stopped **so** *the old lady got off.*

The final version of this game moves into working on varying openings to sentences. In this game, the children are provided with two sentences and they have to join them by using the verb in its *ing* or *ed* form (non-finite).

He ran down the road. He fell over. = Running down the road, he fell over.
Jim was interested in the idea. He rang his friend. = Interested in the idea, Jim rang his friend.

Now try joining these sentences:

The cart came to a wheezing halt. Gandalf strode into the hobbit hole.
The thunder roared. The hobbits hid.
Bilbo ate a snack. The goblins attacked the dwarves.

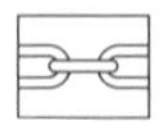

Sentence combination

This game has been researched and shown to improve children's writing. It is well known in America and Australia but is not universally used. There are various ways to play the game. Try giving children a series of statements about a topic. The children have to blend the information and create a single sentence:

> *The cat crept.*
> *It was a marmalade cat.*
> *It went along the wall.*
> *It crept cautiously.*

This could be turned into a single sentence: *The marmalade cat crept cautiously along the wall.* Start by asking children to turn two or three related sentences into one. The more information provided, the more demanding the problem:

> *The fox slept.*
> *It was very tired.*
> *It had travelled far.*
> *It dreamed of sunlit forests.*
> *It slept for hours on end.*

An alternative to listing a few sentences to combine is to provide some instructions in this way:

> *The teacher stopped* (where?), *picked up the book* (how?) *and ran* (where/doing what?).
> *The teacher stopped in the car park, picked up the book cautiously and ran into the staffroom crying.*
> *The car accelerated* (where?), *drove round the corner* (how?) *and came to a halt* (where/doing what?).

Remember to base the sentences on the text and content that you are working on – here is a simple example based on information writing about the Victorians.

> *Queen Victoria escaped many assassination attempts. She escaped seven attempts in all. She was seemingly invincible.*

This final example is more challenging. The sentences do form a mini paragraph but because they are all the same length and pattern, they sound like machine gun fire. How can some of them be linked to gain flow? Which should be left as short, dramatic sentences? Below, on the right-hand side, you can see one way of combining sentences to create a paragraph.

The Skoda shuddered to a halt. *Bill leapt out.* *He ran for cover.* *A car shot round the bend.* *It skidded to a standstill.* *Three men climbed out.* *They began to search Bill's car.* *He waited.* *He clutched the suitcase.*	*As the Skoda shuddered to a halt, Bill leapt out and ran for cover. A car shot round the bend, skidded to a standstill and three men climbed out. Bill waited, clutching the suitcase, as they began to search the car.*

Here is a paragraph to try and inject more flow into the sentences:

> *The car came to a halt. He climbed out. He walked across the road. He went into the shop. He looked for ages. He found a toy. He had wanted it for ages. He bought it.*

Change

This is a simple game to develop the skill of sentence manipulation. The teacher provides a sentence, eg *The old king sat down.*

Then the children are given an instruction, eg turn this into a question. *Did the old king sit down?*

Try other instructions, depending on the text type:

- Make it longer/shorter;
- Add adjectives;
- Add an adverb;
- Change it so that it alliterates;
- Change the words;
- Change the beginning, middle or end;
- Turn it into a newspaper headline;
- Write a fact about it …

Change the opening

To work on varying openings, try providing a sentence and ask the children to change the opening using a different tactic. Use:

- an adverb (how);
- a temporal connective (when);
- a prepositional phrase (where);
- an *ing* verb;
- an *ed* verb;
- a simile using *like;*
- a simile using *as;*
- a single word;
- an adjective.

Now experiment with changing these sentences, modelling the first one for them as below:

The old king sat down.
The caterpillar went along the wall.
Sharks are not all dangerous.
The cat sat on the mat.

Varying openings	Example
How – adverb	*Angrily, the old king sat down.*
When – time connective	*In the afternoon, the old king sat down.*
Where? – prepositional phrase	*On the hilltop, the old king sat down.*
ing verb	*Giggling, the old king sat down.*
ed verb	*Excited, the old king sat down.*
Simile using *like*	*Like a Buddha, the old king sat down.*
Simile using *as*	*As thin as a whippet, the old king sat down.*
Single word	*Weary, the old king sat down.*
An adjective	*Tall trees shaded the old king.*

A different way to emphasise the openings to sentences is to select a powerful paragraph and just present the opening phrases. The children can play this in pairs – each taking it in turn to say the next sentence, using the provided opener. On the left-hand side are openings for a suspense paragraph – on the right is a possible solution.

Suspense sentences	
She/ he crept …	*She crept into the abandoned warehouse.*
At that moment …	*At that moment, she heard a low moan.*
Hardly daring to breathe …	*Hardly daring to breathe, she crouched down and waited.*
Without warning …	*Without warning, a rat scuttled across the dank floorboards.*
Horrified …	*Horrified, she stood up.*
Silently …	*Silently, she made her way towards to door.*
Something was …	*Something was following her.*

Change the mood

This is a more subtle game than the above game of change. Provide the children with a sentence or paragraph and then ask them to change the mood or intention. For instance, change this sentence to alter the character:

> *Mrs Strict glared at the class and clenched her fists.*

This could become: *Mrs Smiley grinned at the class and waggled her fingers.*

Try changing character as well as settings:

> *The wind moaned in the trees and darkness engulfed the lane.*

This could become: *The wind whispered in the trees and sunlight brightened the lane.*

Now, try using this in non-fiction writing. For instance, alter the viewpoint (bias) of the journalist in this piece:

> *Last week United played a disastrous game in which they were lucky to scrape an extra goal putting them only just ahead of Forest Wanderers.*

This could become: *Last week United played a tremendous game, winning by a heart-stopping goal giving them a well-deserved lead ahead of Forest Wanderers.*

Try providing several sentences or paragraphs. Ask the children about the mood created. Underline which words create the mood and explain why the word works. Try swapping key words and listen to the difference. For instance in this sentence, what is the mood and which words create that mood?

Joanna hopped into the room, tickled the cat under the chin and giggled.

An alternative is to take a paragraph and once again ask the children about the mood or effect being created – but slip in one or two words that do not quite 'fit in'. Which are they and can the children suggest better alternatives? In this example, I think that there are two words that do not quite fit in (*skipped/glowing*).

Tina wiped a tear from the corner of her eye, crouched down on the chair and waited with her head in her hands. Time crept by, whilst tear after tear skipped down her cheek. She sniffed occasionally, dabbing at her glowing face with a tissue. Everyone else busied themselves and no one dared come near.

Adding on

Play this game to develop the ability to extend sentences. Begin with a simple sentence, eg *Bob was happy.*

Provide a list of connectives: *because, while, whenever, although, despite, after, even though, as, however, who, which, that.*

The game is for the children to create as many different complex sentences as they can within a given time, by adding a chunk before, after or within the sentence you have provided:

After eating a turkey drumstick, *Bob was happy.*
Bob was happy ***because he was watching Ant and Dec.***
*Bob****, who was watching 'Celebrity Teacher',*** *was happy.*

Try these more demanding tasks. Look at the examples first.

- using 'why' – *They wondered* ***why*** *Bob was happy.*
- using 'what' – *They wondered* ***what*** *had made Bob happy.*
- using 'how' – *They wondered* ***how*** *Bob had got so happy.*
- using 'when' – *Bob was happy* ***when*** *he giggled.*
- using 'if' – *Bob was happy* ***if*** *he won at games.*
- using 'once' – *Bob was happy* ***once*** *he had won.*
- using 'with' – *Bob was happy* ***with*** *the news.*
- using 'that' – *Bob was happy* ***that*** *he was eating a doughnut.*

Ask the children to make as many complex sentences as possible, using any of the words in the box, working with the sentences given below.

because	*while*	*whenever*	*although*	*despite*
after	*even though*	*as*	*however*	*who*
which	*that*	*but*	*so*	
,	*.*	*!*	*?*	

Try using these sentences:

The dragon grinned.
The alien sneezed.
The superhero ate his packed lunch.
Tracy was angry.

Tagging on a question

Provide the children with a sentence and show them how to tag on a question: *She ran home, didn't she?* Show how this can be used in non-fiction, such as argument: *Eating too much fat is dangerous, or is it?* Collect examples from texts and discuss how the tagged on question makes the reader think.

Drop-in

This game can be played in a simple or more complex manner depending on the amount of support that is given. Provide a simple sentence, eg *The queen picked up the shark.*

The children are then asked to drop in extra detail (a collection of adjectives and adverbs can help less confident language users). Try the following, using banks of words or the children's ideas:

- **Adjectives** – *The* ***young*** *queen picked up the* ***dead*** *shark.*
- **Adverbs** – *The queen picked up the shark* ***carefully.***
- **Relative clause** – *The queen,* ***who was frightened,*** *picked up the shark.*

There are three types of clause pattern worth playing with. Show the children a sentence and then add the clause in or onto the sentence: *The shopkeeper picked up a bag of doughnuts.*

- Drop in a relative clause (*who, which* or *that*): *The shopkeeper,* ***who was hungry,*** *picked up a bag of doughnuts.*

- Drop in an *ing* clause (non-finite): *The shopkeeper,* ***hoping no one would notice,*** *picked up a bag of doughnuts.*
- Drop in an *ed* clause (non-finite): *The shopkeeper,* ***excited by the sugary topping,*** *picked up a bag of doughnuts.*

Try these sentences to practise drop-ins:

The elf waited by the house where the giant lived.
The spaceship landed on top of the teacher's shoulder.
Barry picked up the book, the hat and the parrot.
The castle was covered in slime that had fallen from the clouds.
Sir Percy managed to stay on the dragon's back until they reached the forest where he fell off onto the ground.

Boring sentences

Provide the children with a list of dull sentences. The task is for the class to rewrite the sentences to create a stronger image for the reader. It is worth categorising the different sorts of things that you can do to make a sentence more lively, descriptive or dramatic. This could be turned into a wall poster or put into the children's writing journals.

Take this simple sentence: *The bird flew on to the car.*
Here are some ways that you might use to make this more interesting:

You can:	How the sentence changes
• Add words	*The scarlet bird flew on to the shabby car.*
• Drop chunks in	*The bird, which was scarlet, flew on to the car.*
• Add on at the end	*The bird flew on to the car because it was shiny.*
• Add at the beginning	*As it was tired, the bird flew on to the car.*
• Change words	*The parrot settled on the Mercedes.*
• Add in a simile	*The bird flew like a dragon on to the car.*
• Alliterate	*The brave bird blundered on to the cool car.*
• Reorder	*On to the car flew the bird.*

Now try making these sentences more interesting. Here are some more sentences to try:

The cat went along the wall.
The dog ate the bone.
The man got the thingy.
The worm went.

You can:	**How the sentence changes**
• Add words	
• Drop chunks in	
• Add on at the end	
• Add at the beginning	
• Change words	
• Add in a simile	
• Alliterate	
• Reorder	

Here is another way of playing around with sentences by altering them.

Take another simple sentence:

The dog sat on the mat.

Detail to be added	**Example**
• **Who is it?**	*Percy the dog sat on the mat.*
• **What are they doing?**	*The dog sat on the mat, scratching its ears.*
• **Where are they?**	*The dog sat on the mat in the café.*
• **When did it happen?**	*Yesterday, the dog sat on the mat.*
• **Why did it happen?**	*The dog sat on the mat because it was tired.*
• **Which one is it?**	*The old dog sat on the red mat.*
• **Whose is it?**	*The captain's dog sat on the mat.*
• **How did it happen?**	*The dog sat down carefully on the mat.*
• **Change words**	*The poodle slumped on the Persian rug.*
• **Use a special effect**	*The dirty dog dug a ditch as deep as Devon.*

Try using these prompt questions:

How did it happen?	Who is it?
What are they doing?	Where are they?
When did it happen?	Why did it happen?
Which one is it?	Whose is it?

A word of warning! It is easy enough to teach children how to vary a sentence. However, this can lead to children thinking that adding in adjectives or extending sentences instantly makes them 'good' sentences. It is worth constantly talking through what makes an effective sentence. This is to do with the impact on the reader.

Interestingly, you cannot really tell whether a sentence works until it is in a paragraph. The sentence, *The man ran.* might seem to be rather dull but put inside an action paragraph, it might be exactly what is needed. For example:

> *Jake spun round and leaped over the wall. Instantly, his pursuer grabbed hold of the suitcase, turned and began to dash back up the alleyway. With a yell of anguish, Jake turned and stared. The million dollars was still inside the case. 'Come back!' yelled Jake at the top of his voice. The man turned and laughed as Jake scrabbled up the wall but it was too late. There was a screech of brakes as the police car tore down the street towards them. Jake was speechless as he watched. The man ran.*

Once you have worked on single sentences then move onto pairs of sentences and paragraphs. Take this paragraph and discuss with the children why it does not work well. The main problem being that the sentences are all too similar and the text lacks flow:

> *Tom was waiting. Tom heard the phone. He picked it up. It went silent. He put it down. He crossed the room. He tugged at the door handle. It was hard to open. He slammed the door shut. He left.*

Here is a ten-year-old boy's rewriting of the paragraph. It would be interesting to show a class his version. Can they spot the different sorts of sentences and the varying of the openings? The young writer has manipulated the grammar – but it is done to create an effective story. Not just for the sake of it.

It was a bitter winter evening. Thick snow had consumed the street. In the dimly lit living room of the house on the corner, Tom waited restlessly. Suddenly, the startling tone of the telephone cried out for attention. Cautiously, Tom lifted the receiver to his ear. Silence. Taking a deep breath, he slowly replaced the phone, rose from his battered chair and strode across the room. Did he really have to do this? Brutally, he tugged at the temperamental door handle. As expected, it took a few tries to open. Slamming the door shut, Tom departed into the shivering shadows of the night. Phase one complete.

Reordering

Moving bits around in a sentence can create different effects. Try moving adverbs or prepositional phrases:

Quietly, *she crept into the room.*

She crept into the room ***quietly.***

Into the room, she ***quietly*** *crept.*

Try moving *ing* chunks about:

Hurrying home, ***Tim tripped over.***

Tim, ***hurrying home,*** *tripped over.*

Tim tripped over, ***hurrying home.***

Try to see how many different ways you can reorder the following sentence. It can help to put the words and punctuation onto cards for children to move around:

The rain fell like diamonds, sparkling on the leaves in the sunlight.

The	*rain*	*fell*	*like*	*diamonds*
,	*sparkling*	*on*	*the*	*leaves*
in	*the*	*sunlight*	.	

Now try reordering these sentences:

The snow drifted along the wall like a white coat.

The thunder rolled overhead, grumbling like an angry troll staggering towards the distant forest.

Sentence doctor!

This is a simple idea. Provide sentences that contain mistakes. Feed off the sorts of errors that the children make. There are obvious things such as:

- spelling;
- punctuation;
- missing words;
- shifts in tense;
- speech structures rather than written patterns;
- word order;
- misuse of words.

If you work with children who have English as a new language, it may be useful to highlight specific differences between English syntax and that of their own language. Younger children should begin with looking at a few sentences. Older children should be able to work on paragraphs.

Joe ran as he did so a hand snatched at his shirt and grabbed him lashing out with his arms he kicked as hard as he could someone seized his hair and tugged him back he screamed fell backwards and rolled on the ground at the same moment his attackers smashed into each other without thinking Joe leaped up and started to run fortunately he had managed to escape

You could play the game orally, focusing on changing dialect into Standard English or missing words, eg:

He runned down the lane.
Will you pass sandwich to me?
I don't want no pudding.

Or play it by writing up sentences with spelling or punctuation errors, eg:

He ran down the lain.
We seed the trane, it wos two late.
I put on the hoarses' sadel.

Compare

A more advanced version of 'Sentence doctor!' and Improve it activities is played by providing two or three sentences or paragraphs for the children to compare. Ask the children which is the best, why and what can be done to improve the weakest, eg:

The big dog sat on the big mat.
The sly poodle perched on the fluffy carpet.

Try comparing paragraphs – which works best and why? What advice would you give to the weaker sentence writer?

Kezzi went into the shed. It was messy, dark and dirty. There was a load of stuff in there. She hid.	*Kezzi stared round the shed. A fly crawled up the dusty windowpane, cobwebs hung from the rafters and a broken chair lay beside a pile of old carpets. The air smelled musty.*

Hooks

This game invites children to think carefully about the effect of the words in sentences. Writing that grabs our attention, hooks the reader, often by raising a question that the reader wants to solve. For instance, in the sentence below, the adverb instantly makes us wonder why Sam is desperate – but the verb is also making us wonder why he is running – together the words are hooking us in and making the reader want to read further.

Desperately, Sam ran.

Start by discussing the possible hooks in a few sentences. Select from the type of writing that you are working on with the class.

a. *She tiptoed along the city wall, keeping to the shadows.*
b. *'Who's there?'*
   'It's me. Have you got the map?'
   'No. I thought you had it.'
c. *The lights of a passing torch-bearer lit up the faces of the two pirates for a moment. Rustbucket Jake scowled.*
d. *No-one saw a tall figure merge noiselessly into the crowd.*
e. *She was already half an hour late.*

Move on to considering how the hooks pile up in a paragraph:

> *Reluctantly, Skater waited by the bridge. The storm waters rushed underneath, tugging relentlessly at the wooden arches. In the distance, he could hear the sound of the ambulance approaching.*

Making sentences of three

The power of three is a well-known device used by writers. In this game, the children have to produce sentences with three chunks. Begin by writing sentences of three for description of objects, character and setting, eg *The queen was bony, hairy and badly dressed.*

> *The queen was …*
> *The dragon was …*
> *She was dressed in …*
> *The candle was …*
> *The room was full of …*
> *In the distance he could see …*

Now try sentences of three for action: *She ran down the lane, turned the corner and giggled.*

She …/He…/It …/They …
The old man …/The dog …/The troll …/The policeman …

Finally, move on to writing sentences of three for ideas or points of view or facts: *In the end, we must remember that healthy eating, plenty of activity and a good night's sleep all add up to a feeling of well-being.*

In the end, we must remember that …
It is not right that …
We believe that …
Finally, we know that …

Sentence types

Through constant teaching, it is possible over the years for children to build up a basic repertoire of sentence patterns that they can use in their writing. It is worth remembering that good writers:

- Vary sentences to create different effects and rhythms.
- Vary sentence openings to create different effects and rhythms.

Here is a list of the basic sentence patterns that children need to practise many times till they can use them in their writing automatically:

Sentence type	Reason for use	Example
Short	Drama and to make a point	*Humans need food.*
Long	Plenty of action, information, ideas	*Sunlight glinted on the motorbike at the side of the road where Terry stood, waiting for the morning bus to school, its handle bars jutting up invitingly like a cow's horns.*
Simple	Clarity	*The bus pulled up.*
Compound	Flow	*The cat sat down and the dog stood up.*
Complex	To tag extra information onto a main idea or to explain	*After the cat sat down, the dog yawned.*
Question	To make the reader wonder	*Was it too late?*
Statement	To say what we know	*Cats make good pets.*
Exclamation	Emphasis	*It was enormous!*
Command	Tell someone what to do	*Run for it!*
Sentence of three for description	Build description	*The clock had rusted hands, a silver base and a wooden cherub on top.*
Sentence of three for action	Speed up action	*The horse cantered over the corn field, leapt the fence and flew above the tree tops.*
Sentence of three to make points	Pile up viewpoints	*A new supermarket would bring jobs to the town, provide a focal point for shoppers and ease the local car parking problems.*
Drop-in clause (or phrase)	Add in information	*Mr Rivermist, who was normally quite calm, seemed to steam with anger.*
Tagged-on question	Leave the reader with a question	*He was cross, or was he?*

***Ed / ing / ly* opening**	Tell the reader up front what or how	*Exhausted from running, Mr Benn sat down.* *Hoping for silence, he waited.* *Carefully, he opened the strange door.*
Minor sentence	Verbless expression of emotion to speed up action or add drama	*Great!* *Rain!*

It would be tempting to provide many different patterns for children to learn and try to remember – however, the danger of this work is that children end up varying sentences without listening to the impact that is being created. Our advice is to keep this work simple and clear.

Innovating on texts

Part of Talk for Writing involves learning model texts orally and then reading them carefully and closely. All of this helps children internalise the key patterns that they can then use when writing. The model texts can then be used as a basis for innovation – writing a new version. Less confident writers can be shown how to hug closely to the basic sentence pattern. If the story begins with the words, *Bob ran down the lane, round the corner and dashed into the forest*, then the child could be shown how to innovate on the pattern, copying the underlying syntactical pattern:

Tina tiptoed down the path, across the lawn and crept into the house.

Here is an example from a story. On the left is the original model and on the right is the child's version, written by hugging closely to the original pattern, written sentence by sentence:

Original model	***Child's version***
'Hurry up,' shouted Joe as he climbed over the rocks. Carefully, Rahul followed. The two boys stopped at a rock pool and began to search for shells. 'Hey, what's this?' shouted Joe to Rahul. In the rock pool was a small, black	*'Chop, chop!' yelled Charlotte as she ran to find the cake shelf. Slwoly, Honey followed making sure that none of the money on her pocket fell out. The two girls halted and began to esarch for the perect cake to give to their Grandmother for her*

box wrapped in plastic. The boys tugged it loose. What was inside? Joe pressed the silver catch and the lid popped open. The box was full of sparkling jewels!	*birthday. 'Hey, Honey, what's this?' shouted Cjarlotte to her sister. ehind one of the double chocolate cakes was a small, cushioned box that read C.A.K.E. on the lid. Charlotte pulled it out as Honey rushed over. What lay inside? Honey dig her nails under the lid and pulled the box open …*

More confident writers also benefit from such close attention to the patterns of a model. In this instance this version shows a more confident writer, using the underlying pattern but embellishing more adventurously:

Child's version

'Come on,' yelled Derek as he hurried towards the shimmering river.

Cautiously, Bob followed, staring at the glowing sunset. Shifting shadows of trees seemed to scatter ahead like a snake coiling the air, blocking their view. The wind bit brutally, pressed against Bob's frozen face.

'I don't think this is a good idea,' muttered Bob, trembling anxiously. 'Whose idea was this anyway?'

'This was my idea because I really wanted to go searching for precious shells and unusual fossils!' shouted Derek in the distance. 'Keep up! Don't stop now, we're really close,' Derek said, charging ahead. Dashing on, finally Derek arrived. For a moment, he paused by a beaten down boathouse on the river edge. Shafts of steaming light seemed to break the seams of dusk. The shimmering water warned. It was only then he saw it! Out of the corner of his eye, Derek spotted something… something moored against the sloping bank. Could it be a ragged cloth or a jagged stone? Staring, without hesitation, Derek stepped nearer, looking furtively around before picking up the crumpled package.

Trim

One of the problems with working on sentences is that it can lead into 'overwriting'. Children get the idea that using plenty of adjectives or adverbs or writing complex sentences is a good thing in itself. This can lead to children 'bunging in' words and chunks of writing so that their sentences become overwritten, eg *The whirling, swirling, curling, twirling snow fell on the frail fragile bleak barren crisp and crunchy landscape.*

Of course, the advantage of this is that the child has a vocabulary at their fingertips and can easily generate plenty of language. The issue is that the young writer has to also write with the reader in mind. Inside every good writer is an inner reader, an inner critic who is helping the writer to choose the right words – to sift the possibilities and think about which combination works well. If you have children who overwrite, then provide them with some lengthy sentences to 'trim' back:

The tired, weary, exhausted, old man struggled, staggered and trudged down the dark, gloomy, eerie, spooky lane.

The number plate game

Send several tiresome children to collect number plates. You will need the letters. List these and then challenge children to create sentences. My current plate has the letters 'SRL'. This could be:

> *Simon reads letters.*
> *Softly repair lists.*
> *Send Ricky love.*
> *Squirrels ruin lamps.*

Try starting with a name, an animal, an adverb or a verb to get your sentences flowing. It is harder than you think!

Alphabet and counting sentences

Try writing 'counting' sentences from one to ten. You might provide some sort of instruction such as alliteration, similes, include a proper noun, an adverb or drop in a relative clause etc.

One wild wombat, which was white and weary, waited wisely.
Two tired toucans, which were tiny and tousled, tried to tiptoe tastefully.
Three threadbare thimbles, which balanced theatrically, threw a thrusting thoroughbred …

Another simple way to frame sentences is to use the alphabet. One challenge would be for each letter to start a new sentence. A harder constraint would be for each letter to start the next word. Who can write the fewest sentences, using the whole alphabet in order?

A big cat dug eagerly for gold, hourly in jealous kinship ...

Chinese whispers

Pass a sentence round the class by whispering. Once it has travelled the full distance, listen to what it was when it began and how did it end up?

In the city of Rome

This game is a fun memory game that is also about building a picture. In the same way that *In Mrs Mginty's handbag I found...* or *At Mr Mguffle's shop I bought...* the game involves adding another item to a list. You could ask children to make an action for the comma to reinforce punctuation.

Consequences

This is an interesting way to compose sentences where each word is chosen randomly. It was played by the surrealists who enjoyed the strange combinations that random methods create. Occasionally, these throw up surprising and beautiful sentences. Most of us have played Consequences. The game is similar. The children take it in turn to write a predetermined type of word down on a strip of paper that is then folded to hide the word that has been written, and then passed on. The order of words could be:

- A determiner: *a*
- An adjective: *cautious*
- A noun: *kettle*
- A verb: *chased*
- An adverb: *cunningly*
- A preposition: *beside*
- An adjective: *dark*
- A noun: *radio*

The resulting sentences may need slight tweaking:

> *A cautious kettle chased cunningly beside the dark radio* could become, *A cautious kettle cunningly chased the dark radio beside the elegant flamingo.*

determiner	adjective	noun	verb	adverb	preposition	adjective	noun
the	*unwelcome*	*soup*	*returns*	*freely*	*in*	*brief*	*vision*

Use a grid for children to complete. They could work in groups of six listing words randomly – one person per word class. Then complete the grid and turn it into sentences:

The unwelcome soup returns freely in the brief vision.

Cut ups

Cut up a newspaper or pages from an old book. Create piles of words or phrases. Select a few randomly and then use these to invent sentences that MUST include the chosen words. This forces creativity in writing but it rehearses the notion of the sentence in a lively and creative manner.

Play the same sort of game by just taking a really well-crafted sentence from the sort of text that you are working with, type it out in a large font, print it and cut it up into individual words. Children then have to recreate the sentence. Can the sentence be recreated in different ways? Which sounds most effective?

Story sentences

Everyone thinks of a story that they know and writes down a key sentence. These are then read aloud in the round, moving from child to child. Depending on the combination of sentences, this can sound evocative, eg:

- *At that moment the wolf leaped.*
- *The dwarf chuckled.*
- *You can't catch me.*
- *The Queen stared into the mirror.*
- *'Not I!' said the bull.*
- *In a distant land lived a princess who had never smiled.*

An alternative is for everyone to think of a sentence from a story and write the sentence down. Who can guess which story it comes from and what were the clues?

Sentence poems

A simple and creative way to rehearse writing interesting sentences is to write list poems where a phrase is repeated in each line and a fresh idea is tagged on. The repeated pattern acts as a coat-hanger for innovative ideas. There are countless examples and ideas in *Jumpstart! Poetry* (Routledge, 2008), but just to get you into the mood, here is an example based on a poem of my own. You will notice that to write effectively, each idea needs to be fresh and, of course, each idea is a sentence. Helping children to write interesting sentences does not have to be tedious – it can be very creative.

A poem to be spoken silently

It was so silent that I heard
the last cry of a cloud
as it crash landed.

It was so silent that I heard
the first breath of a hurricane
as it breathed deeply.

It was so calm that I noticed
a thistle bristling
and a money spider tickling
the redbrick wall.

Here are some other poetry starting lines that you could use:

Listen can you hear …
In my magic box there is …
Silence – and I dreamed …
Through the open window I saw …
It was so quiet that I heard …
My dream is made of …
I wish I could …
It may be a lie but …
A rainbow is made of …
In my head is …
Open the door …

Years ago, I worked with the poet Brian Moses in a challenging school. We used to invent poetry list ideas to address different sentence issues. For instance, to focus on the difference between, *I could of* and *I could have* we invented a writing idea. A noise is heard in the night – what could it have been?

It could have been a distant car crawling by.
It could have been the last train whistling in the distance.
It could have been a fox rummaging in the bins.

More recently, I have used this idea to introduce key patterns. For instance, to practise using relative clauses, I made a list of objects to write about.

The key, which was golden, fitted the lock.
The window, which was rusty, opened with a squeak.
The pool, which was iced over, glistened.

HOW DIFFERENT TEXT TYPES REQUIRE DIFFERENT SENTENCE STRUCTURES

Different text types, written for various audiences and purposes, use different grammatical structures – the sentences 'sound' different. Experiment by providing a list of sentences from different text types. Can the children say which text type they come from – how did they know?

Sentence	Text type	Typical features and clues
Last night, we went to the cinema and saw a good film.	Recount	Temporal connective, past tense, first person; about something real that happened.
First, turn the red switch.	Instructions	Imperative, temporal connective, brief, precise; tells you what to do.
It turns cloudy because the water content grows heavier.	Explanation	Impersonal, 3rd person, present tense, causal connective; tells why something happens.

Buy this amazing watch.	Persuasion	Imperative, directed at 2nd person (you), exaggerated adjective; seeks to persuade the reader to do something.
Sharks rarely attack human beings.	Information	Impersonal, 3rd person, present tense, generalises, precise; informs the reader.
Furthermore, it is essential to provide extra assistance for older people.	Discussion	Impersonal, 3rd person, present tense, connective used to add in another idea; providing the reader with evidence to support a viewpoint.
The gnome sat down and watched as the giant sneezed.	Narrative	Past tense, 3rd person; invented events to entertain.

Crazy explanations

Provide a list of questions like the ones below – all need a *how* or *why* answer, offering an explanation. Provide a variety of causal connectives on cards. The children must use a causal connective when offering their explanations. They can rehearse orally in pairs – then come together as a class to listen to different explanations. Make sure that you model orally how to use the connectives so that they have heard them.

when	*this results in*	*because*	*so*	*so that*
this causes	*this means that*	*as a result*	*if*	*therefore*

How do stairs work?

Why is it dark at night?

Why did the wolf pretend to be granny?

Why should Jack be imprisoned?

Why was the troll so angry?

Why is a banana curly?

Why does a banana have a skin?

Why do trees have bark?

Why are rainbows coloured?

Why don't rainbows wobble in the wind?

Why do mice live in holes?

Why do flowers smell sweet?

Why do cats purr?

Why does the moon change shape?

Why do some teachers shout?

Why do ostriches bury their heads in the sand?

Where do teachers go at night?

Information reports

Here are some quick-fire ideas for talking games and activities to practise using language to present information:

- Make an information broadcast about a subject that you are studying or know a lot about.
- Give a one-minute presentation eg life in ancient times.
- Present a fact-finding mission – passing on five amazing facts about tornadoes and twisters, sharks and snakes or spiders.
- Role-play Professor Know-it-all – use information about invented creatures, dragons, mermaids and unicorns, giants and trolls.
- Play What I know about, Did you know? and Ask the expert.
- Present your own hobbies and interests.
- Play Mastermind – 20 questions on your chosen subject.
- Present a TV or radio broadcast; or use an IWB or overhead projector to make a presentation.

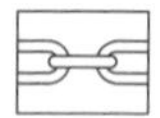

Professor Know-it-all

Choose a subject that most of the children know something about. They could choose a card from a hat and have to say a factual sentence using it. It can be fun to invent information about unicorns, dragons, mermaids, pirates, aliens and so on.

Did you know that ...	*In addition ...*	*... are found in ...*	*Do you think this is true or false?*	*Finally ...*
It is true that ...	*It is known that ...*	*... like to ...*	*If ...*	*It is ...* *It can ...* *It will ...* *It does not ...*
Amazingly ...	*The first thing to say about ... is that ...*	*... is where ...*	*Scientists know that ...*	*Unlike ...*
The most extraordinary thing about ... is ...	*You may not know but ...*	*Have you ever ...*	*Historians say that ...*	*Generally ...* *Usually ...* *Normally ...*

Discussions – the great debating game

When practising for a class debate, provide connectives on cards and dish them out. Decide on a focus for the debate, eg *Should crisps be allowed at break time?* Children have to use their connective to create a sentence. Try moving the argument back and forth.

Good debating topics include:

- *Should we eat kangaroo meat?*
- *Should smoking be banned in all public places?*
- *Should you be able to buy better food in schools?*
- *Should school uniform be banned?*
- *Should animals be used for testing?*
- *Should mobile phones be allowed in school?*

An interesting version of this is to use persuasive language to persuade an audience that *I'm a Year 5 – get me out of here!* In this game, you pretend that the children have been dumped in the jungle or a snake pit, for example. They have to use the connective card selected for them to offer a persuasive reason for why they should be rescued. I suppose it is a more modern form of a balloon debate!

Persuasion games

Here are some quick-fire ideas for talking games and activities to practise using persuasive language in sentences:

- Role-play persuading someone to guard the troll's bridge; go to the ball or not; or walk through the forest.
- Persuade someone to travel to the end of the rainbow.
- Design, make a toy and sell a board game.
- Persuade the class to adopt an environmental issue, eg *Save the panda!*
- Hold a 'keep active' assembly.

Radio phone-in

The aim of this game is to use persuasive language coherently in sentences. One child (or you) role-plays being the minister in charge of something. The others are able to 'phone in' and each has one minute to persuade the minister to adopt their viewpoint. First, agree on a topic. The children then work in groups, brainstorming ideas and points of view. Cards can be handed out so that children have to use a connective somewhere within their persuasive minute – or see who can use the most within a minute without destroying the meaning and thrust of their argument.

I believe that	*There are three reasons*	*Finally*	*Nowadays*	*However*
I think this because	*Most people believe that*	*It is true that*	*It will help*	*Also*
In our area	*First of all*	*Experience has shown that*	*We can improve*	*Furthermore*
Where I live	*Next*	*In other countries*	*If*	*The most important reason*

VARYING SENTENCES TO ACHIEVE DIFFERENT EFFECTS

Through exemplar text and shared writing build up understanding of the following ways of using sentences effectively.

1. *Vary sentences to create effects:*

- Short, simple sentences – for drama and clarity: *Joe hopped.*
- Compound sentences for flow: *Joe hopped and Sally ran.*
- Complex sentences to add in extra layers of information: *As Joe walked along, Sally ate the doughnut.*
- Questions to draw in the reader: *What was it?*
- Exclamations for impact: *Just jump!*
- Sentence of three for description: *She wore a long dress, black shoes and a red hat.*
- Sentence of three for action: *Bill ran down the road, jumped over the wall and collapsed.*

2. *Vary sentence openings:*

- Adverb opener (how): *Quietly, …*
- Temporal connective opener (when): *Late at night, …*
- Prepositional opener (where): *On the other side of the lane …*
- Adjective opener: *Dark trees towered over the house.*
- Simile opener: *As quick as a click … like a ferret …*
- One word opener: *Weary, …*
- *ing* opener: *Running for home, Lee tripped …*
- *ed* opener: *Excited by the doughnuts, Lee ran home.*

3. *Drop-in clauses:*

- Who: *Kevin, who was happy, whistled.*
- Which: *The dog, which looked hungry, eyed the bone.*
- That: *The cow that needed treatment, sat down.*
- *ing*: *Kevin, hoping for a second's peace, lay down.*
- *ed*: *Kevin, frightened by the tiger, crept away.*

4. *The ing clause:*

- Before: *Sneezing violently, Gemma sat down.*
- During: *Gemma, sneezing violently, sat down.*
- After: *Gemma sat down, sneezing violently.*
- Stage direction for speech: Bob: (sneezing violently) Hello!

Practise sentence types that relate to the text type and that will help children to progress. Provide spellings and sentence types on cards and mats etc and in displays. List the key words and sentence features needed to make progress in your plans.

Non-fiction

Through exemplar text and shared writing build up understanding of the following ways of using sentences effectively.

1. Vary sentences to create effects:

- Short, simple sentences for drama and clarity: *Smoking is unhealthy.*
- Compound sentences for flow: *Cats sleep in the day and hunt at night.*
- Complex sentences to add extra layers of information, argument, reasoning or explanation: *While many people eat chocolate, it is not good for you to eat too much.*
- Questions to draw in the reader: *Do most people exercise enough?*
- Exclamations for impact: *Dangerous drivers should be punished!*
- Imperative to instruct or draw in the reader: *Press the red button. Buy now while stocks last.*
- Lists: *You will need a pair of scissors, the red felt and a needle.*
- Sentence of three for description: *Most sharks grow to about one metre long, have rough skin and sharp teeth.*
- Sentence of three to build points or persuade: *It is important to eat a balanced diet, drink a litre of water every day and keep fit.*
- Topic sentences: *Sharks have a varied and unusual diet.*

2. Vary sentence openings:

- Adverb opener (how): *Slowly, open the oven door …*
- Time connective opener (when): *The next month …*
- Prepositional opener (where): *On the other side of the city is …*
- Causal connectives: *Because …*
- Reasoning connectives: *However, …*
- Imperative verb opener: *Turn on the computer …*
- *ing* opener: *Discovering the tomb, Howard Carter …*
- *ed* opener: *Imprisoned for years, Mandela …*

3. Drop-in clauses:

- Who/which: *Harold's army, which had travelled from the North, was exhausted.*
- *ing*: *The Britons, thinking they had won, gave pursuit.*
- *ed*: *Harold, determined to succeed, stood his ground.*

Practising sentence types that relate to the text type will help children to progress. Provide spellings and sentence types on cards and mats etc and in displays. In your plans, list the key words and sentence features needed to make progress.

CHAPTER 5

Punctuation

This chapter provides a wide range of talk-based activities to build children's understanding of how punctuation works and what sort of punctuation is needed where. Some of these are aural activities because a good way to build confidence with punctuation is to read text aloud, pausing appropriately at the punctuation, to help children notice the difference punctuation makes.

WHAT IS PUNCTUATION?

The games below have been designed to help you draw out from the children that **punctuation** is the use of symbols to separate off (or link together) words, phrases and clauses to help the reader follow the intended meaning of a text. The key punctuation marks are full stops and commas: full stops separate one sentence from another, while commas separate off information within sentences. Brackets (commas or dashes) can also be used to separate off dropped in phrases or clauses within sentences. Separating off information in this way is known as parenthesis. Exclamation marks and question marks are a form of special full stop to indicate a different sort of sentence, as their names suggest. Colons introduce information; semi-colons can be used to separate off phrases or clauses, as illustrated in this sentence. Apostrophes indicate missing letters (omission) or possession. Finally, hyphens are used to join words or bits of words together – while dashes can be used informally to separate off clauses or phrases, as exemplified!

Feeling the difference punctuation makes

Young children like physically acting out the punctuation in a text and it's the perfect way to get them to remember that it is important. It's the pattern of the sentence that makes the punctuation meaningful so it is perhaps logical to teach the pattern of the sentences first, and then help the children understand how the punctuation helps make the sentences meaningful.

See page 128 for sound and action activities related to punctuating sentences. The key punctuation mark, the full stop, only makes sense within the concept of sentences, which is covered in Chapter 4.

Musical chairs

Children enjoy the challenge of sharing the reading of a short passage to bring out the significance of the punctuation. This activity both helps children hear the tune of the different sentence types and become more aware of the difference punctuation makes. Select a passage that the class is already familiar with and highlight sections of the text according to how the punctuation breaks the text into clumps of meaning, as in the example below. Ask the children to read the passage aloud to each other, changing reader at each piece of punctuation (one partner reads the highlighted text, the other the plain text).

Fox facts

Foxes are not pets.

What are they like? *They are elegant,* ***dog-like creatures with sharp noses,*** *bushy tails and reddish-brown fur.*

What do they eat? *They eat small furry animals,* ***feathery birds and they are also very fond of tasty chickens.*** *But they also eat squiggly insects and juicy berries.*

Because foxes sometimes kill chickens, *people in the countryside often hate them,* ***but people living in cities often think they are rather charming.*** *As a result,* ***country people often support fox hunting while city people are against it.***

Did you know that foxes are nocturnal? ***That means they come out at night.*** *Foxes are famous for being cunning and pouncing on their prey.* ***Their homes are called dens and their babies are called cubs.***

And they can swim!

Then ask the children what difference it made reading the passage in that manner. Draw out from the children, in book-talk style, that this makes the reader more aware of how the passage has been constructed and the important role of punctuation in helping you understand the text.

COMMAS – UNDERSTANDING THE PAUSES

The comma detective

It makes sense to teach commas alongside the pattern of sentences in which they are used so the emphasis is on the pattern of the sentence. If you just teach commas in disembodied sentences, the chances are that this will lead to a sudden measles-like spread of random commas. Try challenging children to be the comma detective who has to explain why there are or aren't commas within different sorts of sentences. Devise a set of sentences, like the ones below, related to whatever topic you are focusing on. The children work out why some of the sentences have commas and some don't.

1. *We saw a fox.*
2. *We saw a fox and a rabbit.*
3. *We saw a fox, a mouse and a rabbit.*
4. *Foxes are elegant animals.*
5. *Foxes are elegant, alert animals.*
6. *Foxes are elegant, alert and cunning animals.*
7. *The fox ran and ran and ran.*
8. *The fox saw the chicken, pounced rapidly and grabbed it with its teeth.*

Draw out from the children that commas are used to separate off items in a list unless the items are joined by a conjunction (joining word) like *and*. You may want to make this learning visible by displaying the rule, illustrated by some examples, on your learning wall/washing line. Draw attention to the feature through shared and guided writing and reading so that the children internalise the pattern. When you come across a comma that has been placed in front of *and* to prevent confusion, discuss this with the children so they start to understand this subtlety. (Inevitably, some grammarians view this differently and insist that there should be a comma in front of all conjunctions – this is sometimes referred to as the Oxford comma! Modern practice – and the rules for the grammar tests in England – favours no commas in front of conjunctions unless a comma is needed to prevent confusion. The wise teacher in England should, therefore, teach children not to use commas in front of *and* except where they are needed for clarity.)

SEPARATING OFF SUBORDINATE CLAUSES IF THEY BEGIN THE SENTENCE

The games below are designed to help children remember that if a sentence begins with a subordinate clause, the end of that clause is always marked by a comma, to help the reader locate the main clause within a sentence.

The intonation game

Children love playing this game and it is one they don't forget. They like it so much that you can often use the wordless version to warn them of the consequences of misdeeds later on! It not only helps them to remember to use a comma at the end of a subordinate clause, if it begins the sentence, but it also helps them to use intonation appropriately when reading aloud.

Once you have built up the class's understanding of the role of subordinating conjunctions (see pages 91–97), play the game, using sentences like the ones below, so that the children can hear the tune of sentences that begin with subordinating conjunctions.

If *you carry on talking, you will be in trouble.*
Because *it is raining, we won't go to the park.*
As *you've been so good, you can have some chocolate.*
Although *today's story was good, last week's story was better.*

Say the sentences to the class, over-emphasising the way stress and tone is used in such sentences to help convey meaning, and the pause where the sentence breaks in half (indicated by the comma). Ask the children what the purpose of the comma is and draw out from them that the comma marks the end of the subordinate clause to help the reader follow the meaning of the sentence, just as in speech the pause helps the listener understand. Then say the sentences again, in a different order, but this time don't use any words – just make *uh uh uh* sounds in the appropriate pattern and tone, and ask the class to guess which sentence you are speaking.

Do this several times, in different combinations so they get to hear the tune of the sentences. Then ask the children to invent four sentences of their own beginning with subordinating conjunctions each conveying a different mood, like the examples above. Ask them to read their sentences to a partner, first with words and then change the order of the sentences and just use intonation. See if the partner can work out which sentence is which.

Spinning your sentences

Model for the children how to begin complex sentences with a subordinating conjunction as illustrated below.

Because *the kitten was hungry, it waited by its bowl.*
If *the kitten is hungry, it waits by its bowl.*
Until *the kitten has been fed, it waits by its bowl.*

After *the kitten has been fed, it goes off to play.*
Since *the kitten has been fed, it has gone off to play.*
As *the kitten has been fed, it has gone off to play.*

Read the sentences aloud together with the class so everyone hears the intonation and where the pause comes at the end of the subordinate clause (indicated by the comma). Now ask the class to help you spin the sentences the other way around so the main clause comes first. Explain that because the main clause comes first you don't need to put a comma in between the clauses. You will probably end up with sentences like these.

The kitten waited by its bowl ***because*** *it was hungry.*
The kitten waits by its bowl ***if*** *it is hungry.*
The kitten waits by its bowl ***until it has been fed.***

The kitten goes off to play ***after*** *it has been fed.*
The kitten has gone off to play ***since*** *it has been fed.*
The kitten has gone off to play ***as*** *it has been fed.*

Help the children hear the difference in the way the sentences sound if the main clause begins the sentence. Now ask the children to make up their own sentences (about whatever topic you are currently focusing on) beginning with the same subordinating conjunctions and including a comma where the sentences break in half. When they have written their sentences, see if they can recast them orally with their partner so the main clause begins the sentence. You may want to ask a few children to present their sentences to the class so the class can hear the different pattern of the sentences. Make certain that some of the sentences in shared writing begin with subordinating conjunctions to help embed understanding of this type of sentence within the children's writing repertoire.

The ed/ing/ly *challenge*

The ed/ing/ly challenge helps children understand that sentences beginning with adverbial clauses or phrases (fronted adverbials!) follow exactly the same punctuation pattern as sentences beginning with subordinate clauses: the phrase or clause is separated from the main sentence by a comma.

Display a range of sentences, related to whatever topic you are focusing on, beginning with *ed, ing, ly* starters. Ask the children to discuss with their partner why there is a comma in each sentence:

1. *Hoping the weather would improve, the Daleks set off early the next morning.*
2. *Having decided the weather would be good, the Daleks prepared a picnic.*
3. *Bored by endless rain, the Daleks planned to go swimming anyway.*
4. *Encouraged by a cloudless sky, the Daleks left early.*

The children devise similarly constructed *ed/ing/ly* sentences. Ask a few children to feed back their best sentences and flip-chart some examples for display. Illustrate *ed/ing/ly* starters in shared writing within the same unit of work and ask the children to include the approach in their writing.

The case of the missing punctuation

Once children have started to understand the function of punctuation, they'll like being punctuation detectives. Provide the children, in pairs, with a copy of a short passage from a story, preferably one they have already internalised, so reading it will not cause a problem. For example, use the opening section of *Monkey see – monkey do!* Ask them to decide how to read the passage aloud so that it makes sense and then put in the missing punctuation.

> ***Monkey see – monkey do!***
> *once upon a time there was a man who sold hats one day he was travelling through the forest when his cart hit a stone in the road unfortunately all the hats spilled out onto the road as soon as the monkeys in the trees saw the hats they swung down and grabbed them as quick as a click first the man shouted at the monkeys but all that the monkeys did was to shout back because what a monkey sees a monkey does next the man shook his fist at the monkeys but all that the monkeys did was to shake their fists back because what a monkey sees a monkey does*

Once the children have had a go at punctuating the passage, display the unpunctuated passage and get children to feed back their suggestions on how to punctuate it. Draw out from the children that the lack of full stops makes it hard to make sense of the words as you don't know where to pause. Help them see that a full stop is needed after each piece of complete information and that they mustn't use commas where a full stop is needed. Then display a properly punctuated version and read it together bringing out the pattern of the sentences.

> ***Monkey see – monkey do!***
> *Once upon a time there was a man who sold hats. One day, he was travelling through the forest when his cart hit a stone in the road. Unfortunately, all the hats spilled out onto the road. As soon as the monkeys in the trees saw the hats, they swung down and grabbed them as quick as a click. First, the man shouted at the monkeys. But all that the monkeys did was to shout back because what a monkey sees, a monkey does! Next, the man shook his fist at the monkeys. But all that the monkeys did was to shake their fists back because what a monkey sees, a monkey does!*

Reinforce their growing understanding through shared and guided reading/writing so that children become increasingly familiar with the role of full stops, question marks and exclamation marks to separate off sentences, and commas to indicate a pause within a sentence when one is needed to help the reader make sense of the words.

DROPPING IN EXTRA INFORMATION

The games below are designed to help children use drop-in clauses to vary the structure of their sentences and make their writing more engaging. Playing these games helps children see that the dropped-in clause or phrase could be picked up by its commas, brackets or dashes, like ears, and removed from the sentence; the remaining clause makes complete sense on its own. The more the children can understand how good writers select punctuation to avoid confusing their reader, the more they will be able to apply this approach to their own writing.

Drop in a mood

Model how to drop information (phrases or clauses) into simple sentences separating it off with commas. For example, model how to change the mood of a character, as illustrated by the feelings grid below, using a simple main clause like *Zeki the cat sat on the mat.*

The children's first task is to identify the main clause and the dropped-in information.

Different moods	Examples
happy	*Zeki the cat, purring contentedly, sat on the mat.*
sad	*Zeki the cat, sadly wishing that the rain would stop, sat on the mat.*
bad-tempered	*Zeki the cat, crossly waiting for his next meal, sat on the mat.*
friendly	*Zeki the cat, with whiskers like a smile, sat on the mat.*
cunning	*Zeki the cat, waiting for the moment to pounce, sat on the mat.*

The children then construct similarly patterned and punctuated sentences using another simple sentence as a starting point – *The parrot clung to the bars of its cage.* Ask them to share their sentences with a partner and explain how to drop information into a sentence. You may want to ask one or two children, in teacher role, to present their sentences to the class.

Through shared writing, model how this technique can be used to drop in information in phrase or clause form so that the children become increasingly familiar with the technique.

The brackets/dashes alternative

Once the children have understood how to use commas to mark off the dropped-in clause or phrase (known as parenthesis), show them that dashes or brackets could be used instead, as illustrated below.

The parrot, which had been waiting hopefully, desperately, despairingly, for the right moment to escape, clung to the bars of its cage.

The parrot (which had been waiting hopefully, desperately, despairingly, for the right moment to escape) clung to the bars of its cage.

The parrot – which had been waiting hopefully, desperately, despairingly, for the right moment to escape – clung to the bars of its cage.

Ask why the writer might choose to use brackets or dashes to separate off a drop-in clause rather than just commas. Draw out from the class that dashes or brackets are sometimes used when the sentence includes several clumps of meaning separated off by commas. Since too many commas would be confusing, an alternative to the comma is useful. Draw attention to such features through shared and guided writing and reading.

Advanced roving reporters

This game involves finding out how many different places adverbial connectives (*however, therefore, nevertheless, unfortunately, a few days later* etc) can be placed within a sentence. It is much more meaningful if the sentences are related to a topic the children are actually working on. The sentences below are based on work on the Fire of London.

How many places?

Model for the children how adverbial connectives can move around a sentence separated off by commas if it begins the sentence or is dropped into the sentence. When added at the end of a sentence, it is a question of choice. Often a comma isn't needed and sounds odd. Read each group of sentences aloud to the children and ask them which sound the best.

1a. ***However***, *the wind on the day of the fire was very strong.*
1b. *The wind on the day of the fire,* ***however***, *was very strong.*
1c. *The wind on the day of the fire was very strong* ***however***.

2a. ***Therefore***, *the fire quickly got out of control.*
2b. *The fire,* ***therefore***, *quickly got out of control.*

3a. ***Unfortunately***, *the mayor added to the problems by refusing to take any action.*
3b. *The mayor,* ***unfortunately***, *added to the problems by refusing to take any action.*
3c. *The mayor added to the problems,* ***unfortunately***, *by refusing to take any action.*
3d. *The mayor added to the problems by refusing to take any action* ***unfortunately***.

Now challenge the children to move the highlighted adverbial connectives in the sentences below to as many other places within each sentence as possible, and to punctuate the sentences appropriately.

A. ***Moreover***, *the houses were made of wood and built closely together.*
B. ***Fortunately***, *after two days, the wind ceased and the fire died down.*
C. ***Nevertheless***, *there were some benefits as the fire helped to wipe out the remains of the plague.*

You may want to get one or two children to present their sentences in teacher role, explaining to the class how adverbial connectives can move around sentences and how they are punctuated.

DIRECT SPEECH (INVERTED COMMAS)

Children usually like learning about direct speech, probably because of its links with cartoon bubbles. The games below have been devised to bring out this link.

How many paragraphs?

Once children have grasped that they must start a new paragraph for each speaker, working out who is saying what is relatively easy. Begin by drawing attention to how speech is laid out in any nursery rhyme or story that the children know well. Display the first verse and ask the children in pairs to decide why there are so many paragraphs. Draw out from the children that you start a new line (paragraph) for each speaker.

Once upon a time there was a little red hen who lived on a farm. Early one morning, she woke up and went outside. There she found some corn.

'Who will help me plant the corn?' said the little red hen.

'Not I,' said the bull

'Not I,' said the cat.

'Not I,' said the rat.

'Oh very well, I'll do it myself,' said the little red hen – and so she did!

Ask the class to say the next verse together and ask them how many speech paragraphs there are.

The speech detective

Children love this game and it's one that they won't forget. You will need as many balloons as you have speech paragraphs in your example. Each balloon should have the words spoken in each paragraph on it.

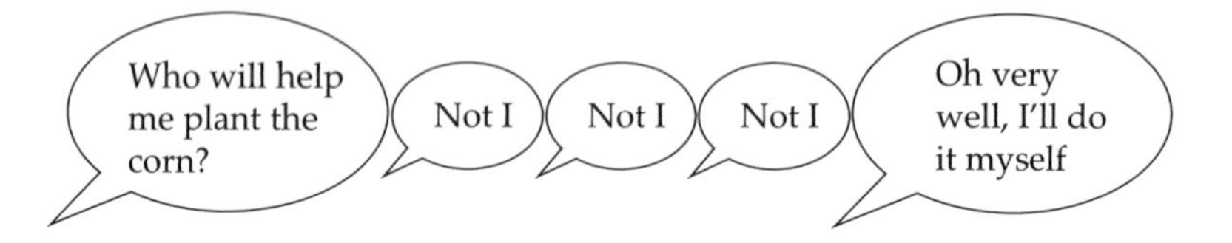

Using your How-many-paragraphs? text, ask the class how they know which words are actually spoken while displaying the balloons to help the children work out the answer. Draw out from the children that the actual words have speech marks at the beginning and end of them to show that they have actually been spoken. 'Burst' a balloon or two to illustrate how speech marks are like the remains of the speech balloon.

Over time, through shared writing and reading, draw attention to how commas are used to separate off the speaker from what is said.

Revisit this game regularly for any story they are internalising that includes speech so that they remember the fact that you need to start a new paragraph every time someone starts to speak and the actual words spoken are separated off by speech marks.

(**Note:** In the grammar tests in England, the term 'inverted commas' is liable to be used rather than speech marks. Over time, introduce this more formal term so that the children are familiar with both.)

How many paragraphs?

To reinforce understanding of speech paragraphs, set up a quick-fire conversation. For example, secretly let a child know that you are going to ask them to return a toy that you know they haven't borrowed. The resulting conversation might go something like this.

Teacher: Can you remember to bring back the teddy you borrowed?
Child: I never borrowed a teddy!
Teacher: You know you did.
Child: I didn't!
Teacher: You did.
Child: I didn't!

Then ask the class how many paragraphs you'd need if you wrote the conversation down. Repeat this sort of quick-fire game until the concept is firmly in their heads.

Direct speech doctor

Being in role as the direct speech doctor who can work out what is wrong with text reinforces understanding. With young children you may want to begin with a story they have already internalised. Help the children understand by providing them with an extract from a story with direct speech (at the right level for the class) that has no new paragraphs for each speaker and no speech marks. The children, in pairs, see if they can:

- work out how to read it so it makes sense;
- mark up where the new paragraphs should be;
- put in the speech marks and commas.

Once upon a time there was a little girl and a little boy who went to stay with their Grandma. Last thing at night, Grandma said goodnight, children, gave them a kiss, turned out the light, and closed the door. But the children said it's too noisy! So Grandma said what you need is a cat. So she said goodnight, children, gave them a kiss and a cat, turned out the light and closed the door. But the cat said meoooow. So the children said it's too noisy.

From cartoon to direct speech

Children love this approach to understanding the different ways a writer can express speech, moving from cartoon to play script, to direct and then indirect speech. Any suitable cartoon strip, preferably without words, that is easy to sequence would work well but a tried-and-tested favourite is the *Who's the bully now?* cartoon.

(Many thanks to the illustrator Malcolm Bird – www.malcolm-bird.co.uk – for permission to reprint this cartoon.)

1. Story as a cartoon:
Display the images and ask the children to decide what the big person is saying to the small person in each stage of the cartoon. In shared-writing style, select the best ideas (making certain they are short) and show the children how to add the words to the cartoon. Then give all the children a copy of the cartoon and ask them to add their version of the story as speech bubbles. (Show them how to write the words in first and then put the speech bubble round them.)

2. Story as a play:
Display your completed version of the cartoon on screen. In book-talk style, ask the children how they know that the big person in each of the pictures is furious with the small person who is being told off. Draw out from the children that the images tell us how the people are feeling. Then

explain that we want to turn the cartoon into a play. We already have the speech but how will we let our audience know how each character is feeling? Draw out of the children that we have to let the actors know what expression to have on their face (through bracketed off stage directions) so the audience can see how the characters are feeling, just as the cartoonist uses an image to let the audience know.

Through shared writing, illustrate for the children how to turn the cartoon into a short play with stage directions. Model for the class how to use colons to introduce the words spoken and brackets to indicate stage directions and then ask the children to turn their cartoon into a play script.

3. Story with direct speech:
Display the cartoon version on screen, with the play version on your working wall or washing line. Ask the children how, if we now wanted to write what happened as a story, would we let our reader know how each person is behaving and feeling as well as what they are saying. Draw out of the children that we have to paint a picture with words to show the feelings and actions just as the cartoonist uses an image, as well as using the actual words that the characters speak.

Through shared writing, illustrate for the children how to turn the cartoon into a good story with direct speech. Model for them how to do all the related punctuation. Remind them that the speech marks are just like the speech bubble in a cartoon: they surround the words actually spoken; the words actually spoken remain the same in the cartoon, the play and the story.

Then ask the children to write their own versions as a story. Display the best of the cartoon versions, alongside the play and story versions to act as a visual reminder of how to write and punctuate direct speech within a story and how to lay out a play script.

4. Story with indirect speech:
When the children have grasped direct speech, you could model for them how to change the direct speech into indirect speech. This time, display the story version on screen and, through shared writing, show them how to rewrite it so that the speech is reported rather than using the actual words spoken. Since excessive use of direct speech ruins many potentially good stories, the earlier children can grasp this, the more likely they are to be able to use speech effectively.

Get the children to write their own indirect speech version of their story and display some of the finished versions. Constantly reinforce understanding through referring to this feature in stories as you read them and through shared writing so that the children practise how to use speech effectively as well as how to punctuate it.

The professor of direct speech

Model for the children how to be the Professor of Direct Speech who can explain all about how to lay out and punctuate direct speech. To help them in this role you may want to provide the children with cut-up strips of advice on how to lay out and punctuate speech. Remind them to choose either single quotes or double quotes for speech marks, and then stay consistent with that choice.

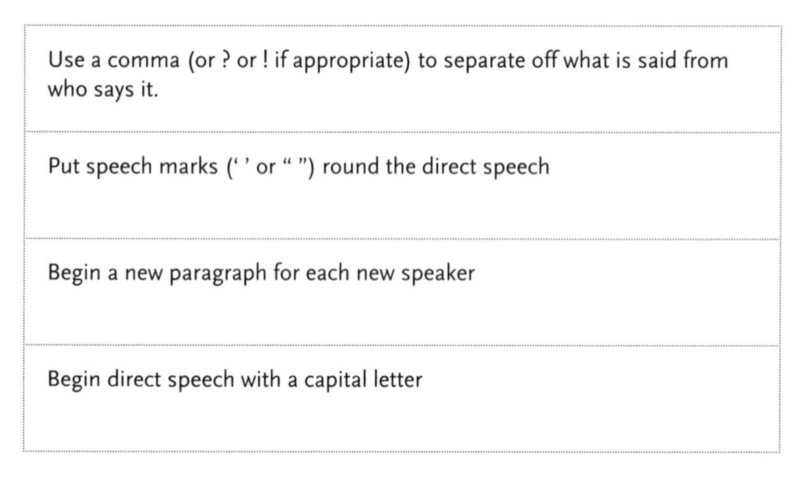

Use a comma (or ? or ! if appropriate) to separate off what is said from who says it.

Put speech marks (' ' or " ") round the direct speech

Begin a new paragraph for each new speaker

Begin direct speech with a capital letter

Ask them in pairs to:

- order the advice so that the most important points come first;
- link their advice to any piece of direct speech they have recently read;
- decide how they would use this extract and the advice to help a child a year younger than themselves understand how to layout and punctuate direct speech properly;
- take it in turns to be visiting professor.

Now ask a budding professor to present their explanation to the class. Display the advice in logical order (ie paragraphs first and speech marks second) as a reminder to the class.

DASHES, HYPHENS AND ELLIPSES

The dash detective (–)

A word of warning: Be sure to distinguish between the look of hyphens (-) and dashes (–) when presenting text to children. There should be no space around hyphens (which are short) while there should be a space on either side of a dash (which is longer). Display a number of sentences like the ones below that include single dashes – preferably linked to a topic the class is working on. Challenge the children to explain why dashes are needed in the sentences.

1. *The girl decided there was only one way out – swim!*
2. *And today's finalist is – Harry!*
3. *Mammals – see page 59.*

Draw out from the children that dashes can be used to indicate a break in the flow of a sentence. Concurrently, through exemplar text and shared writing, demonstrate how dashes can be used in this manner, and draw attention to them when reading, so the children start to use dashes effectively.

The hyphen detective (-)

Display a number of sentences like the ones below that include three different uses of hyphens – preferably linked to a topic the class is working on. Challenge the children to explain the three different ways in which hyphens can be needed in sentences. You may want to ask pairs to compare their conclusions with another pair.

1a. *The baby bear was feeling uncom-*
fortable sitting on such a large chair.
1b. *The terrible floods arrived, unfor-*
tunately, at night.
2a. *A fox is an elegant dog-like creature.*
2b. *The cute-looking child smiled endlessly.*
3a. *His father-in-law had been ill for some months.*
3b. *The police received a tip-off about the burglary.*

Draw out from the children that hyphens can do the following.

- They can show that a word has been split across two lines (model how this has to be at a syllable break that enables the reader to read the word easily).

- They can join two adjectives together that don't make sense on their own. (Model that the way to test whether you need this sort of hyphen is to take away the other adjective and see if both single adjectives make sense on their own. For example, *A fox is an elegant dog creature* doesn't sound right. *A fox is an elegant like creature* sounds even worse. Only when the two words are rolled together does the sentence sound right, *dog-like creature*. The hyphen tells the reader to do precisely that.)
- They can link some compound words together, for example, *step-mother.* (You might want to point out that over time compound words often lose their hyphen. For example, *email* used to be written as *e-mail.*)

Through exemplar text and shared writing, demonstrate how hyphens can be used in these ways, and draw attention to them when reading, so the children start to use them effectively.

The Is-it-a-hyphen-or-a-dash? challenge

Once the children have understood the different functions of dashes and hyphens, challenge them to complete this simple explanation of the key difference between the functions of dashes and hyphens.

Hyphens … while dashes …

Draw out from the class that hyphens join bits of words or words together while dashes separate off clumps of meaning within sentences.

The ellipsis detective (…)

Present the class with a few alternative endings to a paragraph that includes examples of ellipsis – possibly linked to a topic like suspense since ellipsis is useful here. Challenge the children in pairs to explain when ellipsis (…) should be used, and which of the three sentences they think is the most effective.

1. *At that moment, the door opened …*
2. *As the door opened, he froze …*
3. *Without a sound, the door mysteriously opened …*

Ask some of the children to present their conclusions and draw out from the children that ellipsis is three full stops to indicate that some words are deliberately missing from a text.

UNDERSTANDING APOSTROPHES

Children sometimes delight in becoming apostrophe detectives and working out the logic for when they are needed or not needed. Once they have played these games successfully, they will be well on the way to becoming Apostrophe Apostles who can wonder at the errors of many adults who seem to find the mystery of the apostrophe beyond them. They will enjoy being able to correct their elders and to explain clearly that the apostrophe has two functions: one to indicate possession; the other to indicate missing letters (omission).

Apostrophes of omission are easier to understand so it makes sense to start with these.

The missing letters

It is worth teaching the apostrophe for omission early on as an aspect of spelling. It is useful to play quick games where you provide a few instances of apostrophes for omission and the children have to write down the original, eg *don't = do not*. Here are some examples of omissions to use.

don't, I'll, we're, isn't, you're, can't, shan't, won't, shouldn't, couldn't, could've, you've, he'd, she'd, didn't, won't, she's, he's, they've, we've, hasn't, there's, mustn't, I'm

The mysterious case of the missing letters

Display a short text, preferably from a text that the children are currently reading, that is full of a range of different apostrophes of omission. Read the text aloud to the children so they can hear how the elided words sound. The children work out:

- why apostrophes have been used in this extract;
- why people tend to merge some words together when they speak;
- what the full version of each highlighted phrase would be.

'If **we're** not careful **it'll** be dark before we get there. **Don't** you think we should hurry up so **we'll** get to their house before five **o'clock**? **I'd** hate to be late,' she added, fussing as usual.
'**Let's** not worry about that,' her friend replied. '**It's** not late and **they're** always late, **aren't** they?'
'I **would've** left earlier if **you'd** asked,' she continued, still worrying.

Draw out from the children that:

- apostrophes can be used to indicate missing letters (explain that these are called apostrophes of omission);
- it's convenient to join regularly used words together as it's quicker.

Ask the children to explain what the abbreviated words in the text would be in full and create a poster like the one below. (Explain that *o'clock – of the clock* – is never now written out in full but has become a permanent abbreviation. Over time, this comma may disappear, just as *bus* has replaced *'bus* – short for *omnibus*.)

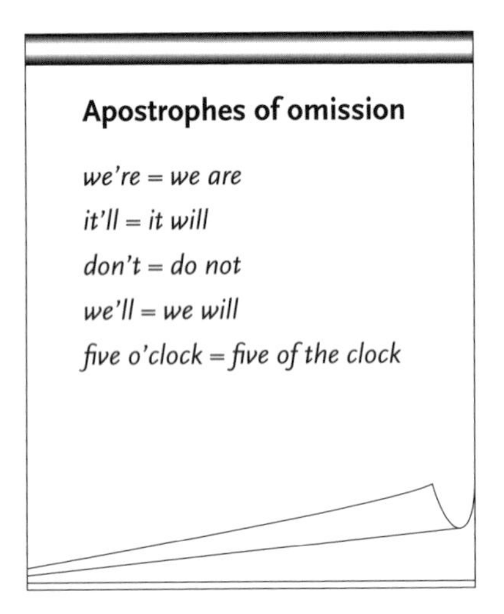

The *could of* confusion: Point out that it is not possible to construct a correct sentence in English containing the phrase *could of, should of* or *would of*. It should be *could've, should've* or *would've* which stand for *could have, should have* and *would have*. The trouble is that the pronunciation sounds the same – hence the confusion. Try to cure children of this before it becomes a habit (see page 154).

Demystifying apostrophes of possession

I can still remember half a century ago being taught apostrophe for possession. The example *the dog's bone* was written up and then turned into *the bone of the dog*. This helped me to gain a sense of ownership – whose was it? Who did it belong to? Try listing these and use the model provided:

	Whose is it?
The king's crown	The crown belongs to the king.
The teacher's apple	The apple belongs to the teacher.
The builder's sandwich	The sandwich belongs to the builder.
The boy's doughnut	The doughnut belongs to the boy.

The way to use the apostrophe is simple for possession:

a. Write down the noun – *the dog*
b. Add on the apostrophe – *the dog'*
c. Add on the letter *s* – *the dog's*
d. Add on the object that is owned – *the dog's bone ...*

Let's imagine that there are lots of dogs which all have a bone. The approach is similar though the extra 's' is not needed.

a. Write down the plural noun – *the dogs*
b. Add on the apostrophe – *the dogs'*
c. Add on the object that is owned – *the dogs' bones ...*

Play a game where you provide some phrases such as *the bone of the dog* and the children have to turn it round, using an apostrophe – *the dog's bone.* I have supplied the answers.

Original	**With apostrophe**
The bike of the girl	*The girl's bike*
The jewels of the queen	*The queen's jewels*
The tyres of the car	*The car's tyres*

The mystery of when s needs a friend

Try presenting the children with a few sentences like the ones below, preferably from a topic they are working on, and ask them to discuss what the function of the *s* is in the highlighted words in the first three sentences and why, in the last three sentences, the highlighted words have an apostrophe in front of the *s*.

1. *The* ***girls*** *walked to school.*
2. *The* ***teams*** *scored two* ***goals*** *each.*
3. *The* ***dragons*** *grew bored of terrifying* ***villagers****.*
4. *The* ***torch's*** *battery had run down.*
5. *The* ***cat's whiskers*** *were long and silky.*
6. *The* ***girl's*** *bag was missing.*

Draw out that in the first three sentences the *s* indicates a plural but in the last three sentences the *'s* is not indicating a plural but shows that the noun owns (possesses) the following word. Explain that this apostrophe is known as an apostrophe of possession and that the *'s* indicates possession. You may want to show how the *possessive s* sentences (4–6) could be spun round to get rid of the apostrophes:

4. *The battery of the torch had run down.*
5. *The whiskers of the cat were long and silky*
6. *The bag belonging to the girl was missing.*

Mini whiteboard apostrophe challenge

Try playing quick games where the children use their mini whiteboards to punctuate sentences, placing apostrophes in the right place. Here are some that have both possession and omission – as well as the odd plural thrown in for good measure.

Mrs Jenkins didnt mind cutting the donkeys beard because it wouldnt look good.

Bobs dog growled as it couldnt chase the cats owners.

Youre about to eat the dogs dinner.

All the soldiers rucksacks were stolen.

Well never find the pirates treasure.

Note: Many children (and adults) get muddled with the spelling of *its*. This has to be revisited many times and is worth putting a reminder in children's writing journals. The rule is as follows. **When you are shortening *it is* (or it has) to *it's* then you use an apostrophe. The apostrophe takes the place of the letter 'i' in *is*. On all other occasion there is no apostrophe.** Play quick games where you provide sentences and the children have to decide which it should be.

Circle the correct punctuation

a. It's/Its a nice day.
b. Have you got it's/its collar?
c. I wonder if its/it's going to rain?
d. Look at it's/its feet!
e. The dog showed me it's/its paw.
f. I will ask if its/it's a good idea.

Is it its *or* it's?

Once you've taught that *its* (like the other possessive pronouns) doesn't need an apostrophe, whereas *it's* with an apostrophe always stands for *it is* (or *it has*), the children will enjoy proving their expertise as detectives in the *its/it's* challenge.

- Give every child a mini whiteboard (or a piece of blank paper) and ask them to write *it's* in large letters on one side and *its* on the other.
- Then say a number of *its/it's* sentences and challenge them to hold up the right version:

> *Oh dear. It's started to rain.*
> *Oh dear. The tree is losing its leaves.*
> *It's a good thing you brought your umbrella.*
> *I think it's stopped now.*
> *Reaching its burrow, the rabbit paused.*
> *The toothpaste is missing its cap.*

You can instantly see who will need to attend a mini-lesson on getting this right. If most of the class is struggling with this, keep revisiting *its/it's* until they know to automatically check if the *its* they are using stands for *it is* or *it has* and, if it does, then it must have an apostrophe. Otherwise, it doesn't need one.

The plural possession challenge

Once the children have begun to grasp the basics of the singular *possessive s*, introduce what happens with nouns that are already plural and what happens to irregular plurals. (It is best to do this after you have taught the spelling patterns related to forming plurals.)

Display some possessive sentences showing how to indicate possession for regular singular and plural nouns, and ask the children to explain how they know which is singular and which is plural.

1a. *The girl's bedroom was untidy.*
1b. *The girls' bedroom was untidy.*
2a. *The cat's food was in the bowl*
2b. *The cats' food was in the bowl.*
3a. *The bike's tyres were all flat.*
3b. *The bikes' tyres were all flat.*

Draw out from the children the rule that to indicate possession you:

- add *'s* to regular singular nouns;
- just add an *'* after the *s* to regular plural nouns.

The irregular possessive challenge

Ask the children to give you some irregular plurals. You may end up with a list like this:

man/men
child/children
sheep/sheep
mouse/mice
woman/women

Display one or two examples of how to make these nouns indicate possession, for example:

The thief stole that man's luggage.
The thief stole the men's luggage.
The cat ate the mouse's cheese.
The cat ate the mice's cheese.

Using the same approach as outlined for the standard apostrophe of possession above, draw out from the children that you just add *'s* to irregular plurals that don't end in *s*, just as you add it to singular words.

Ask the children to make up examples for the other irregular nouns in the list. Then challenge them to work out how you show possession for words that happen to end in *s* in the singular (for example *boss/bosses; glass/glasses*). Draw out from the children that it's just the same as with the normal nouns. You just add an apostrophe after the final *s* for the singular words ending in *s* (*the boss's office, the glass's colour*) but for the plurals ending in *es* you just add an apostrophe (*the glasses' box, the bosses' meeting*). Model these features in shared writing and refer to them in guided reading so that children build up their understanding of how the possessive *s* works.

The great apostrophe challenge

Once the children are beginning to grasp how apostrophes of possession and omission work, devise an engaging sorting activity like the one below for the children to complete in pairs. If possible, use sentences related to work that the children have been involved with. Give every pair or small group of children a set of apostrophe cards. Ask the children to:

- place the shaded heading cards above all the other cards;
- sort the sentence cards into the right category.

Sentences that need an apostrophe of possession	**Sentences that need an apostrophe of omission**	**Sentences that don't need any apostrophes**	**Wrongly punctuated/ written sentences**
The children's playground is being rebuilt.	It's going to rain.	The cats never play with the dogs.	I could of told you that.
Mini skirts were a popular 1960's fashion.	I'll finish this tomorrow.	The tree has lost its leaves.	Fashions changed rapidly in the 1960's.
Donkeys' ears are long.	The station's ahead on the right.	I have forgotten its name.	Its a long way to walk.
The boys' results were better than the girls'.	There's nothing to worry about.	Have you seen my glasses?	I can't see the dog but it's kennel's over there.
The donkey's ears were long.	The girl's looking for her cat.	The oranges look better than the apples.	The dirty cup's and saucer's are in the dishwasher.
The boy was looking for the girl's lost cat.	I should've gone home.	Sam is always losing his glasses.	Donkeys' ears' are long,
Her daughter's results were better than her son's.	That would've hurt!	He was born in the 1960s.	The cliff's looked lovely in the morning sun.

This activity can be downloaded from www.talk4writing.com

The Great 'S Challenge

Ask the children to rise to the Great *'S* Challenge. Explain that lots of people (young and old as illustrated above) get confused by the *'s* and suddenly every *s* has to have a friend. Now ask the children to be *'s* detectives and to make certain that they only use the possessive *'s* when they know the word with the *'s* owns the following word. Tell them to look out for evidence that adults often misuse apostrophes of possession and start to build up examples for everyone's entertainment. The wise teacher checks displays in their school carefully before inviting a class of detectives to hunt out adults' errors!

You might want to tell them that the plural *s* is very common while the possessive *'s* is much less common so, 'If in doubt, leave it out!' and remind them that possessive pronouns like *his, its, yours* don't need any apostrophes because the word itself signals possession (see pages 42–43).

WHEN TO USE COLONS AND SEMI-COLONS

Colons are easier to fathom than semi-colons so introduce these when you think the class is ready for them. Present the children with a range of sentences like the ones below, some of which include colons, and ask the children to discuss in pairs why some of the sentences include a colon and some don't.

1. *Baby Bear: Who's been eating my porridge?*
2. *This is one of the most famous lines that Shakespeare wrote: 'To be or not to be? That is the question.'*
3. *She went to the shop and bought apples, pears and bananas.*
4. *She bought the following items: apples, pears and bananas.*
5. *It snowed all night: the children knew the trip would be cancelled.*
6. *It snowed all night. The children knew the trip would be cancelled.*

Draw out from the discussion that colons are used to introduce something:

- in plays, after the names of the characters, to introduce the words they speak;
- a quotation;
- a list that has been formally introduced (that is why there is no colon in sentence 3 but there is one in sentence 4);
- to join two sentences together when the first sentence introduces the other (a full stop could be used instead or a dash).

Include colons in exemplar text and in shared writing, as well as drawing attention to colons when reading with the class, so that the children build up confidence in using this feature.

The semi-colon challenge

Only when you are sure that the children have really understood how and why to use full stops, commas and colons is it wise to see if they can rise to the semi-colon challenge. If they are not secure about the key punctuation marks, the semi-colon will suddenly sprout up everywhere. Also, although the English exam marking system would have us believe that to write at 'level 6' you have to have used a semi-colon, this is not actually true. There's masses of superb high-quality writing out there where semi-colons have not been used but obviously if it is an examination requirement, you abide by the rules of their game.

Try presenting the children with a range of sentences that use semi-colons correctly and get them to discuss when you would use a semi-colon.

1. *Listen carefully: the green team, led by Fred, should stand by the door; the blue team, led by Jo, should stand by the windows; the red team should stand by the radiator and choose their leader, and my yellow team should stand by my desk.*
2. *Some people prefer tea; some people prefer coffee.*
3. *The rain poured; the wind howled; lightning lit up the sky.*

Draw out from the children that semi-colons are useful for:

- separating off sections of complex lists where commas might be confusing;
- linking closely related statements. Such statements could be separated by a full stop or joined by conjunctions but the semi-colon serves to separate the clauses while showing that they are closely related.

Again draw attention to where semi-colons are well used in text and include the feature in shared writing so that the children start to use semi-colons appropriately.

The great semi-colon/colon challenge

Once the children have understood the different functions of colons and semi-colons, challenge them to complete this simple explanation of the key difference between their functions.

Colons … while semi-colons …

Draw out from the class that colons introduce things while semi-colons separate closely related things within a sentence.

The sentence construction and punctuation game

Once the children have been taught all the different types of sentences there are, present them with a wide range of different ways of expressing the same information. To help them understand the differences between the sentences, underline the main clauses. Again, this works best if you relate the sentences to a topic that they are currently focusing on. Ask the children to discuss the following questions.

- What type of sentence has been used in each of the examples?
- Why do some of the sentences have commas in them and some don't?
- Which sentences work best and why?

1. *The teacher entered the room. The girl quickly closed down the web page.*
2. *The teacher entered the room and the girl quickly closed down the web page.*
3. *The teacher entered the room: the girl quickly closed down the web page.*
4. *The girl quickly closed down the web page because the teacher entered the room.*
5. *Because the teacher entered the room, the girl quickly closed down the web page.*
6. *The girl, who had seen the teacher enter the room, quickly closed down the web page.*
7. *Seeing the teacher, whom she'd always disliked, enter the room, the girl quickly closed down the web page because she didn't want him to see what she had been doing.*
8. *Teacher! The girl quickly closed down the web page.*

Ask some children to feed back their conclusions.

The great punctuation challenge

Once your class has understood how to structure and punctuate more sophisticated sentences, see if they can complete this challenge. Write a paragraph, preferably related to a topic that they are currently doing, that includes most of the different sort of punctuation marks like the one below, and then remove all the punctuation. Provide the children in pairs or small groups with a copy of the unpunctuated paragraph and ask them to:

- read the passage aloud and try to make it make sense;
- decide how to punctuate it (stress that some of the punctuation could vary depending on personal preference and desired effect).

> ***waiting for the bus***
> *charge from nowhere hordes of school children surround the bus queuing long forgotten in the frantic fight to get on board if you don't join in you wont get on this bus or the next or the next so head down elbows out and voice screaming you hurl yourself into the scrum like king canute the conductor tries to control the relentless waves red for grangewood blue for northfields and the full traditional monty for snotty selective Baskerville on board the first battle won you await the bigger battle to come will you be one of the lucky few to board the number 39*

Once the class has had a go at punctuating the passage, display the punctuation-free text on screen and ask a group to take on the role of the teacher to illustrate and explain how they have punctuated it. The final version might look like this:

> ***Waiting for the bus***
> *Charge! From nowhere, hordes of school children surround the bus – queuing longforgotten in the frantic fight to get on board. If you don't join in, you won't get on this bus or the next or the next ... So head down, elbows out and voice screaming, you hurl yourself into the scrum. Like King Canute, the conductor tries to control the relentless waves: red for Grangewood; blue for Northfields and the full traditional Monty for snotty, selective Baskerville. On board, the first battle won, you await the bigger battle to come. Will you be one of the lucky few to board the number 39?*

You know more than you think you know

Use this activity to build up the children's confidence with what punctuation to use where. Display these punctuation marks prominently on screen and ask the children to explain the order in which these have been placed:

,   ;   :   .

Then ask them where they would place a single dash – .

This is a good way to help the children understand that different punctuation marks indicate different strengths of pause within a sentence/text. The single dash can function as a rather informal colon whereas the double dash would function like a double comma that separates off dropped-in text, functioning just like brackets.

AVOIDING AMBIGUITY

What a difference a comma makes

One of the best ways to get children into the useful habit of taking care with punctuation is to model for them in shared writing how important it is to read what we have written aloud, both to see whether it works and to check if the punctuation is correct. Build in useful checking habits into the editing and self-marking systems that you use with the children so it becomes second nature to check their own work for accuracy and clarity.

Once the children are becoming good at punctuation, challenge them to spot examples of where the comma or lack of it completely changes the meaning, as in the great old gag, *'What is this thing called, love?'* The comma instantly transforms the sentimental lyric into an everyday question.

In the exemplar test material provided for 11-year-olds in England, the children are asked to 'Explain how the comma changes meaning in the two sentences below.'

- *Are you coming to see, Ali?*
- *Are you coming to see Ali?*

To answer such a question the children not only have to be able to spot the difference but also need to be able to articulate that difference clearly so the more oral work that is done in preparation for this the better. Paying attention to such detail will at least help them build good proof-reading habits. What better place to help children with questions like this than with the old anecdote that Lynn Truss's book of the same punch line has made famous.

> *A panda walks into a cafe. He orders a sandwich, eats it, then draws a gun and fires two shots in the air.*
> *'Why?' asks the confused waiter, as the panda makes towards the exit.*
> *The panda produces a badly punctuated wildlife manual and tosses it over his shoulder. 'I'm a panda,' he says, at the door. 'Look it up.'*
> *The waiter turns to the relevant entry and, sure enough, finds an explanation:* ***Panda. Large black-and-white bear-like mammal, native to China. Eats, shoots and leaves.***

Display and read aloud the anecdote and ask the children to discuss in pairs the difference the comma makes to the last sentence. Once they have understood the joke, focus on getting them to explain the difference the comma makes.

Build up a display of such howlers like the ones below, encouraging the children to come up with examples, and use these to help children explain the difference the punctuation makes.

- *Let's eat, Fred. / Let's eat Fred.*
- *Call me Sam. / Call me, Sam.*
- *He loves cooking his family and his dog. / He loves cooking, his family and his dog.*
- *Stop clubbing baby seals! / Stop clubbing, baby seals.*

The five-minute punctuation TV slot

Once the children are confident users of punctuation, you could try challenging them to devise a five-minute TV slot on punctuation that will help children one year younger than themselves understand all about punctuation. Inform them that they can use any of the approaches you have used or devise their own and then ask a group or two to present their TV slots.

CHAPTER 6

Cohesion

Including subject and object, formal and informal, active and passive

This chapter provides a wide range of talk-based games to build children's understanding of how to make text flow coherently. It includes activities on understanding the difference between the subject and object within sentences as well as the difference between formal and informal text.

WHAT IS COHESION?

These games have been designed to help you draw out from the children that cohesion is all about making certain that what you write flows logically so the reader or listener can easily grasp what is being expressed. Through a range of engaging activities, the children will be helped to see that cohesion in writing is a complex mix of the following:

- maintaining a consistent good sense of audience and purpose;
- ensuring that the content is logically ordered so that one section builds on another to guide the reader through the text;
- using paragraphs appropriately so that each paragraph has a clear focus;
- using topic sentences within each paragraph to guide the reader through the text;
- using linking devices well (conjunctions, connectives and other sentence signposts) to signal to the reader the direction in which the text is going. These can link text within paragraphs and link paragraphs together;
- using pronouns effectively so that something referred to earlier can be quickly referenced without any confusion;

- punctuating the sentences properly so the reader knows how the text is divided into clumps of meaning;
- staying in the same tense so that there are no unintended jumps from past to present etc;
- reading work through to check that it flows and makes sense.

Combination games are key to coherence. See Chapter 4, Sentence combination, page 134.

Text doctor

These activities will work best if you adapt them to reflect the content that the children have been working on and the type of errors they are making. In pairs the children identify the main problem with each of the extracts and what needs to be done to make each paragraph coherent.

1. *Foxes are very intelligent creatures but sadly they are not liked by lots of people. They are actually very cunning and cute. They look a bit savage but can be really friendly. But suddenly something terrible happened when they went for a walk in the garden.*
2. *Foxes eat chickens and ducks and other birds. When they do this they don't like them and they want to hunt them because they have killed all of them.*
3. *Foxes like eating chickens and ducks and stuff like that and they like jumping on their prey so it doesn't see them coming and if they can't find a chicken to capture they eat insects and berries and sometimes they eat mice or small furry animals like that and they eat little birds.*
4. *Foxes are liked by some people and not liked by other people. They live in dens. They like eating chickens and so lots of farmers want to shoot them. They look a bit like dogs and have got long pointy noses and long bushy tails. They like eating insects and squiggly stuff like that too. And they like coming out at night. Anyway I like them.*
5. *There are lots of reasons why some people don't like foxes. The main reason is because they eat chickens and then there aren't any. But the biggest problem is they make a lot of noise howling and that frightens people. Also the worst thing is they can make awful smells so that's the reason why people think they should be hunted.*
6. *Foxes have eaten any small animals or small birds but they were very fond of chickens. When they haven't found any animals to eat they eat insects and juicy berries.*

Draw out from the children what the key problems are.

Creating Writing Toolkits

You may want to use these key points to start to co-construct a coherent text toolkit. (This is also a good opportunity to model how any bullet-pointed list needs to flow coherently from the statement that introduces it. In this case each point begins with the imperative.) The points that might arise from discussing the paragraphs above could be as follows:

The coherent text toolkit

- Remember **audience and purpose** – don't change the type of writing half way through; maintain the right level of formality for the audience.
- Plan your writing and divide the information into **paragraphs** with a different topic for each paragraph.
- Organise your points within a paragraph logically and use **connectives** well so the reader can follow what you are trying to say.
- Check you have used **pronouns** properly so the reader knows who or what they refer to.
- Write in **well constructed, varied sentences**. Don't just join everything together with *and then*.
- Use **conjunctions** to link parts of sentences together clearly.
- Use **tense** consistently – don't jump from one tense to another.
- **Read your work aloud** to check that it flows.

Display the toolkit on your working wall or washing line and refer to it regularly, adding to it as other features arise.

Build on this by devising text-doctor activities like the ones below, preferably related to the topics that the children are writing about and constructed to remedy the types of cohesion errors they are making, to help reinforce any aspects of cohesion that they have difficulties with.

HOW PRONOUNS CAN AFFECT COHERENCE

Sequencing text coherently

Sequencing text helps children understand how a whole range of features like conjunctions, other sentence signposts and pronouns help make text coherent.

Select a short text that the class should be able to read, preferably related to a topic they are working on, and cut it up into sections. (Remember to rearrange the paragraphs on screen before printing them off to cut up into sections. In this way, the children can't reassemble the order of the text from the cut lines.) Give groups of children a cut-up version of the text and ask them to:

- sequence the text;
- read the sequenced text aloud to check it is coherent;
- identify the linking phrases and/or pronouns;
- explain the order in which they have placed the text.

Ask a group to present the order in which they have placed the paragraphs explaining why they have decided on this order. Use the resulting discussion to bring out the key role of the conjunctions, connectives, pronouns and other sentence signposts in guiding the reader through the text. Flip-chart the key linking phrases to encourage the children to use similar phrases.

Fill the gaps

A useful but more difficult alternative puzzle is to present text as a cloze activity. Using focused cloze procedure is an excellent way of helping children understand the centrality of connectives and other sentence signposts in making text coherent.

Take any coherent short text related to the unit you are teaching and remove the key words or phrases that make it coherent. Ask the children in pairs to see if they can fill in the gaps.

The pronoun detective

Display a very short story that doesn't read well because no pronouns have been used, like the example below. Read the story to the children so they can hear the rather awkward phrasing and clumsy repetition that the absence of pronouns causes. Then give the children a copy of the story in pairs, and ask them to edit the story so that it now reads well because pronouns have been used in appropriate places. You may want to model the opening section for them so they know what to do.

> ***The Hodja's cat***
> *One day the Hodja bought a large fish for his dinner. All day the Hodja thought about how lovely the fish would taste. But in the evening his wife only gave the Hodja bread and soup. 'Where's the fish,' the Hodja asked rather crossly.*
> *'Ah, your cat ate the fish. The Hodja knows how the Hodja spoils that cat,' his wife replied somewhat unsympathetically.*

The Hodja was very angry and, grabbing the cat, weighed the cat carefully. The cat was exactly two kilos. Then the Hodja turned to his wife saying 'My fish weighed two kilos too. Since my wife says that my fish is here, where's my cat?'

The children read their amended version aloud to hear if it works. Point out that if they use too many pronouns, the reader may lose their way so they may want to edit their version. You may want to ask one pair to present their final version, in teacher role, explaining their choices.

Pronoun text doctor

Adapt sentences that children have written that are ambiguous because of a poor use of pronouns, or write your own examples like the ones below, and explain that there is more than one possible interpretation for each text. The children discuss how they could be rewritten to make the meaning clear – choosing any interpretation as long as the text is no longer ambiguous.

1. *She asked Sarah if she had seen the purse and then she asked Jo but she said she hadn't and she said she had. Suddenly she left.*
2. *He looked at his friend and decided he would do exactly what he wanted to do regardless of how much pain he caused others. He was always like that.*
3. *She stared at her for as long as she had stared at her and then declared that she had won.*

You may want to use a visualiser or tablet to enable some groups to feed back their improvements in teacher role, explaining the reasons for their choices.

The What connects to What? game

Construct a few sentences that relate to whatever text the children are currently focusing on and use them to develop the children's ability to link text coherently. This activity would be particularly good as a warm-up game for information text since it focuses on using generalising language as a link.

Model the first task for the children and then ask them in pairs to discuss what each word in bold refers to. They should be prepared to present their explanations.

1. Most trees, such as oak and plane, shed their leaves in winter. **Some**, like holly, keep their leaves.

2. Most dragons are green and hibernate in the winter. **A few** spend the winter ice skating.
3. Typically, trolls lurk under bridges. **Some** are known to hide in hollow trees.
4. Unicorns are distinguished by a single white horn in the centre of their foreheads. **This** is usually spiral and over 40 centimetres long.
5. The fronted adverbial can be added to the beginning of a sentence. **It** can be used to help the writer guide the reader through a text.

WHY UNDERSTANDING SUBJECT AND OBJECT MATTERS

Games can turn what could be a befuddling grammatical nicety into an engaging activity that also builds children's confidence in identifying the subject of sentences. Pronouns are a good place to start building understanding of the difference between the subject and the object of a sentence as most of them have a different form to distinguish the subject from the object.

Pass the parcel

This game helps children implicitly understand the difference between the subject of the action and the object of the action. Select an object from the classroom like a book and model how to play the game with a small group of children using as wide a variety of personal pronouns as you can. For example:

Person 1 (teacher):	*I'm giving **this** to **you**.*
Person 2 (boy):	***She** gave **me this** but now **I'm** passing **it** to **him**.*
Person 3 (boy):	***He** gave **me this** so **I'm** giving **it** to **you**.*
Person 4 (girl):	***You** gave me **this** and **I'm** passing **it** to **her**.*
Persons 1 and 2:	***We** gave **this** to **them** but **they** gave **it** back to **us**.*

The children play the game in groups using as many different correct versions as they can.

The I/me, he/him *detective*

To move from implicit to explicit understanding, involve the children as pronoun detectives solving the puzzle of why the pronouns change. Display a range of simple sentences showing how most pronouns change depending on whether they are the subject or object of the sentence. For example:

1a. ***I*** *saw* ***him.***	1b. ***He*** *saw* ***me.***
2a. ***I*** *texted* ***her.***	2b. ***She*** *texted* ***me.***
3a. ***I*** *followed* ***you.***	3b. ***You*** *followed* ***me.***
4a. ***She*** *asked* ***us.***	4b. ***We*** *asked* ***her.***
5a. ***They*** *laughed at* ***us.***	5b. ***We*** *laughed at* ***them.***
6a. ***They*** *phoned* ***me.***	6b. ***I*** *phoned* ***them.***

The children discuss why sometimes *I* is used and sometimes *me*; why sometimes *he* is used and sometimes *him* etc. If a group seems to have got the right idea, ask them to feed back their conclusions and, as they feed back, flip-chart their findings.

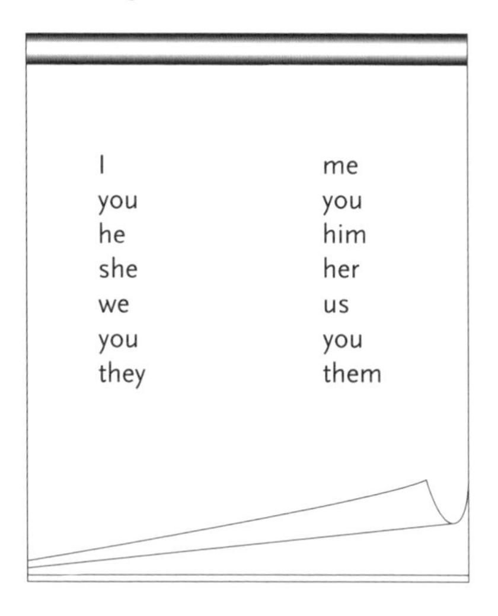

Through open-style discussion draw out the following from the children.

- The **subject** in a sentence is the person or thing doing something, and the **object** is the person or thing that is having something done to it. (Add these headings to your flip chart.)
- Most personal pronouns change depending on whether they are the subject or the object of a sentence.

The I/me *puzzle*

Present the class with some sentences like the following, explaining that all the sentences are correct. Challenge the class in pairs or small groups to come up with an easy way of helping people remember when it's correct to use *I* and when it's correct to use *me* when writing this type of sentence.

1a. *I waited at the bus stop.*
1b. *My friend and I waited at the bus stop.*
2a. *The last person to get on the bus was me.*
2b. *The last people to get on the bus were my friend and me.*

3a. *My friend and I saw the man.*
3b. *I saw the man.*
4a. *The man saw me.*
4b. *The man saw my friend and me.*

Co-construct with the class that you remove the other person, see whether *I* or *me* sounds right (ie *I* if it's the subject and *me* if it's the object) and then put the other person back into the sentence. Out of politeness, you should always mention the other person before yourself.

Subject/object games

Once the children are becoming confident with the concept of subject and object, provide them with a few simple sentences relating to their classroom like the examples below and ask them how they know which noun is the subject of the sentence and which is the object:

- *Ali is talking to Mehmet.*
- *Jo is writing a story.*
- *The hamster likes apples.*

Draw out from the class that the **subject** in a sentence is the person or thing **doing something**, and the **object** is the person or thing that is **having something done to it**. Refer to the flip chart that you displayed when the class established this with the pronoun sentences (see page 197).

Sentence doctor: the subject verb agreement game

The verb of a sentence should agree with the subject. *I, you, we* and *they* ***walk*** *to work. He* ***walks*** *to work*. This is pretty straightforward in English. As you can see from the example above, apart from the third person singular of the present tense, verbs do not change except for the very irregular verb *to be* (see page 209). If children are saying *he sit* instead of *he sits* or *she say* instead of *she says*, recast their sentences for them and emphasise this pattern of agreement when reading aloud. If the local dialect uses different forms of the verb *to be*, emphasise that that is fine for informal speech but that formal English must be used when writing and speaking formally. Reinforce the pattern by playing Sentence doctor. The children have to sort the sentences into those that are correct and those that need correcting and then work out how to correct them.

- *I play with the dog.*
- *The child play with the dog.*
- *You sing in the morning.*
- *We sing in the morning.*
- *She sing in the morning.*
- *They like chocolate.*
- *He like chocolate*
- *I goes to school.*
- *He goes to school.*
- *We were going.*
- *You was there.*
- *I is going.*

Look out for errors in agreement in the children's work and create passages for them to improve. Challenge them to explain why this sentence frequently seen on computer screens is correct: *Windows is shutting down.*

The active/passive game

Display a few pairs of sentences like the ones below, preferably related to topics you are actually teaching. Ask the children, in role as subject/object experts, to discuss what the difference is between the sentences.

1a. *The dog chased the cat.*
1b. *The cat was chased.*
2a. *Clouds hid the moon.*
2b. *The moon was hidden.*
3a. *We heated the test tube.*
3b. *The test tube was heated.*

Draw out from the children that in the a. sentences it is very clear who is doing what to whom (you know who is carrying out the action and who/what is having something done to them/it). However, in the b. sentences the person or thing carrying out the action is not mentioned. You just know that something/someone has had something done to it/them.

Explain that the a. sentences are active – the subject of the sentence is carrying out the action and that this is the usual way of expressing English. But the b. sentences are passive. What was the object of the sentence has now become the subject of the sentence and it is having something done to it; the agent of the action is not mentioned at all.

- Ask the children in pairs to turn a few active sentences about familiar subjects into passive ones so that the thing that was done to in the active sentence (the object of the sentence) becomes the subject that is done to in the passive sentence. For example:

Active	*Passive*
4a. *Errol was reading* ***a book****.*	4b. ***A book*** *was read.*
5a. *The headteacher organised the fire practice.*	5b.
6a. *The hamster was staring at the children.*	6b.
7a. *The children were laughing at the hamster.*	7b.

- Now ask the children if they can think of a way of adding a few words onto the b. sentences so that we know who/what is carrying out the action in each case.
- Ask for feedback. Hopefully, someone will suggest using the word *by*. Model for them how to add the actor into each of the passive sentences. *The cat was chased by the dog* etc. Ask the children to add the actor into all of the sentences above and see if the whole class can say the complete passive sentences in turn together to help build the children's confidence with the tune of the passive.
- Draw attention to the passive when you come across it in text and discuss why it might be used, for example, to make text more formal and less immediate (useful for describing processes as in science – *The beaker was filled with water*), or even to make text more mysterious – *A body was found next to the canal by a man out walking his dog*. Also draw attention to the fact that many tenses can be in the passive: *A report* ***was written****. A report* ***will be written****. A report* ***is being written****. A report* ***should have been written****.* etc.
- Demonstrate when to use the passive through shared writing.

Selecting the right register

Non-fiction writing is an excellent way of building up children's understanding of levels of formality. Provide the children with an audience and purpose for their writing and help them select the right level of formality by modelling how to make the language selected appropriate for the audience. When assessing children's work, note down errors relating to levels of formality and build them into activities. For example, if the class had been involved in groups representing different bids for how to develop the local town centre, the unit could begin with a focus on a more informal persuasive register. For the role play of the council meeting there would be the formality of council procedures contrasting with the more informal register of the bidders. This could then be followed up by a formal third-person passive report. Apart from providing exemplar text, so they know what a good one looks like, try a Not suitable for …/Suitable for … sorting activity to develop children's understanding of the appropriate register:

Not suitable for a formal 3rd person report	**Suitable for a formal 3rd person report**
I decided to vote for the Spendulike bid because ...	The meeting was held to discuss ...
You hear each of the bids in turn and then you make a decision about ...	Presentations were made on behalf of ...
We sort of heard all the bids and then ...	The first organisation to present its bid was ...
The daftest point they made was ...	The main arguments supporting this bid were ...
Well, that made everyone laugh and then ...	Following the presentation of all the bids ...
Anyway, I explained to the meeting ...	After much discussion it was agreed that ...
My friend Jacky thought the best bid was ...	A minority of councillors supported the view that ...
It was the most boring sort of meeting you could imagine ...	The conclusion reached by the Council ...
Well, in the end, the Council decided that ...	The key reasons why X bid was successful were ...

Use the activity to draw out from the class the typical features of formal report writing: formal, impersonal, passive, abstract and general. A useful follow-up role-play activity could be to turn the report into an item for the regional evening news. Children could magpie useful informal phrases while watching regional news.

EMBEDDING UNDERSTANDING OF COHESION

The cohesion challenge

Present this challenge once your class has a good grasp of cohesion. Write/select/adapt a coherent complex passage (see below) so that it includes a number of paragraphs, many different types of punctuation marks, and a range of techniques to achieve cohesion. Remove the paragraphs, punctuation and capital letters, then give a copy of this text to each pair of children and ask them to do the following.

- Read the passage aloud to try and work out what is happening and where the sentence breaks should be. (Point out that there are several ways that some of the sentences could be punctuated and different ways in which the passage could be paragraphed.)
- Decide where the paragraph breaks should be. (Show them how to use two short parallel lines to indicate a new paragraph.)
- Punctuate the text using the full range of punctuation marks.
- Finally, annotate the text to bring out what makes it coherent.

For example:

first day at school

and do your tie up properly as he finally made it out of the front door the last of a long line of desperate instructions rang in stuarts ears his mother watched him until he was out of sight nervously hoping that a new school would make a difference separate him from those so called friends that had led him astray at st marys was her solution hoping the bus would take forever stuart proceeded miserably towards spencer high tie firmly in pocket he made it to school just as the bell rang the headteacher beaming at the new intake pointed pupils in the direction of their tutor rooms at spencer high we wear our ties he observed glaring at stuart all the other children in his tutor group seemed to know each other old friends from primary school reuniting stuart sat alone a neat little girl clutching a teddy bear and arranging her sharp multi coloured new pencils almost made him smile easy prey but he would wait the tutor called the register scanning faces for those who might cause bother lost in his own world of resentment stuart didn't hear her call the name kevin pearce or see her look up edgily having been warned about him by st marys at that moment kev swaggered in kev his great friend until theyd been expelled and hed had to move estate as soon as their eyes met both knew that the old partnership was about to be renewed his mother waited nervously for her sons return how was school she asked hesitantly as soon as he reached the door ok he mumbled on his way to skulk in his room mrs smith sighed with relief so far so good for her solution a smile played over stuarts face he was looking forward to the next day

Once they have completed their versions, display the punctuation-free text on screen and get pupils in teacher role to explain how they have punctuated it and how the text is coherent. Use open discussion techniques to draw the more subtle cohesion points out of the children. The final annotated version might look like this:

First Day at School

'And do your **tie** up properly!' As **he** finally made it out of the front door, the last of a long line of desperate instructions rang in Stuart's ears. His mother watched **him** until **he** was out of sight nervously hoping that a new school would make a difference. Separate him from those so-called friends that had led **him** astray at St Mary's was her solution.

Hoping the bus would take forever, Stuart proceeded miserably towards Spencer High. **Tie** firmly in pocket, he made it to school just as the bell rang. The headteacher, beaming at the new intake, pointed pupils in the direction of their tutor rooms. 'At Spencer High we wear our **ties**,' he observed glaring at **Stuart**.

All the other children in his tutor group seemed to know each other: old friends from primary school reuniting. Stuart sat alone. A neat little girl (clutching a teddy bear and arranging her sharp, multi-coloured, new pencils) almost made him smile: easy prey. But he would wait ...

The tutor called the register, scanning faces for those who might cause bother. Lost in his own world of resentment, Stuart didn't hear her call the name Kevin Pearce or see her look up edgily, having been warned about him by St Mary's. **At that moment**, Kev swaggered in. Kev! His great friend until they'd been expelled and he'd had to move estate. **As soon as** their eyes met, both knew that the old partnership was about to be renewed.

His mother waited nervously for her son's return. 'How was school?' she asked hesitantly as soon as he reached the door

'OK,' he mumbled on his way to skulk in his room.

Mrs Smith sighed with relief; so far so good for her solution. A smile played over Stuart's face; he was looking forward to the next day.

Repetition of *he* and *him* glue paragraph together and help reader see how mother is worrying about son

Good use of paragraphing to reflect different stages of story: leaving home and setting up story, reaching school. First experience of tutor group etc.

Reader is shown that Stuart is a bully – undercuts mother's early illusion that her son is led astray and helps link story

'Tie' serves as useful link between first two paragraphs and helps reader understand tensions between mother and son over school rules and what the headteacher values

Use of Stuart's name so reader doesn't confuse the *he* that refers back to the headteacher with Stuart

Connective phrases help link the action

Final balanced 2-clause sentences help builds tension of battle between mother and son and hints that mother's solution won't work

Change the register

A good extension activity to the cohesion challenge is to ask children to think of the way in which they would change their register – the way that they speak and the words that they use – depending on audience, for example, an eight-year old audience versus an audience of primary teachers. Select two very different audiences that your class will be familiar with and model for them how to change the register. The children can then practise changing register, feed back and discuss the difference that audience makes to the words and sentences that we use.

The each-one-teach-one cohesion challenge

Once you think the class has understood the different elements that can contribute to text cohesion, challenge them to work out how to explain what cohesion is to their partner. They can choose any of the examples that they have already worked with or devise new examples. Once they have each had a go at teaching their partner, ask them to swap partners and explain to someone new. See if any child wants to rise to the Professor of Cohesion challenge and explain cohesion to the whole class.

The naming of parts

Understanding grammar is all about understanding the function of a word or phrase within a sentence: what is it doing? All the research evidence would suggest that the best way to develop such understanding so that it improves the quality of writing is to integrate the understanding into writing activities, which in turn work best if children have talked the text first and can talk about the text. In England, the disembodied naming of parts is increasingly becoming a key feature of grammar tests so 11-year-olds are asked questions like this:

How do the words *At that moment* function in the sentence below?

At that moment, she didn't care if yelling made her look silly: she just wanted her purse back.

	Tick one
• as a noun phrase	☐
• as a relative clause	☐
• as a fronted adverbial	☐
• as a conjunction	☐

Source: Sample 2016 KS2 grammar test, DfE

Warning: If your class, or groups within the class, have reached test age in England and are not at the stage when this would be a feasible activity, then do not torture them with it; that would only sap their confidence. But, in these circumstances, you might want to use this bit of advice for tackling such questions: just tell them that if *fronted adverbial* is one of the choices and the selected phrase begins the sentence, then it's a fronted adverbial. This is pleasantly easy and has a very high chance of being right!

If such naming of parts is relevant to the tests your class has to face, and you think they have enough understanding to tackle the question, you might want to try giving them some multi-clause sentences to analyse in small groups, as an entertaining challenge. The more they have to discuss these issues, the more likely they are to understand them and not be daunted by them. For example, expand the question above as illustrated below.

Ask the groups to see if they can identify all the features listed here in the sentence and explain why they know they are right:

- an expanded noun phrase;
- a relative clause;
- a fronted adverbial;
- a conjunction;
- the past progressive.

At that moment, the very agitated young woman, who was shouting and screaming, didn't care if yelling made her look silly: she just wanted her purse back.

For those who can tackle the question with some confidence, help them to explain that:

- **expanded noun phrases** are just nouns (naming words) plus at least one adjective to describe them and a determiner to pin them down, for example, *the sleepy cat*
- **relative clauses** are extra information dropped into the middle of clauses or tacked on at the end; they begin with a relative pronoun: *who, whom, which* or *that;*
- **conjunctions** join the bits of sentences together, and subordinating conjunctions introduce clauses;
- *at* is a preposition and it is introducing a phrase so this is a **prepositional phrase** not a **noun phrase**. (All prepositional phrases are also adverbials as the phrase is acting as an adverb and tells us when the action took place. This adverbial happens to be at the front of the sentence and so it is a **fronted adverbial**!)
- the **past progressive** (eg *was shouting/were shouting*) is often used to refer to things that happened at a particular moment in the past to set the context.

If they can do this, it probably won't improve their writing in the slightest but it may make them feel confident, if not smug! Then at least they won't be fazed by such questions in a test.

A final note on the mini-lesson approach

Once you have finished modelling and explaining any grammatical feature, a useful option for all children in all classes is to offer the opportunity for any of them who feel they haven't understood to form a mini group. This group will then immediately receive more opportunity to play games with the concept to build their confidence and understanding so that they can start to integrate the technique into their writing repertoire successfully. Remember that practice only makes perfect if you are practising something correctly. If not, practice just makes permanent.

Grammar glossary and index to grammar games

Grammar provides the rules for joining words and phrases into sentences. Pinning down grammatical terminology is verging on the impossible. The glossary in Bill Bryson's marvellous book *Troublesome Words* (Penguin, 2009) begins: 'Grammatical terms are, to quote Frank Palmer, "largely notional and often extremely vague".' This offers comfort to the perplexed. However, it's useful to have some explicit understanding of grammar to help you express yourself more effectively; having key technical terms in common helps discussion about how to use language powerfully. Moreover, understanding grammar helps you to learn another language, which in turn strengthens your understanding of any language.

Below we have attempted to provide clear explanations for key grammatical terms with an emphasis on their function. After each term are the page numbers for activities related to this term so the glossary acts as an index.

active and passive (199–200)
Most verbs can be active or passive. In English the active is used much more than the passive. Look at these three sentences:

- *The cat* ***saw*** *the dog.* (active)
- *The dog* ***was seen***. (passive)
- *The dog* ***was seen*** *by the cat.* (passive)

In the active sentence, the subject (*the cat*) performs the action. This sentence has the typical English sentence structure of subject, verb, object. In the middle sentence (passive) the dog has become the subject of the action. In this passive sentence, the agent of the action, *the cat*, is not mentioned at all. If the agent is mentioned, it is normally introduced by the word *by* as in the final example above.

All forms of the passive consist of the verb to be + a **past participle:**

passive	active
• *The wallet **was stolen**.*	• *She **stole** the wallet.*
• *The wallet is being stolen.*	• *She is stealing the wallet.*
• *You **were seen** by me.*	• *I **saw** you.*
• *You had been seen.*	• *I had seen you.*

To sum it up, if the subject of a sentence is having the action done to it, rather than being the actor, then the sentence is in the passive. Passive forms are common in formal, impersonal writing:

- *It **was concluded** that …*
- *A body **has been found**.*

adjective (19–35, 37, 77)
Adjectives describe nouns (something or somebody): *the **deserted** beach; an **old wise** man*; or act as a complement to linking verbs (verbs that record a state and need to be completed to make sense) such as *to be, to look, to get, to seem*. For example, *the castle was **old**; the beach looked **deserted**.*

As illustrated above, adjectives come before nouns and after verbs. They can also compare things: *That cat is **fat**; the middle one is **fatter** but the one over there is the **fattest**.* (19–20, 25–26)

adverb (73–80)
Adverbs are describing words that not only give added meaning to verbs, but also to adjectives, another adverb or another clause:

*It **endlessly** rained this summer.*
*It's **really** raining now.*
*It rained **extremely powerfully**.*
***Usually**, it rains more in the winter.*

They frequently end in **ly** but not always – *It rained **very often**.* They usually tell us how, where, when and how often something happened – ***hurriedly, quickly, near, far, inside**.*

adverbial (80–83, 165, 168–169)
This is a term for words, phrases or subordinate clauses that, just like adverbs, modify verbs or clauses. All prepositional phrases are adverbials.

An **adverbial phrase** is a group of words without a verb that function just like an adverb.

adverb	adverbial phrase
• *He spoke* ***hurriedly***.	• *He spoke* ***in a hurried manner***.
• *They are arriving* ***tomorrow***.	• *They are arriving* ***in a few days' time***.

Similarly, an **adverbial clause** is a group of words including a verb that functions just like an adverb.

adverb	adverbial clause
• *It will be sunny* ***tomorrow***.	• *It will be sunny* ***by the time we go back to school***.
• *She shut the window* ***quickly***.	• *She shut the window* ***when it started raining***.

Also see **fronted adverbial**.

agreement (196–199)
The verb and the subject of a sentence should agree, ie the form of the verb sometimes changes because of the subject. For example, *I* ***run***; *you* ***run***, but *he/she/it* ***runs***. In English, apart from the third person singular of the present tense, as illustrated above, verbs don't change. The one exception to this is the verb *to be*:

- Present tense: *I* ***am***, *you* ***are***, *he/she/it* ***is***, *we* ***are***, *you* ***are***, *they* ***are***.
- Past tense: *I* ***was***, *you* ***were***, *he/she/it* ***was***, *we* ***were***, *you* ***were***, *they* ***were***.

ambiguity (195)
This is a phrase or sentence that has more than one possible interpretation. *He asked if he had seen his dog but he said he hadn't and so he left.* Misused pronouns are a great source of ambiguity since it has to be clear which noun the pronoun is referring to for the reader or listener to follow the meaning clearly.

antonym (34)
The name for a word that has the opposite meaning to another word: *hot/cold*.

apostrophe (18, 48, 161, 177–185)
The apostrophe, looking like a raised comma, has two functions: it indicates possession or omission.

Possession (18, 48–49, 161, 177–185): *the cat's food* (one cat); *the cats' food* (many cats); *the women's changing room*. However, **possessive pronouns** don't have an apostrophe because the possession is part of the meaning of the word: *yours, its, hers* etc.

Omission (48–49, 177–178, 180–181): an apostrophe is used to indicate that letters have been missed out from words or phrases: *It is – it's; will not – won't* etc.

article (46–47, 49–50)
A/an and *the* are articles which are a type of **determiner**. Consider the difference between *I saw **a** cat* and *I saw **the** cat*. ***A** cat* refers to any old cat but ***the** cat* refers to a particular, definite cat. *A/an* is therefore known as the indefinite article and *the* is the definite article.

auxiliary verbs (63–71, 121); also see **tense**
These are 'helper' verbs that support the main verb in expressing additional meaning. The most common auxiliary verbs are ***to be, to have*** and ***to do***.

- *I **am drinking** tea.*
- *I **have drunk** my tea.*
- ***Do** you **drink** tea?*

The auxiliary verb *have* is used to construct verbs in the past – *I have eaten. The train has arrived*. The 'had' form is used to refer to earlier situations – *I had eaten all the strawberries before I reached home.* These are referred to by some grammarians as the perfect (have) and the past perfect, also known as the pluperfect, (had) tenses probably because these are separate tenses in Latin with different verb endings. Other grammarians don't use these terms as they don't think they fit English. Basically the term **perfect** is used to indicate that an action occurred earlier than the time being focused on.

The **present perfect progressive** (66–68) (aka the continuous) is used to show that an action lasts up to the present and still influences the present – hence its name as it expresses the action's progression: *I have been waiting for the bus for over half an hour but it still hasn't turned up.*

In a similar way, the **past perfect progressive** (66–68) is used to express the length of an action that took place before a certain point in the past. *He had been playing snooker ever since he could see over the snooker table and hoped to become a professional player.*

The more children read, the more they will implicitly internalise these different tenses. Many excellent teachers of English feel that it is not useful to be able to identify all of the tenses by name as long as the children are using them correctly.

The other auxiliary verbs, sometimes known as **modal verbs**, are all about possible actions that may be within or beyond our control. The modal verbs are ***can/could, may/might, must/ought, will/would*** and ***shall/should***. They are used to express future actions in English and are followed by the infinitive of the verb.

- *I* ***can go*** *out tonight.*
- *She* ***could jump*** *higher than that.*

brackets (161, 167–168)
Brackets (which always come in pairs) are used to separate off additional information that would interrupt the drift of a paragraph or cause confusion if commas were used instead. They are used in scripts to separate off stage directions from the words actually to be spoken. They can also be called **parentheses**:

- *William Shakespeare* ***(****1564–1616****)*** *is the most famous playwright in the world.*
- ***Man****:* ***(****watching the television****)*** *Is dinner ready yet?*

bullet points (193)
Bullet points are a way of indicating separate items in a list. The list should flow grammatically from the introductory statement. Punctuation to separate off the items should be consistent, ie no punctuation (a final full stop at the end of the list is optional) or a comma or semi-colon after each line with a full stop to close the list:

To make your writing scary you can:

- *Begin with the main character (MC) enjoying themselves in a safe place*
- *Put the MC in a dark lonely place …*

clause (37, 39, 43, 72, 80–84, 88–91, 95–101, 123–125, 163–166)
A clause is a group of words that contains a verb and a subject. A main clause makes complete sense on its own and can be a sentence – known as a simple sentence. A **subordinate clause** (43, 88–89, 91–92, 163–166) is dependent on the main clause – as its name suggests. Compound and complex sentences contain at least two clauses.

It is very sunny today. (One main clause – a simple sentence.)
It is very sunny today and I am feeling too hot. (Two main clauses joined together by the conjunction *and* to form a compound sentence – these are sometimes called co-ordinated sentences.)
Because it is very sunny today, I am feeling too hot. (A subordinate clause introducing the main clause in a complex sentence.)

One sentence can contain many clauses of different types, but the more clauses there are, the more difficult the sentence becomes to understand, as this sentence illustrates.

Clauses normally require a subject and a verb but sometimes the subject can be understood, eg command clauses – *Sit!* – where the subject *you* is understood. (See also **adverbial clause**, **noun clause**, **participle**, **phrase**, **relative clause and sentence**.)

cohesion (see 41, 90; Chapter 6: 191–206)
A text has cohesion if its sentences and paragraphs are related together well so that the reader can follow what is being said easily. Pronouns and determiners are key to cohesion as well as conjunctions and connectives to guide the reader. Punctuation also aids cohesion. These features are known as cohesive devices.

The teacher was uncertain what to do: ***this*** *boy was always seeking attention claiming to have lost things that turned out not to be lost* ***but, this*** *time,* ***it*** *might be true.* ***Without further hesitation, she*** *decided to ask the class.*

colon (161, 173, 185–186)
Colons are used to introduce closely-related information where one clause or phrase introduces the next clause or phrase, for example, formally introduced explanations, examples, lists or quotations.

- *The weather was deteriorating rapidly: she would not go out today.*
- *She decided to buy the following items: an anorak, waterproof boots and over-trousers.* (**Note:** *She decided to buy an anorak, waterproof boots and over-trousers.* This sentence does not require a colon because there is no formal introduction to the list.)
- *Samuel T Coleridge wrote the following memorable line: 'Water, water everywhere and not a drop to drink.'*

Colons can also be used to separate off numerals and titles: *The odds were 11:1.*

comma (44, 76, 89, 161–169, 179, 187–190)
Commas are used to separate words, phrases and clauses within a sentence to help the reader follow the meaning. Some commas are seen as essential and others as optional. They should be used as an aid to understanding: too many in one sentence can be confusing. Below is guidance on general uses.

- Commas for lists (162–163): commas are used to break up items (words, phrases or clauses) in a list:

  It was a lovely, warm, sunny morning.

Normally, commas aren't used in front of conjunctions like *and*, *but* and *or*. However, they are sometimes used to help the reader follow longer sentences to indicate a change in direction.

He ate a mound of eggs and bacon plus beans and chips and sausages, and then felt sick.

- Commas to separate off clauses (89, 95, 163–164):

1. Commas are used to separate off embedded clauses within a sentence. *The dog, which was feeling hungry, waited by its bowl.* (These commas could be replaced by brackets or dashes to separate the embedded clause from the rest of the sentence; commas are most often used for this purpose. In speech, voice inflection serves the same purpose.)

2. Commas should also be used to separate off subordinate clauses at the beginning of sentences. They can also be used to separate out the clauses in multi-clause sentences. The standard way of constructing sentences in English is to begin with the main clause and then add other subordinate clauses.

   The teacher looked up nervously when the inspector walked into the room. (In this sentence a comma separating the clauses is optional.)

   When the inspector entered the room, the teacher looked up nervously.

A good rule of thumb when writing multi-clause sentences is to read your sentence out loud and see whether a break helps it make sense and, if it does, put in a comma.

The teacher, who had been up half the night preparing, looked up nervously as the inspector walked into the room, fearing that all his preparation might be in vain.

Remember, the more clauses there are in a sentence, the harder it is to understand.

- Commas to separate adverbs and adverbial phrases at the beginning of sentences (165): Adverbs and adverbial phrases are usually followed by commas if they occur at the beginning of sentences.

  At long last, the speech ended.
  Hurriedly, he packed his bag. (You would probably omit the comma if the sentence were reversed: *He packed his bag hurriedly.*)

- Commas to separate off additional information and interjections (167–168): Phrases providing additional information or interjections are usually separated off just like embedded clauses:

  Oh no, I think I've lost my phone.

- Commas to separate the speaker from what they say (162): Direct speech is always separated from the speaker by commas.

  'It would be great,' she replied, 'if I could go.'

comma splice – see **full stop** (219)

command – see **sentence**

complement (19, 20)
A complement tells you more about the subject or the object of a verb. They are common in sentences using the verb *to be* but are also used after other linking verbs like *become, get, looks, seems.*

He is ***angry****.*
Doing nothing makes me ***bored****.*

compound sentence – see **clause** (88–91, 95–96, 123–124, 147, 159–160)

compound word (14, 176)
A word created out of two words: *football, inbox, timetable*

conditional
A conditional sentence is a sentence in which one thing depends on something else. Such sentences often include the conjunction *if*. Conditional sentences are complex by nature as they have at least two clauses and the *if* clause is subordinate to the main clause. Some other possible conjunctions for conditional sentences are *unless, assuming that, providing/provided, given that* and *as long as*.

- ***If** it rains, we won't go.*
- *I'll arrive early **providing** the bus arrives on time.*

conjunction (88–101, 123, 131–133, 163–165, 187, 191, 193–194, 205–206)
Conjunctions link the parts of a sentence together. They can link words, phrases or clauses together.

> *The boy **and** the cat waited **until** they could visit the magic mountain **because** the pathway only appeared **when** the moon was full.*

- Co-ordinating conjunctions (88–91): (*and, but, or, so*) join clauses of equal weight – each clause could be a stand-alone sentence.

> *It will rain in the morning **and** it will rain in the afternoon.*

- Subordinating conjunctions (91–101, 124, 163–165, 206): (*when, if, although* etc) introduce a subordinate clause.

> *We will light the fire **when** it gets dark.*
> ***Because** it is cloudy, we can't see the moon.*

(**Note:** If the subordinate clause begins the sentence, the end of the clause is signalled by a comma.)

connective (101–110, 129–131)
This is a useful umbrella term to refer to words or phrases that link clauses or sentences together; they are key to making text cohesive. Grammarians tend not to use the term connective. All conjunctions are connectives and link the bits of a sentence together (see pages 88–89). However, many adverbs/adverbials also function as connectives. They act as signposts introducing paragraphs, linking sentences together or introducing additional information into a sentence. They can signal many things including:

- opposition – *however, on the other hand*
- explanation – *for example, that is to say, in other words*

A word of warning: There never was such a thing as a 'level-5 connective' just a connective that is effective or not for the context in which it is being used.

continuous – see **participle**

co-ordinating conjunction – see **conjunction** (88–91)

co-ordination – see **clause**

dash (161, 168, 175–176)
A dash (a longer mark than a hyphen) is used to indicate the break in the flow of a sentence. It is often used in more informal writing.

> *And the winner is – Angela!*

It can also be used instead of brackets or commas to separate off information in a sentence.

> *The lost cat – which had now been missing for three days – looked small, tired and hungry.*

Additionally, a dash indicates range, with the sense of *from...to,* as in: *from pages 82–89.*

determiner (36–37, 46–49)
Determiners are like precise adjectives that help pin down the exact number or definiteness of the nouns: ***a*** *boy;* ***the*** *boy;* ***four*** *boys;* ***all*** *boys* etc. They are always positioned in front of any other words that modify a noun: ***The*** *strangely quiet cat sat still.* They are some of the most commonly used words in English and include **articles** (*a/an, the*); demonstratives (*this/that, these/those*); possessives (*my, your, his, her, its, our, their*); quantifiers (*some, any, few, each, every* etc); numbers (*one, nine, two million* etc); and question words (*which, what, whose*).

Some of these words can also function alone as pronouns that refer to the nouns.

> ***That*** *jug is the nicest. Buy* ***that****.* (The first *that* is a determiner; the second is a pronoun.)

dialect (55, 144, 198)
This is a version of a language spoken in a particular region that has some different grammar or vocabulary. Often the verb *to be* is declined differently – *'I weren't doing it'*; pronouns are used differently – *thee* and *thou* for *you*.

direct and indirect speech (169–174)
Direct speech repeats the actual words that the speaker spoke, and puts speech marks round these words, just like the words in a speech bubble:

The boy shouted, 'Run! The Daleks are coming.'

Indirect speech, sometimes known as reported speech, sums up what has been said:

The boy shouted that they should run because the Daleks were coming …

Typically, indirect speech is in the past tense and the third person.

elision/ellipsis (114, 176)
This is the missing out of a word or phrase which is predictable to avoid repetition:

I might go or I might not [go].

Ellipsis is also the word for three dots (…) to indicate that something has been left out or not been completed:

He stared in horror. Surely it couldn't be …

exclamation mark (114, 120, 121, 147, 161, 167)
These are a customised full stop signalling strong feelings or urgency and are used after emphatic declarations (*You will obey!*), emphatic commands (*Go away!*) and interjections (*Ouch!*). They are frequently used when writing down speech and are usually avoided in formal writing.

Additional note on exclamation marks: Teachers in England may have noticed this most strange and befuddling passage from section 4.5.2 of *English grammar, punctuation and spelling test framework, National Curriculum tests from 2016*:

> ***Sentences with different forms: exclamations***
> *For the purposes of the English grammar, punctuation and spelling test, an exclamation is required to start with What or How, e.g.*

What a lovely day! How exciting!

A sentence that ends in an exclamation mark, but which does not have one of the grammatical patterns shown above, is not considered to be creditworthy as an exclamation (e.g. exclamatory statements, exclamatory imperatives, exclamatory interrogatives or interjections).

This is a very limiting definition of the use of exclamation marks, and we can only assume that it has been defined as such to facilitate the marking of multiple-choice grammar tests, since many sentences are potentially exclamatory. This is not just confusing but potentially damaging because teachers and, therefore, children may begin to think that the correct use of the exclamation has to be constrained by this definition, leading to confusion when reading real text, especially comics. Do not confine children's understanding of exclamation marks to the DfE definition!

extended noun phrase – see **noun phrase**

finite and non-finite verbs (133, 140)
Finite verbs alter depending on tense or subject. They signal contrasts of tense, number, person and mood:

- *He walks to school. He used to walk to school.* (contrast in tense)
- *I walk. She walks. They walk.* (contrast in person and number)
- *Walk! We are walking.* (contrast in mood)

A standard sentence must have a clause that includes a finite verb.

Non-finite verbs do not alter depending on tense, number, person or mood. A clause that begins with a non-finite verb is called a **non-finite clause** and cannot form a sentence on its own. There are three non-finite forms of the verb.

- The **present participle** (*ing*): *She is **running**.*
- The **past participle** (*en/ed*): *I am **tired**.*
- The base form used as an infinitive: *I could **go**.*

fronting/fronted (81–83, 165, 196–199, 205–206)
This term will be new to many of us. It is currently used in the National Curriculum in England to signify that a word or phrase that usually comes after the verb has been moved in front of it. Hence the term fronted adverbial:

- ***Confused*** *by the term fronted adverbial, the teacher made a cup of tea.*

full stop (113–115, 118, 120, 128–129, 161–162, 166–167, 187)
Full stops are key to making text readable. They are the most important punctuation mark because they separate off clumps of complete meaning. They mark the end of each sentence as illustrated in this brief paragraph:

> *Communication has changed completely in the last 15 years. Mobile phones that can access the internet, store all your favourite music and take pictures are now commonplace. Moreover, computers are found in most homes.*

Traditionally, full stops marked abbreviations and contractions but modern style leaves these out. The important thing here is consistency. In any text, all the abbreviations should either have full stops or not have them:

> ***Mr.*** *and* ***Mrs.*** *Hart* or ***Mr*** *and* ***Mrs*** *Hart*
> ***eg*** or ***e.g.***

- The **comma splice** is a common error where a comma is used to separate two main clauses rather than a full stop: *He checked his emails, he looked nervously to see if the message had arrived.* This could have been written correctly in the following ways:

  > *He checked his emails. He looked nervously to see if the message had arrived.* (Two sentences – two main clauses separated by a full stop.)
  > *He checked his emails: he looked nervously to see if the message had arrived.* (One sentence – two main clauses linked by a colon (or a dash) since the first main clause introduces the second.)
  > *He checked his emails and looked nervously to see if the message had arrived.* (One sentence – two main clauses joined by a conjunction.)

- **Question marks** (121, 161, 167) are customised full stops signalling a question (interrogative sentence) and are used at the end of the sentence:

  > *What is she doing?*

future tense (63, 65–66)– see **tense** and **auxiliary verbs**

gender (11–12)
This term is used to refer to whether a noun is feminine, masculine or neuter (neither masculine nor feminine). Approximately a quarter of the languages in the world classify nouns like this; the gender of the noun can then affect the formation of the words like determiners and adjectives that modify the noun. In English, gender is only relevant for a few words, eg prince/princess and it does not affect any related modifiers.

grammar
Grammar is the name of the rules of a language that explain how sentences are structured or words are inflected.

hyphen (161, 175–176)
Hyphens link; dashes separate. Hyphens, which are shorter than dashes, are used to link the related parts of certain words together: *brother-in-law*. New words often begin their lives with hyphens and gradually lose them: *e-mail* has become *email*; *on-line* has become *online*.

They are also used to prevent confusion between words:

> *She is recovering from an illness.*
> *She is re-covering the chair.*

They can be used to indicate the division of a word at the end of a line if there isn't enough room to fit the whole word in, for example *unfor-tunately*. The hyphen must come at a syllable break.

In addition, hyphens are also used to join adjectives which have to be linked to make sense: *a three-inch nail; a never-say-die attitude.*

imperative – see **sentence**

impersonal – see **personal**

infinitive
The infinitive is the base form of a verb that is often written with *to* in front of it – *to swim, to walk, to look* etc. It is used with modal verbs: *He will **leave**; He should **leave***, or as part of verb phrases – *He hoped **to win** but was lucky **to come** third.*

inflection
Inflection is the name for the way a word changes to indicate tense, number etc:

- *eat/eats/ate/eating/eaten*
- *fast/faster/fastest*

interjection
An interjection is a word like *Ouch*! They are used to express sudden feelings of joy, pain, horror etc. They usually stand alone and are followed by an exclamation or question mark. They can also be linked to sentences with a dash: *Oh no! – it's started raining again.*

intransitive verb – see **transitive verb**

inverted commas (169–171)
These punctuation marks signal the beginning and end of quotations (quotation marks) and direct speech (speech marks) as well as indicating titles. They always come in pairs, one to open the quotation/speech/title and one to close it:

- *The opening of 'Pride and Prejudice' sets the tone of the novel: 'It is a truth universally acknowledged, that a single man in possession of a good fortune, must be in want of a wife.'*
- *'I'm not certain if I can be there,' she said, 'but I'll try.'*

They can be single or double; what matters is consistency. If there is a quotation within a quotation, then single and double quotation marks should be used consistently (as exemplified at the start of this glossary – page 207). If a quotation is longer than one paragraph, then speech marks are used to open each paragraph but the speech marks are not closed until the end of the final paragraph.

metalanguage
This denotes the language of grammar – the language we need to talk about language.

modal verb (68–69) – see **auxiliary verbs**

modify (19, 77, 125, 220)
In grammar, if one word modifies another it makes its meaning more specific: *sports hall* – here the word *hall* is modified by *sports* so you know what type of hall it is.

mood (71–72)
You can change the mood of verbs. Technically there are three types of mood to indicate whether the verb phrase in a clause is factual, non-factual or giving an order.

Verb phrases are usually in the indicative mood that is used for stating or questioning factual things: *It's ten o'clock. Why are you still in bed?*
The imperative mood (122–123) (bossy verb) is used to give orders: *Turn right. Run!*
The subjunctive mood (71–73) can be used to express wishes, conditions and other non-factual situations: *If I were to do it again …* See **subjunctive**.

morpheme/morphology – see **root word**

noun (1–19, 21–22, 26–28, 38, 61, 77)
Nouns allow you to name what you are talking about – a person or living thing (*man, rose*), a place (*sea, mountain*) or a thing (*pen, floor*). Abstract nouns (1, 16) name qualities (*happiness, love* etc). Most nouns can be singular or plural: *cat/cats*; but mass nouns (18) don't have a plural: *flour, butter.* The names of people and places are proper nouns (1, 6–9) and begin with a capital letter (Ali, Manchester Road, Buckingham Palace); all the others are common nouns (1, 6–7). Collective nouns (1, 15–16) name what a group of something is called: *a* ***swarm*** *of bees.* If you can put *a/an* or *the* in front of a single word, it's a noun.

noun clause (36–37)
This functions like a noun in a sentence but has a verb within it so it is a clause. A noun clause can be a sentence on its own (***The language you used was rude.***) or a subordinate clause (*I objected* ***because the language you used was rude.***).

noun phrase (36–38, 46, 125, 205–206)
This is the name for the word/group of words that functions as a noun in a sentence – eg, *your dog*. Technically, it can refer to a single noun. A noun phrase can always be replaced by a pronoun , eg ***That very large box*** *is mine.* ***That*** *is mine. I liked* ***the little dog I saw last week****. I liked* ***it***. The DfE in England defines an expanded noun phrase (36, 205–206) as any noun phrase that is more than a determiner plus the noun it determines, eg: *the very old cat. The very old cat in the basket in front of the fire* is still an expanded noun phrase – extended by a couple of prepositional phrases.

object – see **subject**

paragraph (10, 169–171, 174, 176, 191, 202–203)
A paragraph is a group of sentences focusing on the same point. Paragraphs are used to help structure writing by separating off a change of focus, time or place. Most paragraphs begin with a topic sentence that introduces the focus of the paragraph. Topic sentences can conclude a paragraph by summing it up. In dialogue, each change of speaker triggers a new paragraph. Paragraphs should begin on a new line and are often indented.

parenthesis – see **brackets**

participle – present/past (35, 159)
A participle is a **non-finite** form of a verb that can be used to help form the tenses of verbs (like an auxiliary) and can also function as an adjective and sometimes a noun – in other words they can participate!

- The present participle is formed out of the verb stem + the suffix – *ing* (*look+ing = look**ing**, eat+ing = eat**ing***). It might be easier if it was called the continuous participle as it is used in all **continuous** forms (the term used to refer to action that is in progress at a specific point in time): *she is swimm**ing**, she was swimm**ing**, she will be swimm**ing*** etc. They can be placed at the front of sentences: *Swimm**ing** as fast as she could, she reached the shore.* In teaching, this fronted adverbial is often referred to as an *ing* verb.
  These *–**ing*** endings can also function as:
  - *an adjective: The swimm**ing** competition starts at 10.00.*
  - *a noun: Swimm**ing** is an important skill.* This form is sometimes known as a verbal noun and used to be called a gerund.

- The past participle is formed out of the verb stem and usually ends in *ed* or *en*:

  *He finish**ed**/has/had/would have finish**ed** his work.*
  *The work was finish**ed**.*
  *She has had/would have stol**en**.*
  *It was stol**en**.*

They can be placed at the front of sentences:

*Stol**en** just before noon, the painting was smuggled out of the country that evening.*

These *ed / en* endings can also function as adjectives:

*The stol**en** bag was behind the wall.*

Occasionally, if they become part of a compound noun, they function as nouns – as in *stolen goods*.

parts of speech – see **word class**

passive – see **active**

past progressive (63–68, 205–206) – see **tense**

perfect (51, 66–68) – see **auxiliary**

person/personal/impersonal (154–155, 199, 204)
It is useful when discussing sentences to be able to refer to whether something is written

- from a personal perspective (I/we), known as the 1st person;
- as if addressing the reader (you), known as the 2nd person;
- from a more distanced impersonal perspective (he/she/it/they), known as the 3rd person. What person a verb is in can alter how it is inflected – see **inflection**.

Narrative text is normally written in the 1st or 3rd person: the 1st person is selected for autobiographical style since it is more personal; the 3rd person is selected for author-as-'God' – the omniscient author, which can be more impersonal but can also be emotive and engaging depending on the writer's purpose and how they select words:

- *The man glanced at the motorbike.* (3rd person impersonal)
- *Jim gazed longingly at the Ducati.* (3rd person personal)

The 2nd person (you) draws the reader into the text and is therefore much used in advertising. Most non-fiction text is written in the 3rd person and is impersonal. Evaluation text can be personal or impersonal:

- *Van Gogh is my favourite painter because I love the way that his pictures are so colourful and emotional.* (1st person personal)
- *Van Gogh's striking use of bold colour to recreate everyday scenes has made him one of the world's most famous painters.* (3rd person impersonal)

Just as 3rd person fiction writing can be impersonal or emotionally engaging depending on the author's purpose, so can non-fiction when persuasive techniques are used:

- *Everyone loves Van Gogh's paintings because of his striking use of bold colours and charming recreation of everyday scenes.* (3rd person persuasive)

personal pronoun – see **pronoun**

phrase (125–126)
A phrase is a group of words without a verb that form a unit of meaning within a sentence: *the large cat; extremely cold; three years later; beside the canal; without a further thought*. If there is a verb within the phrase, then it becomes a clause.

plural – see **singular**

possessive pronoun – see **pronoun**

prefix – see **root word**

prepositions and prepositional phrases (36, 37, 84–87, 125, 206)
Prepositions are the head word (lead word) in the little phrases that join the phrases of a sentence together often showing how they are related in time (*at, during, in, on*) or space (*to, over, under*).

All prepositional phrases are adverbials because they modify a verb or clause within a sentence. Prepositional phrases technically function as adjectives or adverbs because they tell you more about a particular noun or verb. In the sentence *The cat* ***in a hat*** *sat* ***on the mat***, the first prepositional phrase, *in a hat*, acts as an adjective because it describes the cat and answers the question Which? The second prepositional phrase, *on the mat*, acts as an adverb as it tells you more about how the cat was sitting and answers the question Where?

Prepositional phrases don't link clauses – that is the job of conjunctions. They help you know where or when the action is taking place.

- ***In the morning,*** *the cat usually hides* ***under the table***.
- *The train leaves* ***at three o'clock from platform four***.

present progressive (63–68) – see **tense**

present tense – see **tense**

pronoun (39–42, 121, 181, 191, 193–196)
Pronouns can replace nouns or noun phrases as a short way of referring to someone or something that has already been introduced. They're useful for helping join text together avoiding repetition.

> *The boy was stroking the cat making* ***it*** *purr.* ***That*** *made* ***him*** *happy.*

- Possessive pronouns (39, 42–43, 48, 181, 185) express ownership:

> *mine, yours, his, hers, its, ours, theirs*
> *The books have arrived.* ***Yours*** *is here. Have you seen* ***mine?***

These words signal possession and so they do not need an apostrophe of possession.

- Personal pronouns (39–42, 194–195), as the term suggests, are the pronouns (*I, you, he/she/it, we, you, they*) that tell you which person is being referred to (as in first person, second person etc – see **person**). These pronouns change (inflect) to show whether they are acting as the subject of a clause or the object. The list of personal pronouns above all represent subject. When representing the object within the clause, they would be written like this: *me, you, him/her/it, us, you, them*:

> ***I*** *saw* ***him. He*** *saw* ***me.***
> ***We*** *saw* ***her. She*** *saw* ***us.***

(Note that *you* and *it* do not change. ***It*** *saw* ***you. You*** *saw* ***it.***)

All personal pronouns except for *you* change to indicate whether the person is singular (***I, he/she/it***) or plural (***we, they***). Only the third person singular pronouns have different forms to indicate gender (***he/him, she/her***). *It* does not have a gender so it stays the same.

- Relative pronouns (39, 43–44) are used to introduce clauses that relate to the person or thing that they refer to, hence their name. The clauses they introduce are similarly known as relative clauses.

There are five relative pronouns: ***who, whom, whose, which, that***

- ***who*** *and* ***whom*** *refer to people (****who*** *for the subject and* ***whom*** *for the object – increasingly this is only used in formal English):*
  - *The woman* ***who*** *phoned yesterday will arrive today.*
  - *The doctor* ***whom*** *I saw yesterday is an eye specialist.* (**Note:** This could have been written as, *The doctor I saw yesterday is an eye specialist*. The use of ***whom*** here is optional.)

- ○ ***whose*** *indicates possession:*

  The man ***whose*** *car was stolen was very angry.*

- ○ ***which*** *only refers to things:*

  The car, ***which*** *had been parked in front of his house, was a Mercedes.*

- ○ ***that*** *refers to things:*

  The car ***that*** *was stolen was a Mercedes.*

Note: ***that*** can refer to people as well as things when the clause it introduces is essential to the meaning of the sentence (technically a defining relative clause) rather than simply adding extra information:

The man ***that*** *you want to see is sitting over there.*

- Reflexive pronouns (44) reflect back to a previously mentioned noun or pronoun:

She asked ***herself*** *if it was worth it.*

They can refer forward to a noun or pronoun within the same sentence:

In ***itself*** *it did not appear difficult.*

Just to make life complicated, when pronouns are used on their own in place of a noun, they are pronouns, but when they are used like adjectives to pin down the nature of the thing being described, they are determiners as in ***that*** *book,* ***this*** *hat*. See **determiners**

punctuation (see 117–120, 126, 128–129; Chapter 5: 161–190, 202–204)
Punctuation is a way of marking text to help the reader follow the meaning. Symbols are used to separate off (or link together) words, phrases and clauses to help the reader follow the intended meaning of a text.

question mark – see **full stop**

quotation marks – see **inverted commas**

register (200–201)
When relating to use of language, register describes the level of formality within a conversation or text. Most people select the language that they use to suit the situation they are in, using one sort of language for chatting with friends and another when answering questions at an interview etc. This is known as *register*.

relative clause (43–44, 205–206)
A relative clause gives more information about somebody or something in a sentence, in other words they modify nouns. Typically they begin with relative pronouns (*which/that/who/whom/whose*):

> *The shoes* **that I bought** *are not comfortable.*
> *Our sofa,* **which is still extremely comfortable**, *looks rather old and tatty.*

As illustrated above, *that* should be used to introduce additional information that is key to the meaning of the sentence and *which* to introduce a drop-in clause separated off by commas, which adds additional information but is not essential to the meaning of the sentence. See **clause**.

root word (77)
A root word is the basic unit of meaning of a word from which other words can be created by adding **suffixes** (77–78) (letters at the end of the root word – *ful/ing/less/ly* etc) or **prefixes** (62) (letters at the beginning of the word – *un/dis/mis/ re* etc):

> ***help**, **help**ful, **help**less, **help**lessly, un**helpful***

The study of the structure of words is known as morphology and all the separate bits are known as morphemes.

semi-colon (161, 185–188)
Semi-colons are used to separate off closely related items within a sentence:

- *The following people have been selected: Jane, whose work has been outstanding; Dwayne, who has shown leadership, understanding and talent throughout; and Ali for his ability to ensure the team finishes on time.* (Just using commas would have been confusing.)
- *It was the best of days; it was the worst of days.*
- *The sun shone; birds sang; insects buzzed contentedly.* (These clauses could be separated by a full stop or joined by conjunctions but the semi-colon serves to separate the clauses while emphasising that they are closely related.)

sentence (44–45; Chapter 3: 88–101; Chapter 4: 111–160; Chapter 5: 161–190)
A sentence is a group of words in grammatical order that makes sense on its own. Written sentences begin with a capital letter and end with a full stop to help the reader make sense of the words in between.

The structure of sentences can be:

- simple (single **clause**) (88, 90, 94, 123) – ***The dragon sat by the kettle.***
- compound (two clauses or more joined by a co-ordinating conjunction) (88, 123) – *The dragon sat by the kettle* ***and*** *waited for it to boil.*
- complex (more than one clause joined by a subordinating conjunction so that there is a main clause and a subordinate clause) (91–101, 124, 206) – ***Because*** *the dragon was waiting for it to boil, the dragon sat by the kettle.*
- multi-clause sentences (a mix of compound and complex clauses) (124) – ***Because*** *the dragon was waiting for it to boil, he sat by the kettle* ***and*** *texted a friend.*
- minor (148) (verbless expressions, often of emotion, that make sense in context) – *Thanks! Snow! Hey!*

There are four main types of sentence:

1. Declarative (121–122) – statements providing information or suggestions:

   In wintertime the nights are longer.

2. Interrogative (121–122) – for questions or requests.

   What is the date today?

3. Imperative (121–122, 160) – for commands and instructions.

   Put your pens down.
   Stop! (Sentences in the imperative can just be one word as the subject – *you* – is understood.)

   The imperative is also a verb mood – see **mood**.

4. Exclamative (121–122, 160) – for exclamations.

   Thank goodness for that!

sentence signpost (101–110, 191, 193–194)
This is a useful non-grammatical catch-all phrase for any group of words within a sentence or paragraph that tell the reader the direction in which the text is going. They include connectives: *After this …, As a result …*, but they can also include introductory statements that may not be adverbials like: *This caused …/This led to …/The main reason for…*

singular and plural (1, 2, 11, 18, 39–41, 42, 180–185)
These are the terms used to show if there is just one of something (singular) or more than one (plural). The plural is usually indicated by adding an *s* to the noun: *dog/dogs; apple/apples*. A few plurals are irregular: *man/men; child/children*.

speech marks – see **inverted commas**

Standard English (xvii, 55, 144)
This refers to the grammar, vocabulary and spelling of English that has become the national norm. It differs slightly depending which English-speaking nation is being referred to. It is the type of formal English used for all formal public communication and is taught in schools in the UK.

subject and object (40, 191, 196–200)
The subject in active sentences is the person or thing doing something, and the object is the person or thing that is having something done to it. See **active**.

A typical simple sentence in English begins with the subject followed by the verb followed by the object, eg *The girl ate the apple.*

Most **personal pronouns** change depending on whether they are the subject or object of the verb:

I saw him. – He saw me.

subjunctive (71–73): Also see **mood**.
The subjunctive, which is important in Latin grammar and some living languages, is now rarely used in modern English. Constructions like *If* ***I*** ***were*** *to do it again* have largely been replaced by *If I did it again.* It is a mood of the verb used to express wishes, conditions and non-factual situations. There are three types of subjunctive in English:

- **The hypothetical subjunctive** (the *were* subjunctive):
  If he were more sensible, he would get into less trouble.
- **The mandatory subjunctive** (the *bossy* subjunctive):
  I insist that he be more sensible immediately.
- **The formulaic subjunctive** (for certain set exclamatory phrases)
  God save him!

subordinate clause – see **clause**

suffix – see **root word**

synonym (34)
The name for words that have the same meaning – *large/big*.

syntax (144)
Syntax is the study of sentence structure.

tense (51, 54, 63–71, 192–193, 198)
The tense of a verb indicates the time at which an action took place. In English there are two basic tenses, the present (54–56, 63–64, 154–155, 192) and the past (55–57, 63, 154–155, 192), and each of these can either be simple or progressive (also known as continuous). The perfect tenses are used to indicate that something has already happened, or happened even earlier. These tenses can also be used to show that the past action is continuing.

Present	Past
I dance (simple)	*I danced* (simple)
I am dancing (progressive)	*I was dancing* (progressive)
I have danced (present perfect)	*I had danced* (past perfect)
I have been dancing (present perfect progressive)	*I had been dancing* (past perfect progressive)

There is technically no future tense in English but it is commonly referred to as such by all but grammarians. Future actions are expressed by the modal auxiliary verb *will/would*:

I will dance.
I will be dancing.

or by using the present tense and then words to describe when in the future the action should occur:

He is dancing in two days' time.

Auxiliary verbs support the main verb in expressing additional meaning. The most common are *to be*, *to have* and *to do*. (See **auxiliary**.)

topic sentence – see **paragraph**

transitive and intransitive verbs
Verbs are divided into transitive and intransitive. Transitive verbs are action verbs that need an object to complete their meaning (*like, want, hold,*

support). In other words they need someone or something who is affected by the action of the verb:

> *I want a cup of tea.*
> *He's holding the cat.*

Intransitive verbs do not require an object to make sense (*arrives, goes, smiles*):

> *The bus arrived./The bus arrived late.*
> *She smiled./She smiled secretly.*

Inevitably, some verbs can be transitive and intransitive, it just depends on the sentence, eg *eats*:

> *She eats eggs.* (transitive)
> *She eats slowly.* (intransitive)

verb (18, 19, 34, 49, 51–66, 77, 195)
Verbs are doing words that show what someone or something is, has or does. For example, *It* ***is*** *hot today. He* ***has*** *a dog. She* ***walked*** *to school.* Verbs are the only words that can be altered to show the time when the action took place. *I run* (present tense), *I ran* (past tense). Most verbs in English form their tenses in a regular pattern but there are a few irregular verbs (55–57). The verb *to be* is the most irregular. Often several words form a verb phrase: *is leaving, had been running, were waiting*. See **tense**, **mood** and **auxiliary verbs**.

voice – see **active** and **passive**

word class (also known as **parts of speech**) (xv, 61, 152)
The role a word plays within a sentence gives it its grammatical category. The key word classes are **noun**, **pronoun**, **verb**, **adverb**, **adjective**, **conjunction**, **preposition** and **determiner**. The opening terms of this list are normally seen as the words that provide the content – the bricks of meaning – and the last three are the cement that glues the key words together. Often, naming the parts is tricky because many words change their class depending on the role they play in the sentence: *I skate* (verb) *to work. I've lost a skate* (noun).

word family (77)
Word family is the term given to a group of words related to each other by the same root word: *direct, director, directed, direction, indirectly.*

Get ready to...

Jumpstart!

The *Jumpstart!* books contain 'quick-figure' ideas that could be used as warm-ups and starters as well as possibly extended into lessons. There are more than 50 games and activities for Key Stage 1 or 2 classrooms that are practical, easy-to-do and vastly entertaining.

To find out more about other books in the Jumpstart! series, or to order online, please visit:

www.routledge.com/u/jumpstart/

David Fulton Books

www.routledge.com/teachers